TRAUMA
Beyond Time

TRAUMA
Beyond Time
Temporal Constructs in Holocaust Testimonies

Sarah Seiselmyer-Snyder

Purdue University Press / West Lafayette, Indiana

Copyright 2025 by Sarah Ellen Snyder. All rights reserved.

Cataloging-in-Publication Data on file at the Library Congress.

978-1-62671-205-8 (hardcover)
978-1-62671-206-5 (paperback)
978-1-62671-207-2 (epub)
978-1-62671-208-9 (epdf)

Cover design by Chris Brannan.

To my mom and my husband

CONTENTS

	Preface	*ix*
	Acknowledgments	*xvii*
1	**THE MULTIGENERATIONAL HOLOCAUST TESTIMONIAL** The Story of the Tabak Family	1
2	**WRITING HISTORY WITHOUT HINDSIGHT** The Impossible Task of Living Without the Holocaust Through the Eyes of Diarists	43
3	**THE CONTINUATION OF TRAUMA THROUGH TRANSCRIBING** First-Generation Survivors' Memoirs	77
4	**RETHINKING THE "POST" IN "POST-HOLOCAUST"** Trauma in Generational Survivors' Memoirs	115
	CONCLUSION	**155**
	Bibliography	*161*
	Notes	*171*
	Index	*177*
	About the Author	*195*

PREFACE

Understanding Survivorship Through Holocaust Literature

My interest in the idea of the traumatic "after" and the term "post-Holocaust" began when I first volunteered at the Memorial and Museum Auschwitz-Birkenau. I made all the arrangements for volunteering prior to my arrival, including living arrangements for the entirety of the time. I assumed that I would be staying in a hostel or something similar as I would be paying a small weekly rent. When I arrived in the main building where the tourists and visitors arrive, I was told to give the receptionist a moment. It was then that I found myself ushered through one of the main pathways of Auschwitz to the other side of the camp with my large suitcase in tow. It was not clear the reasoning, because at the time I did not speak Polish and the guard did not speak English, but we arrived at security and picked up a key. More trekking. There was a horrible noise that my suitcase made, drawing a great deal of unwanted attention. We finally arrived in front of the *Kommandatura*. Having climbed a set of stairs that clearly showed where others had stepped repeatedly, I arrived at what I would call home for the next few months. I think I was in shock. Here I stood, alone, in what was the office of the commandant of Auschwitz-Birkenau during the genocide. It was a different type of alone—one that I struggle to put into words. There were about ten beds in the room, a table, a mini refrigerator, and a bathroom. I picked a bed in the far corner of the room so that I had my back and side facing walls. I imagined some sort of safety, but from what I'm not sure. My view to the outside would be the place where the orchestra played for the Nazis and the gas chamber. Thankfully, throughout most of my stay I had rotating roommates; I never knew when a new one would arrive, but it was always a blessing. During the times that I did not have a roommate, I met people at the museum and attempted to maintain some sort of social interaction beyond work.

The *Kommandatura* was cut off from tourists and visitors by a white gate and barbed wire. This isolation creates a different sense of the place and a disconnect from the heavily visited former concentration camp. I remember the first time that I saw a small tricycle laying on the ground, the friendly cats that kept me occupied, or the small dog who greeted me. This small dog was particularly important to my journey. He led me to a family that lived on a different floor of the *Kommandatura*. They were an elderly couple who I had the pleasure of saying "hello" to and sharing some wonderful moments with. I was invited into their home and, despite not being able to verbally communicate, we socialized just fine. Eventually, I met some of their extended family who spoke English, and I learned that the couple had lived there for years. I later attempted to interview them, but at the last moment they declined. I was curious how they could live there, but as time went on a part of me understood. I too laughed, ate, slept, and made that corner of the world my home, albeit temporarily.

However, I had not suffered there, nor had any of my family suffered there, and that made my stay a little bit easier. That is not to say that I was not aware of the immense suffering that had occurred at that location, or that I did not have close friends who had survived the Holocaust, but it is different not to have a familial connection. A few years after my first stay, I was once again in the same room waiting to take part in the seventieth anniversary of the liberation of Auschwitz-Birkenau. I learned that survivors had been placed in the same building that I was in as a means of lodging. I could not comprehend it. A part of me understood that logistically it made sense as they would be close to the event, but it seemed to ignore the continuation of the trauma these individuals experienced. I heard that some survivors refused to stay there, and others accepted the arrangements with a feeling of pride. The situation sparked my interest into how academics, including historians and museum workers, view survivors of genocide. Academically speaking, the Holocaust ended in 1945 with the marking of the liberation of the various concentration, extermination, and labor camps. I started to question this finite construct of time that ignored the continuation of trauma and asked, "For whom did the Holocaust really end in 1945?" and "Is this not just a convenient stop time for historians to focus on?" and "Why do we not view trauma and history from the perspective of those who experienced it?" This does not mean that we must or should solely rely on survivors' understanding of events, but that by defining an event or events in this case, is dangerous to our understanding of history. Additionally, I wanted to analyze how trauma lives on beyond the survivor generation and as a watershed moment(s) in history through a micro analysis of survivor's family members. It was through this curiosity that I began questioning of the notion of "post-Holocaust," which can also be applied to the concept of "post-genocide." This would lead to what I call a survivor-focused approach to history.

As a part of the overarching theme of my research, I delved into various theoretical frameworks that could assist my understanding of trauma and the impact it has on both survivors and their descendants. I began with Helen Epstein's *Children of the Holocaust: Conversations with Sons and Daughters of Survivors*, whose pivotal work features various voices of the second-generation of Holocaust survivors. She approaches the topic from her professional lens as a psychologist, but she quickly finds that she cannot disconnect from the conversations that are unfolding. The conversations reflect much of how she felt growing up in a household with a mother who was a Holocaust survivor. This led me to question what is trauma and how can trauma be shared?

In the case of these second-generation survivors, trauma is and was a part of their everyday lives, although not necessarily at the forefront of their experiences. Throughout her work, Epstein points out various psychological issues that stem from trauma, including paranoia, post-traumatic stress disorder (PTSD), and physical ailments that manifested in this group; however, I still wanted to know what exactly this trauma was for the second-generation, and, in turn, what was this trauma for survivors and how do we as scholars interact with this knowledge.

I looked at Dina Wardi's *Memorial Candles: Children of the Holocaust* to find my answer. Her work as a therapist focused on a group therapy setting of mostly second-generation survivors to understand emerging patterns. It is within Wardi's research that I began to realize the burden that was placed upon the second-generation, whether intentionally or not. This group of individuals were now living, as she calls it, a "double-reality" (Wardi 108). They are living in the present as themselves, working to build their lives, all while balancing their parent(s)' past. These "memorial candles"—or individuals who have taken up this role within their families—must contend not only with their parent(s)' trauma, but now with their own trauma.

Although trauma is evident in both Epstein's and Wardi's research, I still did not have a firm definition of what trauma is. Cathy Caruth, a trauma theorist, states that trauma is "a response, sometimes delayed, to an overwhelming series of events, which takes the form of repeated, intrusive hallucinations, dreams, thoughts or behaviors stemming from the event" (Caruth 2), while the American Psychological Association (APA) claims that "trauma" is an "emotional response to a terrible event" (Alter n.p.). These two definitions represent some of the conflict that is present in trauma studies, as the former represents the physical toll and the latter represents the emotional toll. This calls into question if it is the event that is traumatic or the response that is traumatic, as individuals have differing experiences. In the context of this research, it is both the lack of response (the annihilation of the possibility of a response), as well as the continuation of the experience.

To reach back further in trauma studies, Henry Krystal, a pioneer of trauma studies from a psychoanalytical perspective and a survivor of Auschwitz, claims that the term "trauma" has been overused and thereby made "useless" (Krystal 113). If this is the case, is there a limit to how many individuals can experience trauma? He continues to explain that individuals can misuse the term "trauma" for experiences that are "near trauma." If considering this at a macro level, which historians frequently do, does surviving genocide not constitute "trauma" rather than "near trauma"? Additionally, as Krystal is a survivor himself, does his definition of trauma prevent him from being classified as traumatized? The author, in his groundbreaking work, claimed that trauma was only one element of what was at that time termed "concentration camp syndrome (KZ syndrome)." Eliazar de Wind, a Dutch psychiatrist and survivor of Auschwitz, coined this term in 1949 in response to the psychological impacts of the Holocaust, including defense mechanisms and adaptations for survival. It is always important to note that not all victims of the Holocaust were in camps; however, de Wind's syndrome could be linked to other victims, not just those in the camp system. He also led the way in arguing that trauma has a direct link to intergenerational survivors (Sak and Suchodolska 1). Considering de Wind's stance on intergenerational survivors, it is evident that trauma and the concept of *after* does not and cannot exist for survivors.

When analyzing primary sources, including diaries, memoirs, and oral testimonies, I began to see patterns of how trauma was conveyed in these texts, including the theme of time. As such, I deeply reflected upon Elie Wiesel, who frequently wrote about time in his publications. Why was time so important to his stories? It was from there that I found David Patterson's *Along the Edge of Annihilation: The Collapse and Recovery of Life in the Holocaust Diary*, in which he commented that time is the measure of humanity (Patterson 85).

This measurement of humanity via time would begin to answer my question of what trauma is. Genocide is a rupture of time as it strips away the individual's ability to maintain time, relationships, and selfhood. If time is the connecting piece to the other, and individuals are no longer able to structure who they are through time constructs, they lose part of their humanity. The Nazis accomplished this distortion in the erasure of time, thereby traumatizing those that they targeted and those that were descended from that group. The Nazis' goal was to make the Jew less than human—a disease, a contagion, a bug—and by rupturing time, they could achieve their goal.

To look at specific examples of this rupture of time, I began my research with writing a case study of the Tabak family. In 2018, I was assigned to document the Holocaust survival story of Philadelphia resident Frieda Tabak. Through this project, I had the privilege of meeting both her brother and her children. The first chapter weaves together the powerful testimonies of two survivors—Frieda and her brother, Stanley—alongside the perspectives of two second-generation survivors—Mark and David, Frieda's children. The purpose of this chapter is to provide evidence that memory does not function on a linear pathway as some scholarship would suggest via the concept of "post-Holocaust." In order to emphasize the lack of a linear path in memory, I intentionally avoided chronology, with the exception of the rehearsed parts of Frieda's presentation, and I intertwined the various family members' storylines. The methodology utilized to obtain these testimonials is what Henry Greenspan has called the "multiple interview process," which helps to build rapport and to scratch beyond the surface, especially in the case of Holocaust survivors who have presented their stories many times in public settings. The public presentation can lead to an edited recap of their experience and a distancing of the emotions that come with recollecting genocide.

Next, I viewed Holocaust diaries with the understanding that most diarists did not survive the Holocaust. Despite this, I believe that diarists set the stage for historians' ability to analyze what was occurring during the Holocaust and how the Holocaust outlived the individual. The diarists I researched were of varying ages, genders, and experiences, although the majority were imprisoned in the Warsaw Ghetto. This is where a great variety of diaries were written—and more importantly preserved. By looking at different demographics, it becomes clear that there are various patterns that occur in diaries. For example, the idea of childhood and the changed meaning because of the Holocaust, or the disruption of holidays and how each one took on a new meaning. Essentially, each piece of the chapter focusing on Holocaust diaries tears a thread from the woven fabric of time constructs and the preconceived notions historians have about time.

The following chapter analyzes what it means to be a Holocaust survivor from 1945 onward via the Holocaust memoir—the act of writing a memoir as a continuation of the trauma. The events that have stayed in survivors' minds and the need to write about the experience conveys a connection to the Holocaust that is inescapable. It is directly through the words of the survivors in their memoirs that I consider the idea of "after" and what clearly becomes an impossibility. It is not only through the moments in which they are awake that survivors reflect that a "post-Holocaust" does not exist, but also in their dreams or nightmares, which are analyzed in this chapter. Many survivors' dreams are linked to the idea of home and being able to return home. The reader will find that this is also an impossibility as their homes no longer exist or the people that made the location a home have been murdered. The tragic truth is more than some can live with, and they decide to end their lives. It is in this moment that a survivor might be able to experience a "post-Holocaust," but the analysis will consider if it is ever possible to escape the Holocaust, even in death.

Lastly, the group of individuals who are written about are those who experience intergenerational trauma—the second—and third-generation, that is, the children and grandchildren of survivors. I began this research by considering a survivor who was born at the start of the Holocaust and what category he is placed in, questioning whether it is, in fact, an accurate representation of his experience via his own words. Transitioning to the words of the second—and third-generation, I look at how their words reflect the trauma of the Holocaust, how memory functions for these groups, and, in turn, how trauma continues beyond 1945. For example, the concept of a pilgrimage is dissected as a means of connecting to the experiences of their family members but also as a method to connect to themselves. I argue that the second—and third-generation have their own form of trauma that stems from the Holocaust, in addition to the trauma passed on to them from the direct survivor(s).

One important note is that the word *after* is not utilized with the exception to be disproved. This was done to maintain the philosophy that is present throughout my research. My intention was to provide evidence that the Holocaust is not only an event anchored in time that is researched in terms like "past" or "post," but that it continues throughout time, preventing these terms from accurately representing the survivor experience. It is my hope that scholars and others become more conscious of what the definition of a survivor is and how it is a lasting title that has been involuntarily imposed upon them.

Throughout this book, readers will journey with me as I dismantle the artificial construct of a "post-Holocaust" period—a concept that I argue fundamentally misrepresents the lived experiences of survivors and their descendants. The chapters that follow will demonstrate how the Holocaust transcends conventional historical periodization, continuing to shape lives across generations in ways that defy our traditional notions of historical events with clear endpoints.

Readers will gain not only a deeper understanding of how trauma manifests across generations, but also methodological insights for approaching traumatic history more ethically and accurately. By reconceptualizing the Holocaust through the lens of those who lived through it and their descendants, this book offers a framework that respects the continuing reality of trauma rather than relegating it to a concluded historical period. My research stands as both a challenge to conventional Holocaust periodization and an invitation to historians to develop more nuanced approaches to traumatic history—approaches that acknowledge how the past continues to live in the present for survivors and their families. In rejecting the false construct of a "post-Holocaust" era, we honor the true experiences of survivors while advancing a more humane historical scholarship, one that may be applied to understanding other genocides and collective traumas as well.

ACKNOWLEDGMENTS

Thank you to those who offered advice, ideas, and support throughout this process; to those who have listened to me read a paragraph; or those whom I have bounced an idea off. You have been the backbone to my ability to continue presenting, researching, publishing, and completing my work.

To the Tabak family, thank you for letting me into your family and sharing your stories.

Last, but certainly not least, the biggest thank you goes to my friends and family, especially my editor-in-chief, who has always supported all my endeavors, and to my junior editor, who has always stood by my side.

1
THE MULTIGENERATIONAL HOLOCAUST TESTIMONIAL
THE STORY OF THE TABAK FAMILY

"You who weren't there no matter how much you study . . . you'll never fully understand it."
— FRIEDA TABAK

Through multigenerational interviews and testimonials, this chapter demonstrates how the Holocaust remains ever-present, living on through generations of survivors. In this chapter, the lasting impact of the Holocaust is analyzed through a series of interviews with the Tabak family. The Holocaust shaped who they are as individuals and who they are as a family unit. It is within their story that each member of the Tabak family experiences the Holocaust to this day; therefore, the term "post-Holocaust" is inaccurate and cannot be used. Although this chapter primarily focuses on Frieda Tabak's testimonial, there are various sections in which her family members have contributed about their lives, Frieda's character, and other facets of their history.

The Holocaust molded who Frieda became and impacted the future generations of her family. Frieda's story is not presented in a timeline, as her memories do not naturally present themselves in that manner. This chapter serves as a case study to establish concepts for future chapters and the understanding of memory and time. Throughout this chapter, Frieda's life is not written chronologically with the intention of representing my experience as a listener. Thereby, in order for a historian to begin to understand how survivors are still impacted, we must understand how they remember. It must also be considered that it is not simply "remembering," but it is also living in the present that the Holocaust impacts survivors and their families. This means that the events of the Holocaust are not past, but present.

METHODOLOGY

In September of 2018, I began a project with the Holocaust Awareness Museum and Education Center in Philadelphia, Pennsylvania. The museum paired me with Frieda Tabak, and what a blessing that would turn out to be. The interviewing process began with Frieda Tabak and branched out to her children and her brother. Following Henry Greenspan's approach in *On Listening to Holocaust Survivors: Beyond Testimony*, I conducted multiple interviews with Frieda and her family, allowing formal interviews to evolve naturally into conversations. To start the process, I utilized a formal interview method, but following the first set of questions altered my methodology to an informal interviewing process.

We emailed back and forth in an attempt to find a coinciding period of time that we were free. The holdup was usually on her end as she is always on the go. It took two weeks until we finally sat down on Skype. While Skype enabled visual communication, the digital interface created barriers to establishing genuine human connection. The screen inhibited the ability to read subtle body language and build the trust essential for such personal conversations. It is easier to hide behind a screen, whereas in person there is no way to obfuscate oneself. One cannot hide the bouncing leg or the fretting hands; they are simply there as a part of the process. Also, the confrontation of history can be minimized by the technological issues that arise, and this new technology seems to modernize the conversation, which adds a layer of disconnect.

I came prepared with questions, a note pad, pen, and a recorder. A member of the museum set up the technology and the interview began. I didn't have to say a word—Frieda just began speaking. The story that she told me that day was well rehearsed and distant. Frieda frequently speaks at schools and at other events in person and, more recently, virtually.

Telling her story to strangers is a part of who she is; however, the story that she tells her audiences is rehearsed and less painful than her reality. This is not unique to Frieda. Survivors who present testimonials, both orally and in writing, provide the details that they presume others want to hear—details that are not too upsetting, and often do not blame or cause shame.

That first interview was the hardest. Frieda and I knew nothing about each other, and we were attempting to discuss a topic that brings to light an array of emotions, for both of us. Skype became a hindrance to the process, so I decided to fly out to Philadelphia and meet Frieda in her home, a choice that would forge a lasting friendship.

The story that you will read here is not the same as the one that she tells when visiting schools. Her story was told to me as memories came to her, not just as she rehearsed. Many moments during the multiple interviews, I did not pose a question; she would simply offer a story that she had recollected.

MEMORY AND NARRATIVE STRUCTURE

Though Frieda presents her public testimonies chronologically, this structure does not reflect how she actually remembers or experiences these memories. William James coined the term "stream of consciousness," which links the individual's temporality and flow of thought to what Georg Northoff described as one's "inner time consciousness." Northoff's model distinguishes between *explicit time*, where consciousness directly engages with temporality, and *implicit time*, where temporal awareness serves as a background framework while specific details occupy the conscious mind. Implicit time helps us to understand the flow of thought and links that one makes to experiences despite the potential discrepancy in explicit time (Northoff 185–186).

This chapter analyzes how Frieda and her family members express their continued trauma through their stream of consciousness, examining both how they represent it in their lives and the various forms in which they remember it. Jakub Jonkisz argues that consciousness is a way of processing information that is unique to the individual or "individuated" (Jonkisz 3). Giorgio Marchetti expands this concept, arguing that while universal emotions like fear are commonly experienced, their meaning and manifestation vary significantly based on individual memory and experience (Marchetti 436). In turn, this must be considered when conducting interviews as the perspective of the interviewer must understand how a person has developed and transformed, and how new meaning has been derived (439). In this case study, it is how the individual(s) have produced meaning in connection to the Holocaust.

WRITING APPROACH

When I wrote this chapter, I had already written one version of her memoir in chronological order, starting from her birth date until present day. This was a challenging task as our conversations were not in any order, and altering the order made the story sound inorganic and forced. It lacked an emotional connection because it could not show how Frieda recalled memories or how her recollections were sometimes directly linked to what she was experiencing at that given moment.

The version in this volume is written with chronological portions. These are often the stories that Frieda includes in her presentations to schoolchildren. They are riddled with historical facts and figures and do not connect her to the outwardly emotional portion of her story because they are rehearsed. Surrounding these chronological portions are recollections that she shared during the interview process. Many of these stories are presented in the place where she recounted them in the interview. These are not chronological; they are spontaneous and often emotional.

It will become evident in further chapters that survivor memoirs are presented chronologically until the modus operandi shifts for the descendants' memoirs, which often abandons the chronological timeline, and an intertwining of stories is created. This aids in our understanding of trauma and how it continues beyond "liberation" and into future generations.

This chapter serves to showcase that it is feasible to write history nonlinearly while remaining coherent. Structurally, it also excluded the subsections featured in future chapters. This deliberate decision was to highlight the continuation of Frieda's Holocaust story, with no abrupt disruptions.

FRIEDA'S LIFE

The day arrived, and I eagerly walked to Frieda's apartment overlooking the Delaware River, with New Jersey visible across the river. It was a short distance to the historic area of Philadelphia. I would later learn how Frieda and her husband came to live in this apartment, and how it was the home's natural light that led them to move in. We sat down at her table, I turned on the recorder, got out my pen and pad, and Frieda began to tell me her story. She brought out an array of books on the Holocaust in Romania. Some were macro histories of Romania and the Holocaust, while others were specific to where she had lived in Czernowitz, and she said, "Here I have two copies. You keep this one." This is who Frieda is. Frieda has a deep need to expand her knowledge of the Holocaust, and more specifically, her own Holocaust experience, along with teaching others about her history. Her research into Romanian Holocaust history helps fill the gaps in her childhood memories, helping her better understand her own story. Much like other children survivors, like Joseph Polak, who is referenced in the intergenerational memoirs chapter, Frieda seeks out information by researching her own story to fill in anything that is missing. This prevents a sense of impostor syndrome that plagues the children survivors who do not remember as vividly as the adults who survived. Although she has memories directly connected to the Holocaust, there are many details she cannot recall without assistance. Through her work, Frieda is forming new memories of trauma from the Holocaust throughout time, making it impossible to escape.

Having given me the book, she mentioned the story of arriving in America as a teenager with only the clothes on her back and what she could carry in a bag and a satchel. Frieda said, "One thing about being a survivor is if I lose something, as much as it is bothersome, especially after my husband died, it's just a thing." Frieda's complex relationship with material possessions stems directly from her Holocaust experience. On one hand, she had to leave behind most of her possessions when she fled Romania, but she was able to hold on to her family, which was always the priority. Now she has a beautiful collection of antiques and items from her vast travels strewn around her home. These new pieces will someday become family heirlooms that will be given to her two sons and their children. Carol Kidron argues that heirlooms are meant to breach a wall from the past to the present for those who have experienced trauma, but I argue that they provide a physical continuation (Kidron 4). In the case of Frieda, her possessions are the wall that attempts to barricade her from the Holocaust. It serves as a reminder that she does not have traditional family heirlooms that have been passed down to her, which would have been a continuation of her family.

It was my second visit, a year later in 2019, that I would learn more about her collection of beautiful objects that were always linked to a story. For example, she has a coffee table resting in the middle of her living room. It is a large planting pot with a cut of glass over it. I had mentioned that I thought it was an interesting piece, and she told me that it had always bothered her. The French grammar on the pot, "*mon maison*" instead of "*ma maison*," was wrong. It becomes evident why grammar is important to Frieda throughout her story. I continued to look around her beautiful home and asked her about the light-filled river view, the reason she and her husband had purchased the space. She confessed that there was once a ballpark across the river, and after each game that the home team won, they would set off fireworks in celebration. Of course, having lived there for many years, she knew that this was a tradition, but one night the game ran late into the night. She claimed it was about midnight when she heard the fireworks in her sleep, and she woke up convinced that they were being bombed. For Frieda, it was not a matter of "if" she was being bombed, but a certainty that she was being attacked. Of course, she knows that bombs were not physically being dropped in her area at that specific time, but she was not able to divorce herself from her trauma stemming from the Holocaust.

Following this heartbreaking story, Frieda told me that she also has flashbacks when she sees motorcycle gangs with helmets that resemble

Nazi helmets. The helmets invoke a deep-seated fear. She also shared that even thinking about them gives her a chill. These two anecdotes are brief insights into the lasting impacts of the Holocaust for Frieda. They do not exist in the past, but are present in her home, on the streets, in times of play and in times of relaxation. Her Holocaust experience cannot be placed in the linear past, nor can it be written in terms of the past. For survivors like Frieda, there is an inability to escape the torments of the Holocaust, for there is no *after* genocide, it is a continuation of a genocide, an additional step of torment. If we consider the extreme responses to these torments—the cases of suicide among Holocaust survivors—it is abundantly clear that there is no leaving behind the "past" because the only escape is death.

After these flashback stories, we attempted to pick up right where we had left off from our Skype session, but that was challenging as neither one of us could remember exactly where in the story we left off. This could be in part due to the rehearsed nature of her story. Normally, the story would be told from her birth date of December 20, 1931, and follow a specific timeline of events. She would include how she was born Frieda Weinschenker. When she arrived in the United States in 1947, she became Frieda Wishner, adding that she was not sure if this was done legally or not, but her aunts and uncles had assumed that last name when they immigrated to United States in the 1920s. Changing her last name may have symbolized more than a simplification of spelling. Her last name was a part of her life in Europe; therefore, by assimilating and recreating her last name, she and her family could start anew. With this step to assimilate, there was a removal of the past in an attempt to have a future void of the Holocaust; however, this would prove impossible. By altering their names, they could cut another tie to the Holocaust, and in this case to their Jewishness. As Frieda explains, her first name was Germanic, so it provided a sort of distancing from Judaism, and more broadly, Europe. But she was still the girl in class with a funny accent.

We continued to talk, and although we veered off course numerous times, sometimes discussing my dog or the Yiddish classes Frieda teaches, our conversation always returned to the Holocaust. The return to the Holocaust was not always because of a question posed, but rather because it is a large part of who Frieda is. She cannot escape how the Holocaust has molded her. It is not set in the past, and thereby she has never experienced a "post-Holocaust." At first, I thought this was because she knew I was there for the purpose of interviewing her about her Holocaust experience, but I learned through separate discussions with one of her sons that Frieda frequently reverts to the topic. Arguably, she does this because the Holocaust has influenced how she views the world. With these sporadic off-topic conversations, it only made the memories flood in from random points of her life. Things that she had not recalled in years were suddenly coming back. I listened with great intensity, trying to be prepared with a question in response, but I must admit it was difficult.

When I left Philadelphia, I returned to Dallas where I felt a passionate drive to write down her story, and I started to do just that. There were gaps in her story that I could not possibly fill in myself. Although Frieda was more than happy to share stories (and if she was not, she would tell you), I wanted to meet her family, the people she talks about in great length. Frieda gave me contact information for her two sons and her brother, each of which I had heard a great deal about prior to speaking with them.

These conversations revealed that her younger brother, Stanley, whom Frieda had always referred to simply as her brother, is her half-brother. For Frieda, these details were not important. Stanley is her brother and that was what mattered; however, for me, her family dynamics started to make more sense. Frieda's family structure, although not entirely unique, took on a different meaning because of the Holocaust.[1] Frieda and Stanley have a deep bond that was forged by the Holocaust. Of course, the pair have a sibling relationship, but they were also there for each other in times when the adults did not always believe the children would understand. This ability to be a constant in a world where they did not know what would happen at any given moment impacted their relationship. Their deep connection is linked to the moments when their lives were in danger, continuing into the present day. They cannot escape what the Holocaust has done to their relationship as it created a deeper sense of family.

Another question I pondered was, what had happened to her biological mother, and did it have any relation to the Holocaust? I learned from Mark, Frieda's eldest son, that Frieda's birth mother had passed away when she was three years old, and it would not be until years later when she learned her biological mother's name. Frieda did not discuss many details about her life before the Holocaust. This could be because she was a small child, or perhaps it is the belief that the lasting impact of losing multiple mothers is not relevant to her story. The guilt of not knowing her biological mother's name or any other details about this woman, a stranger to memory, may also be a reason she does not reflect upon this period of her life. After Frieda's mother's death, her father, Chaim, sent Frieda to live with her Aunt Rifka. For two years, her aunt filled the maternal role that Frieda was missing. Frieda never mentioned Aunt Rifka or any other family members who had died during the Holocaust. These were the topics that were not broached during our initial interviews, nor are they mentioned in her presentations. As Henry Greenspan writes, these topics were "unsaid," meaning these are topics Frieda could present on, but "chooses" not to (Greenspan 3). This direct link to Frieda's Holocaust suffering expands upon the concept that she does not experience a "post-Holocaust" in that not only were family members murdered, but their memories cannot be easily recalled without the pain of not knowing details of what had happened, and when information is known, it is too painful to recollect.

Frieda also never mentioned her daughter, Rifka, who passed away a few years before our first interview. I was never privy as to how she passed, and I only learned of her and her passing from Frieda's son. Of what I could gather their relationship was strained, and Rifka suffered the most as a second-generation survivor. It was through this mention of a sister that I learned of the aunt she was named after. As Dina Wardi notes, "Many survivors therefore preserve the memory of family members in their children and name them after dead relatives. They thus decree for their children a double sense of identity and emotional life; the children must live simultaneously as themselves and as the relative they were named after" (Wardi 94). Within the intergenerational survivor memoir chapter, there are ample examples of children of survivors who were named after their parents' loved ones who had been murdered in the Holocaust. There existed a burden of having such a history already attached to oneself before ever having the opportunity to become an individual separate from the Holocaust. This means Rifka never lived a life without a reminder of her family that had been murdered—a life without a "post-Holocaust" because there was no *before*. If I could have, I would have asked her if carrying the name of a murdered loved one impacted her life, but I can only imagine it did. Rifka's predecessor died in Transnistria.

Frieda's omission of those in her life who have died could be linked to the notion of "discomposure," as noted by Ellis Spicer: "When an interviewee 'composes' their narrative, 'shaping and organizing ... temporal experience,' a sense of well-being or composure is usually elicited, evident in both the interview itself and more broadly in the life of the interviewee. On occasion, however, composure is not attained. Discomposure has been defined as 'a kind of psychic unease at their [the interviewee's] inability to align subjective experience with discourse" (Spicer 442). This defense mechanism helps to protect survivors, like Frieda, who took on the burden of retelling their story numerous times.

Throughout the process, Frieda spoke often of her living family. For her, they are everything. This deep sense of family is easily linked to the Holocaust. Frieda lost every item she owned, but her immediate family was lucky and managed to leave Europe together. She often calls her children to tell them of some finding that she has discovered about the Holocaust, as she says it is a link to a part of who they are. She hopes they will someday present the Holocaust as she does, but she knows that this may never be the case. Eva Hoffman wrote, "It demands something from us [second-generation], an understanding that is larger than just ourselves, that moves beyond the private vicissitudes of the inner life" (Hoffman 103). The second-generation carries this burden, which enacts an inescapable toll due to the constant reminders that haunt them, including Frieda's hope that they carry on her legacy in the classroom and community, something that had impacted Frieda and her daughter's relationship even in death.

However, there is hardly a time when I call or email Frieda that she does not mention one of her sons, grandchildren, parents, or brother. This deep connection to her family reflects her own connection to her childhood and what her family means to her. They survived together and because of each other. I remember the first time that I spoke with Stanley on the phone. I was attending a conference on genocide in Sacramento, and he called me. This time I was not prepared and did not have a pen or notebook. Thankfully, I found someone who had supplies.

The stories I heard about Stanley were impressive to say the least. In 1939, Milo Weinschenker was born. He assumed the American name Stanley in an attempt to assimilate. He is eight years younger than Frieda and resides in California where he works as a cardiologist. Stanley arrived in the United States when he was just eight years old, a boy from Romania who lived in five other countries, under different governmental rulers, by the time he arrived in America. He had never attended school as they were too busy staying alive in Romania, Poland, and Germany. At eight years old, he started first grade with no knowledge of English, and, by the end of the year, he was placed in fourth grade. English was the only language Stanley conversed in after this. Language was consequential for his survival, along with his entire family's survival, and this disconnect from his Holocaust experience is a break from his own "childhood"—the erasure of a past—and without a past he cannot have a post. He eventually attended Harvard Medical School and graduated third in his class. Their mother, Clara, was the one who pushed him to graduate. Clara promised herself that when Stanley graduated medical school, she would keep kosher and observe the Sabbath. According to Frieda, she did so until the day she died. For each member of the family, education seemed more than just gaining knowledge, but rather a method to prove significance, a significance that the Nazis tried to rip away. Frieda saw education as the one thing the Nazis could not take away, and she instilled this belief in her children as a form of protection against persecution.

Clara was a strong proponent of education for Frieda and Stanley. Throughout the entire interview process Freida called her "mother." Her father married Clara a few years after her biological mother, Feige, passed away. Clara was the glue that held her family together throughout time, and she continued to be the glue even after she had passed away. Her roles as confidant, protector, and caregiver were with her until her dying day. Here was a woman who later in life wrote to newspapers to give them a piece of her mind and save her family many times from certain death. The way her family describes her, she was fearless and the pillar of the family. Baba, as her grandchildren so affectionately called her, was a cultured,

Austrian Jew whose father was a lawyer. However, Frieda's paternal grandparents were *Ostjuden* by Clara's definition.[2] This created a fundamental divide: Clara came from Western Europe while Chaim hailed from Eastern Europe, and according to Frieda, "[Clara] didn't hesitate to let him know." This East-West cultural divide profoundly shaped their religious practices. Clara was less observant religiously, though she remained superstitious, while Chaim was deeply devout. His religious convictions even influenced major life decisions: while his three siblings immigrated to America in the 1920s, Chaim chose to keep his family in Europe because he had heard that Americans were required to work on Sabbath.

Chaim grew up in a kosher home and found the Holocaust challenged his faith. They ate what they could when they could. He could not believe that God could allow something so profoundly horrid to occur. Frieda says that she is passionately Jewish, but not religious, and she declares herself to be agnostic as she can neither prove nor disprove that God exists. For her, what matters most in Judaism is the culture, the peoplehood, and the traditions. She studies the Talmud as a practice of mental exercise and a continuation of studying philosophy. Maybe this culmination of study and tradition are small parts of her childhood home to hold on to. Stanley, I was informed by Frieda, is not religious at all and never has been. When I asked if this could be in part because of the Holocaust, she said she did not think so because he had never been religious. Interestingly, Stanley would raise his children to be religiously Jewish. Stanley's choice to reconnect to his Jewish roots via his children is indicative of his understanding of his Holocaust experience. For Stanley, as he had learned in Europe, it was dangerous to be Jewish, but in America it was safe. Additionally, as he stated, he is American and is profoundly patriotic because of the freedom America provides. Although he chooses not to practice Judaism, his decision to bring up his children in the faith reflects a hope for a Jewish future for his family.

It was not until Frieda's family lost their home and homeland that they (through the power of Clara) headed to America. The Soviet Union took control over Bessarabia and northern Bukovina in June 1940, establishing an occupation that would last until July 1941 (Carp 18).[3] Very quickly the area transformed: flags were changed, city squares took on new names, and other symbols took shape (Hirsch and Spitzer 2011: 100). Although there was a new government, the Jews were not greatly disturbed by the presence of Communism. At the root of Communism is the belief that everyone is created equal. Despite this being true ideologically, the Soviets wanted to rid the world of the Jewish religion as the Soviets were antisemitic. The Soviets outlawed synagogues, but allowed Yiddish schools, theaters, and other places of culture to remain available. Three weeks after the occupation, Jews were made aware just how unequal they were in the eyes of the Communists. However, being a child seemed to have protected Frieda from the impact for the time being. The common belief was that the Jews were rich, a stereotype that plagued Europe.

The Weinschenker family were kicked out of their home because they were Jews and were believed to be rich. Frieda was just nine years old when she lost her toys, her own bed, and the sense of security that a home provides. However, she was lucky her family remained together for the time being. In 1940, about three weeks after the Soviet invasion, they moved to Czernowitz, Romania (presently in Ukraine), to stay with her uncle, Dr. Salo Koffler. As Marianne Hirsch and Leo Spitzer so poignantly wrote, the town is "a place that cannot be found in any contemporary atlas," and "nowadays, of course, Czernowitz is nowhere" (Hirsch and Spitzer 2011: xiii). This can only serve as a painful reminder of the political erasure of Frieda's home, which disrupts any attempt at having a past. Frieda thinks of Czernowitz as her first home. The city had a population of roughly 160,000, and of those about 60,000 were Jews who worked in professional jobs. Her uncle was a physician who had a spare room that Frieda's family of four shared. His role in Frieda's life, as well as Stanley's, was essential. He filled the void of teacher when the children could not attend school, and of father when Frieda's biological father was sent to a labor camp in central Romania. As I was told, Dr. Koffler's influence would lead to Stanley's choice of profession later in life.

This was information that I learned from the first time we spoke on Skype. The history Frieda shared in our first interview was information that could be found in textbooks that had a direct link to her and her family. It was informational, with the exception of my interjecting questions. Mark, Frieda's eldest son, told me how Stanley became a doctor because of his uncle's work as an obstetrician/gynecologist. It is possible that Frieda told me what she normally presents because often people have not bothered to become deeply informed about the Holocaust; this style of presentation could be due to history being taught in a distanced manner as opposed to the human connection to the event(s). At the time of our first interview, Frieda was not aware of my own background with the history of the Holocaust and approached me not as a Holocaust scholar.

I was essentially a stranger at this point in our interviews. She did not know how much I knew or how I would react to her story. One story that was recited was that of her son and granddaughter. While Frieda's granddaughter was a high school student, between 2004 and 2008, Frieda's son had suggested that Elie Wiesel's *Night* be added to their reading list, and he offered to pay for the books; however, no one at the school ever replied. Frieda also mentioned that she often asks the students who hear her speak what they know about the Holocaust. Sometimes the students have visited the United States Holocaust Memorial Museum in Washington, D.C., or others have read *Anne Frank's Diary* or *Night*.[4] Yet for Frieda, these stories are not remotely like her own. She noted, "if they read *Night* then hear my story, they won't understand mine." Frieda's story was not like that of Anne Frank or Elie Wiesel, but each survivor has a unique story to tell and each history is equally as important. Both Frank and Wiesel's stories have shaped the general public's understanding of what the Holocaust was and is; however, the stories of many survivors and victims do not include imprisonment at a concentration camp or death camp, nor do they write in a similar manner. It is impossible, only one of the limitless impossibilities, to gather every Holocaust story, but each individual story has value.

On June 22, 1941, the Nazis and Romanian governments broke the Molotov-Ribbentrop Pact with Russia (Ioanid 66). Three days after the invasion by the Germans, there was a knock on Frieda's door and Romanian soldiers demanded all Jewish men gather in the courtyard of city hall.[5] Frieda's father was marched off to the gathering, and by luck he returned to tell the tale of the horror that ensued. Machine guns were stationed there and aimed at the men, but by a change of orders, they were saved and released. Frieda would later find out that a different group of two thousand Jews were taken to the forests and shot by the *Einsatzgruppen* D, including the chief rabbi of Czernowitz (Carp 18). Frieda's fear of explosions, like her fear of the fireworks during the baseball game mentioned earlier, could be linked to her father's experience. The intergenerational transmission of trauma worked both ways: just as Frieda's children inherited her trauma, she internalized her father's experiences. She was not present in the courtyard where the men stood and anticipated death, but she now recollects the moment with fear. This fear was caused by her father's memory of events—his life was at risk, and although he came back, he did not return without mental impact.

On October 10, 1941, the Jews were rounded up in a temporary ghetto from which the Nazis intended to move them to Transnistria. This was an area between the Dniester and Bug rivers and was established by the Romanian authorities to be used for mass killings. Thousands of Jews from the ghettos were deported to Transnistria and housed in two concentration camps (Ioanid 195–196). Frieda, along with her parents and younger brother, moved into a three-bedroom apartment with ten other families who were strangers. Fear lurked around every corner. In one of the rooms, an individual had typhus and this, according to Frieda, was the greatest fear aside from being transported to Transnistria. There were other fears in the ghetto as well, such as starvation, being arrested for being out on the streets past curfew, or being shot for exiting the ghetto.

It was only when I interrupted Frieda and asked if or how she maintained her childhood that she remembered having two girlfriends to play with in the ghetto. They were not allowed to attend school and had to find ways to entertain themselves. One way she filled in the time was creating dollhouse furniture from items she found lying around, such as matchboxes and pins. She taught herself to sew and would create doll outfits out of scraps of fabric that she found. This lasted throughout her life, and that skill provided her first income in the United States. Although Frieda was aware of her surroundings, she said her parents never spoke to the children about what was happening. Instead, Frieda listened from around the corner to her parents' discussions.

This was not normally a part of her publicly recounted story. Frieda has presented at schools for about fifteen years. Before that, she did not speak about her experiences. It was at the table during a Passover Seder, with her family surrounding her, when her eldest son wanted to know more. Prior to this, they knew that she was a Holocaust survivor, but the details were limited. From that point on, she said she did not stop talking about it. The Holocaust shaped Frieda, and by inviting her family into that part of her life, she began allowing herself to share her experiences outwardly to the world. Relieved of the burden of hiding helped to heal some wounds within her family, because they were able to better understand Frieda. As a part of her new outward expression, she spoke to USC Shoah Foundation and the Jewish Federation. The two groups contacted her to set up interviews, and then she began speaking at schools. It is her hope that by speaking she will touch at least one person in the group. I know that it worked on me. The hope that she has, stemming from her belief that her story can change the perspective of individuals, is something she holds dear. A part of this need to share comes from the desire to find meaning in her suffering, which for Frieda means preventing such atrocities from happening again. Frieda's mentality is that one person can make the world a better place.

She receives thank-you notes from the groups that she presents to, and there is one letter that she felt compelled to show me. Frieda pulled out a binder filled with cards. A young boy wrote her a poem that proved Frieda had touched at least one person in that group that day. His words were powerful as he wrote about the injustice of it all, and how he was sorry. He was an eighth grader.

Before Frieda began presenting her story publicly, she lived a quiet life married to her husband, Edward. As she put it, he was the driver and she the navigator. Of course, she was referring to the road trips they took, but this may have been true throughout their lives. They married when Frieda was nineteen years old, in June 1951, and their union lasted for fifty years. Their wedding took place not far from where Frieda currently lives. Sadly, the building no longer exists, but her memories do. Her in-laws arranged the wedding, as Frieda and her family had only been in the United States for a short period. They had nothing and no one at the time. After the wedding, Frieda recollects writing thank-you cards for gifts she received at her wedding, but had no idea who each person was.

She told me the story of her wedding day; although she laughs about it now, I imagine it was not entertaining at the time. As she waited at the venue, an hour passed before her fiancé arrived. Without modern technology, she had no way to contact him, something she now finds hard to imagine. Edward had made a wrong turn on the bridge and ended up in New Jersey. All the while, Frieda wondered if he had gotten cold feet. Thankfully, after they were married, Frieda took on the role of navigator, and if they became lost, they were lost together. She particularly remembers a trip to Canada where the couple planned to attend the Shakespeare Festival in Stratford, Ontario. Frieda made the mistake of taking a nap while Edward drove. She slept through forty miles, missed a turn, and they missed the performance. When the GPS was invented, Edward joked, "Perfect, I won't need you anymore." They made these trips twice a year after Edward retired.

Edward was there to support Frieda through her reunion with her uncle. Frieda recalled another significant journey: a family trip to Israel. It was 1969 and Mark was to have his bar mitzvah. Frieda packed up the family to see her uncle, the one whom she had lived with in Czernowitz. He was living in Israel, and she had not seen him since she left Romania at the age of thirteen. For Frieda and her brother, their uncle filled the role of protector and was a link to life that they were forced to leave behind in Europe. For Frieda, reuniting with her uncle stirred deep emotions connected to their shared Holocaust experience.

Tragically, Edward passed away in October 2001, following their fiftieth wedding anniversary. It is evident Frieda's marriage was a blissful one. When she talks about her husband, her face lights up, but interestingly, she never mentioned his name until prompted. He is not a part of her narrative, and I doubt many students ask about him as she does not mention his existence. That is not to say he was not a big part of her life, but rather that he is not directly part of her Holocaust story, because history teaches students that the Holocaust ended in 1945. However, her husband was there through Frieda's nightmares, the paranoia, and other symptoms related to the Holocaust. The role he filled was the connection and reminder that there is life after the Holocaust, though he also always served as a thread linking her to her prior experiences, preventing Frieda from ever fully separating from the Holocaust, even after it "ended."

Edward was an American, born and raised in Pennsylvania. Frieda had arrived two years prior to meeting him and began the eleventh grade with limited knowledge of English. Thankfully, she was well versed in Romanian, German, Yiddish, Russian, Polish, French, and Ukrainian, which provided a solid foundation for learning a new language. As she later joked, though serious, she once went to Italy for two weeks and felt the Italians wondered if she was from Italy. Her knack for languages is a skill that she relies on heavily.

Frieda attributes her ability to learn English in two months to her English teacher, Dr. Jordan. Many students did not like Dr. Jordan because of her strict demeanor, but her dedication to teaching enabled Frieda to become fluent and assimilate into her American surroundings. Assimilation was particularly important to Frieda, not because she did not love her home, but because assimilating was a means of survival. Throughout her journey in Europe, fitting in meant a deeper sense of security, which was the difference between life or death. As a part of her self-preservation, she met Dr. Jordan each day, and the teacher assigned Frieda an essay to write. Every morning, Frieda arrived at school early to review the essay with her teacher. Dr. Jordan was a stickler for grammar, much like Frieda is now. By the time Frieda entered college, she was skipping levels of English. She went on to win an award in English and Latin studies. Despite her fluency, she never lost her accent, though I am told it is less pronounced than it once was.

Frieda did not discuss the Holocaust with her husband; he knew what she had endured, and that was enough. In 2000, together they went to Poland to visit Auschwitz-Birkenau. As she said, "I simply told him we are going." They left Kraków via train to Oświęcim at night. She remembers looking out the window as they made the short journey. When the train halted, she imagined arriving via train to Auschwitz. She thought that reliving the journey that so many people like her took might help her, but it only made things worse. She had survived when so many did not, but her survival came with the price of guilt. As Frieda said, "I didn't suffer like them. That's why I went to Auschwitz. I don't have a number." Interestingly, although she was not a physical prisoner in the Nazi camp system between 1933 and 1945, she remained trapped in the notion of what it meant to not be a concentration camp or death camp survivor. For Frieda, this adds to the complexity of what it means to have survived, and impacts her life and the way she views her own survival.

It was at this point that I asked her if she thought there was a sort of hierarchy of suffering. As Frieda mentioned, she does not have a number tattooed on her arm, and for many people, being in a camp, forever marked by a number was a significant part of being a survivor. She said that she believes there is a hierarchy and for many people, if you were not in a camp, your story is not considered interesting or as valuable. It is her belief that the museum (from which she is assigned schools to speak) would prefer to send survivors of concentration camps rather than those who survived a ghetto and became children wandering through Europe in search of home, as Frieda had. Frieda noted that she had met another survivor who had hidden in France during the Holocaust but never considered herself a survivor because she was taught that you needed to have a certain experience to claim that title. Therefore, this woman never speaks of her experiences publicly because of the stigma that exists. She believes she did not suffer "enough."

As Yehuda Bauer stated,

> Holocaust survivors are only those people who were physically persecuted by the Nazis or their cohorts. This means people who lived in ghettos and concentration camps or compulsory labor frameworks, who hid or who joined the partisan ranks. I don't mean to denigrate the suffering of people who suffered from race laws and anti-Semitic decree, or those who fled with nothing in their possession, but they are not Holocaust survivors. (Barkat 1)

In Frieda's case, she and her family were forced to live in a ghetto, but it is a lesser known location, and Frieda knows that knowledge of Romania and the Holocaust is minimal, which impacts her own identity. Additionally, Frieda was a child when she was liberated from Europe, which affects the way in which she remembers. This will be further examined in the chapter about memoirs and how child survivors experience the hierarchy of suffering due to their age and link to memory, or lack thereof. According to Spicer, "All of the younger survivors, aged fifteen and under in 1945, brought up the notion of hierarchy without prompting and elaborated in extensive detail regarding its manifestations and how this made them feel" (Spicer 443). This deep-seated notion of exclusivity impacts the way in which one presents their own history, including Frieda, who understands what fragments of her trauma the museum would like her to present. It is also important to note that part of the Nazi mission involved exclusionary thinking and action. When historians or survivors create chasms among themselves as part of a hierarchy, irreparable damage can be done: "Suffering becomes competitive, definitions become a means of inclusion and exclusion, and the impact on individuals cannot be overestimated" (Spicer 447). This damage reflects trauma that was endured at the hands of the Nazis and, in turn, could take on a deeper meaning because of the continuation of suffering experienced by those who lived through a variety of atrocities.

In the continuation to ease her survivor's guilt, Frieda and her husband also visited Theresienstadt on their journey, although she did not have the same experience here. It was the ovens, or maybe it was more than that—perhaps it was the knowledge of lost loved ones at Auschwitz-Birkenau. She did not say. I asked how her husband responded to being at Auschwitz, and she said she was sure he was upset, but they did not talk about it. He knew to just move on. I think about this conversation now and wonder how lonely that must have felt.

I cannot imagine this was the first spell of loneliness Frieda felt. This sense of loneliness could be linked to her busy lifestyle and desire to keep in frequent contact with her family. For her, familial connections serve as an escape from herself and her trauma. Also, for Frieda, family is the most important part of life because from a young age that was all she had. She was not lucky enough to have a steady education or long-term friendships, and she spent only six years in school; prior to that, her learning was informal and arranged by her parents. Those six years were not sequential, and each was in different languages. At age fifteen, she would be the one foreign girl in a school of two thousand. I asked if Frieda was bullied during her school years, and she shook her head. In fact, she was unique, and people were curious about who she was, so much so that even today people from her school days will approach her and ask her if she is Frieda Wishner, and she will not recollect who they are. She did say that she struggled with culture shock.

Would it be possible to return to Romania? This is a question that resonates with her family members to the present day. When I first asked Frieda if she had ever been back to her first home, she responded, "I almost did. There was something that held me back, but I can't quite explain what." I asked her if it could be the fear that Romania would not be as she remembered. She said it is possibly a fear; she still yearns for Czernowitz. Frieda felt the concern that the space would not be physically the same, which it is not, and also that the feeling for the place would be gone. The Holocaust annihilated the Jews in Romania and any presence of Jewishness. The pre-Holocaust Romania was what Frieda felt was her home—the feeling of home that she longed for. To a degree, I could understand this. I had lived abroad, and each time I returned home it was always different— not necessarily in a negative way, but never the same. I explained this to her and asked if it was the sense of home that kept her attached to the place she lived for such a brief period of her life. Frieda's memory of the place that she calls her first home no longer exists outside of her memory; it was erased and will never exist again. With the erasure of the Jewish people from Romania, there can be no after because the before was eradicated: this erasure caused an absence that can be felt halfway around the world within Frieda's heart and mind.

This sense of home seems to weigh on Frieda because she has not returned, nor does she ever plan to return; however, there was once a family discussion about visiting, a sort of pilgrimage. Plans were drawn up, including a guide, maps were located, and important locations were marked. David seemed to be the driving force behind the idea. He wanted to go with his mother to the place where she had grown up and eventually escaped from. At the last minute, Frieda backed out of the trip. When I asked Frieda why, she said, "I guess that it was a fear that it won't be as it was." In part, I was told that Frieda likes to be in control, and returning to Romania would be an adventure into the unknown with many uncertainties. But this was not simply an idea that focused on Frieda and David; they wanted the family to go. Stanley, Rifka, Mark, David, and Frieda all had discussed the trip. Rifka did not want to go, and eventually Mark would not either. The different reactions from her children provide insight into the general responses of what it means to be the offspring of a survivor. There is no one persona that exists. For some it becomes a responsibility, for others a burden, and for still others a curiosity—and not always one feeling at a time. Pilgrimages are often crucial to the "memorial candle" of the family. They provide a deeper connection to the individual who is their survivor and contextualize the trauma that individual is still experiencing along with trauma that the child of the survivor is experiencing. When speaking to Mark, it became evident that at one point he wanted to go on the trip, but the idea had entered his mind that if Romania is void of any Jews, why go?

This decision seemed to weigh on David, the most eager to go. It was in 2018, during a search for family documents, when Frieda found a photo of her birth mother's headstone in Lipcani, Moldova (once Romania). Through her searching, she found where her birth mother was buried, and it even included a photo of the headstone. All these years, Frieda did not know where her birth mother was laid to rest, and now one more piece of the puzzle was filled in, and by some miracle the location still existed. This was the information that relit David's desire to visit to his mother's homeland. Frieda seemed interested in going, but she claims her health was not strong enough to travel, and although that may in part be true, I still wonder how much of her decision was influenced by the fear and anxiety that she had mentioned experiencing during her the earlier trip.

David emailed me to let me know he had made the choice to fly out during the summer of 2019 to try and locate the site. JewishGen had previously digitized the stone, and there was hope that it would still be viewable.[6] I received the sad news that the cemetery had grown over and essentially was a "jungle." He was unable to locate Frieda's birth mother's stone. This was meant to be a comforting moment, a physical link for the family to hold on to, but all David got was a reminder of the decimation of the Jewish population in the area.[7]

Maybe Mark was right. If there were no Jews left, what was the point? The place had changed dramatically. Jews were not saved from the horrors of the Nazis despite the pact between Hitler and Stalin; Germany invaded Romania on June 22, 1941, and Russia lost the land that once again became Romania, though now affiliated with Germany. The Romanians were members of the Axis powers and proved instrumental in carrying out attacks against their own people, especially the Jews.

The Weinschenker family was saved by the unlikely courage of the mayor of Czernowitz, Traian Popovici. He became the mayor in July 1941 and risked his life by negotiating the lives of 20,000 Jews whom he deemed necessary. Popovici informed the Nazis that he could not maintain the functioning of his city without these individuals. A system was set in place to distribute certificates to individuals and families that were deemed necessary for the function of the city. Each morning, starting in mid-October 1941 (not long after the decree was set in place for the establishment of the ghetto on October 11, 1941), Frieda accompanied her father to the building where the certificates were assigned and hoped their names would be called.[8] There were 50,000 Jews within the ghetto walls at its peak (Hirsch and Spitzer 2011: 130). According to Popovici's personal notes, the area designated for the ghetto "could not have sheltered more than 10,000 people pressed together.... It had to house 50,000 not to mention the Christian population that was living there" (134). With this large population and competition for survival, the wait became more daunting as each day went by because more and more Jews were being sent to Transnistria, and with that came the shrinking of the ghetto. In the fall of 1941, nearly half of the 30,000 Jews of Czernowitz were deported to Transnistria, where they died from hunger or typhus or were murdered in other ways (163). After six weeks in the ghetto, Frieda's family received their certificate stating that they were part of Popovici's integral Jews.[9] This certificate would be the only item that Frieda mentioned she wishes she still possessed. She is not sure what happened to the document, but she has a theory that it was left behind in Poland after they escaped Romania. Due to Popovici's bravery, Frieda and her family were saved from deportation and moved back to their apartment outside the ghetto.

Like all Jews in Romania and throughout Europe, they still faced restrictions. In August 1941, a curfew was imposed that allowed Jews, in groups of three or fewer, to be on the streets only from six in the morning until eight at night. The yellow star was required to be worn outside their homes, children were not permitted to attend school, and Jews were prohibited from teaching. Additionally, Jews could only go to the market between 9:30 a.m. and 11:00 a.m., making it challenging to receive what little food they were granted (Hirsch and Spitzer 2011: 176). Frieda's parents decided her education was an important part of her life, and they would pay a slice of bread to a teacher for a lesson. It may seem like a small price to pay, but when whole families were receiving limited rations, a slice of bread was essential to life. Her education proved to be sporadic at best because of the circumstances and risk of lessons. They were breaking the law by attending these lessons and being caught could mean death.

Frieda makes it clear that Popovici was her family's savior. She made a point of informing me that at the late Popovici's home, there was a plaque recently erected by a group of 300 people, serving to commemorate what he did for the Jews of his city. In recent years, Frieda's granddaughter wrote a piece about Popovici, which Frieda proudly presented to me while we sat at her table. Frankly, I thought the essay was going to be about Frieda and her life, but I found that the words the young woman wrote were more impactful. The narrative was about Popovici and how despite what he could have lost and what he lacked to gain, he still chose to protect the Jews. In turn, she linked this to the survival of her grandmother, and also to her own survival.

Not so long ago, Frieda's life was just like that of her granddaughter, a schoolgirl writing essays. Of course, as we have read, it was not as simple as that. Still, she received an education, some of which was done in secret by the sheer will of her parents. Education was a topic Frieda talked about with great pride. It is important to her, perhaps because she worked so hard to receive an education, or maybe because it is something that no one can take away once you have it.

This need and desire for education would extend through the various countries that she trekked through on the way to America. Frieda attended a Soviet Ukrainian school in 1944 after Romania signed the Rumania Armistice Agreement.[10] Despite her inconsistent schooling, she was placed in the fifth grade, and every child was required to have military training. "I think to this day I could take apart a rifle and put it back together again," Frieda told me with a bit of a chuckle. This indoctrination was familiar to Frieda, as she attended another Soviet school in 1940. During that period, she recalled having to wear a red kerchief to represent communism. This was one way Frieda remembered the Soviet Union's attempts to persuade Romanian youth to join their political movement.

As the transition of rule occurred in Czernowitz, a terrifying event befell the Weinschenker family. This legend was told in various ways and never fully detailed, but all versions agree that Clara was the driving force behind it.[11] In Czernowitz in 1944, as the Nazis were retreating, the family was home eating chicken soup and potatoes when they heard a knock at the door. A duffel bag containing their most valuable possessions—prayer shawls, prayer books, photos—lay on the bed, a detail recalled by Stanley. Two Ukrainian soldiers from General Andrei Vlasov's army broke in and discovered the "nest of Jews."[12] Frieda's uncle first stepped in, telling the officers that the family owned German books, but the soldiers saw Frieda and identified her as a Jew. She was twelve at this point, with dark hair and light eyes. Frieda admits she cannot recall what happened after this, not because she simply forgot, but because she had blocked it out.

Stanley provided the most details about what happened next. Clara stepped in and removed her children from harm's way, though he could not quite remember how she managed such a feat. Everyone remained safe. Clara took the children away from the room where the soldiers were. Stanley remembers his mother crying and recalls the startling cold as they hid outside without heavy clothing. They feared that Chaim would be taken away, but when the three returned, they found the soldiers took the duffel bag and left Chaim. When Frieda told the story, it was clear that she knew her mother saved her, but did not remember the courtyard where she hid or the stairwell where Stanley found cover. The family knew they were no longer safe, so they took their coats and went to Clara's cousin's house. This was not the first family legend that I had stumbled upon, each of which seemed to be a miracle.

The fear of the war may have ended, but the Soviet regime posed other issues for families. The Russians were welcomed by Romanians. They threw chocolate to the little ones on the streets and played their music loudly as their horses galloped along and tanks lined the thoroughfare. I imagined a fanfare of Soviet parades. When the fanfare died down about two months after the Soviets liberated the area, Chaim went out, to where Frieda can't recollect. He did not come back, and Frieda's family did not know where he had gone. Clara took action to locate her husband. Because

Frieda's father was under forty-five, he was sent to the aluminum mines in the Ural Mountains, where he was forced to work for nine months. His family waited for his return, not knowing if they would ever see him again. Stanley recalled how his mother and a group of other women gathered in their home. Each woman was alone because their husbands had been involuntarily placed in the mines. While discussing matters, the women would smoke. When the other women left, Frieda stole the cigarette butts and hid them in newspapers, and later Stanley and Frieda smoked together. As I listened to this story, I remember chuckling and thinking her little brother was snitching on her by recounting the mischief, a task I proudly took on many times as the younger sibling.

He told me another story about his father. Stanley suffered from an ear infection and could not sleep one night. It lingered due to the lack of available medicine. As he laid awake from the pain of his infection, he heard a knock at the door. Previously, such knocks brought terrible news. This time, it was their father who had returned from the mines, holding two aluminum rings and oranges. Stanley had never seen an orange in his life; maybe that is why he remembers it so fondly, or maybe it is because of this man whom the family at times doubted would return.

Frieda's parents decided to escape the oppressive rule of the Soviets, but to do so they needed to change their citizenship to Polish. Clara managed to have false papers created, and in 1945, they headed to Łódź, Poland, as Polish citizens. Their journey, which Frieda remembers taking place in a cattle car shared with several families, normally a ten-hour train ride, took three weeks due to the high volume of Europeans attempting to return home. It was not viewed as an important train and was often left on the tracks to let other trains pass. In Poland, they lived with an educated family that Clara had befriended. Throughout the year, they shared a small room divided by a blanket.

Bianca was only a year or two older than Frieda and was the daughter of the family that they resided with while in Poland. She went on to become a professor at California Polytechnic State University. Her family would also stop in Germany on their way to America, but they did not travel with Frieda's family. They arrived a few years after. Frieda keeps in touch with Bianca. For Frieda, this family was the one she remembers most regarding living arrangements. She did say that there were many families she lived with, but those memories are a bit hazy.

They stayed there until 1946, following the Kielce pogrom.[13] However, unlike other Jews who were fleeing the country because of the pogrom, her family was set on the goal of traveling to the United States and making a home there. Clara was attempting to secure passage for her family to leave Poland. She traveled to Warsaw to gather the correct papers. Chaim was not able to partake in the voyage because he was circumcised, and the partisans were checking. If a Jewish man was caught, he would be shot; however, Stanley, being a small child, was brought along as a sort of protection for Clara. As he recalls, people still held onto their humanity and would not harm a mother with her child. Just as Stanley was a form of protection for Clara, Clara always protected her children. During an outing, Stanley saw a soldier lying in a gutter with blood streaming from his head. He remembers the stark contrast between the color of the blood and the white snow underneath him. Clara tried to shelter her child from the grotesque sight, but it was too late; Stanley witnessed what humanity was capable of.

The Weinschenker family was fortunate to have family members living in the United States who sponsored their immigration. However, it was not as simple as buying a ticket and moving. Most of Europe was plagued with homelessness and people searching for lost loved ones. Homelessness was something many Europeans would not overcome, even those who found refuge in new countries. Many of their fellow countrymen had betrayed them. There was no one to return home to because they were killed in the war or murdered in the Holocaust. Few physical structures remained due to the bombings.

When speaking with Stanley, I asked about his experiences in Poland and what he remembered. He recalled Clara and her actions related to Poles, though the story did not take place in Poland itself. Clara risked her life and her family's by agreeing to hide two Polish siblings, a brother, and a sister. At this point, they were still living in Czernowitz in Frieda's uncle's home. The two Polish siblings stayed with them for a few months. When a rumor circulated through the city that anyone caught with stowaways would be punished, Clara decided to act. She did not simply evict the pair; instead, she found poison that would make them ill so they could be hospitalized. During this period, the Romanians did not permit the Nazis to enter hospitals and remove patients from their beds. The sister, who left behind a six-month-old child in Poland, could no longer stand the separation and returned to Poland. She was murdered. It is unclear whether the sister ever went through with the poison plan or if she started her journey back to Poland immediately. The brother survived and now lives in America. This heroic act of Clara's was never mentioned by Frieda. When I asked her if she remembered living with them, she said yes, but offered nothing more.

Many details remained mysteries to me. How did Clara managed to arrange for false papers? How did they learn about the pogrom? How did she encounter these siblings? When I asked about antisemitism and whether she had ever felt threatened in any country other than those under Nazi control, Frieda said she was not personally a target of antisemitism in any country where she had lived. This conversation took place just days after the shooting at the Tree of Life Synagogue in Pittsburgh, Pennsylvania. I also spoke to her son, David, during this period. He expressed his sadness about the events taking place. The shooting was only a few hours away from Frieda's home. She felt angered by these events—she lived through the largest campaign of antisemitism to sweep Europe, and now America was becoming more hostile toward Jews.

When speaking with Stanley about America, I sensed his patriotism. This could be because he arrived in America as a young child, and although he has memories of Romania and more broadly Europe, they were mostly scarred by the Holocaust. He mentioned that when he arrived in America, he refused to speak Yiddish or German and spoke only English. The new country was to be his home in every way possible. He maintained that the Holocaust could never happen in America because of its diverse population, thus taking on the persona of the optimistic American.

Frieda also has a sense of pride in being American, but it presents itself differently. She says that she is American and loves her chosen country. However, when Frieda encounters a stereotypically American action, she silently reacts with "Oh, that American." She attributes her feeling of belonging here to having a husband, a family, and a home, but something integral still separates her from being fully American. Like Stanley, she had not used her birth languages, except with her parents who have passed away—German with her mother, who died in 1992, and Yiddish with her father, who died in 1975. She wanted to belong in America, but now she teaches a Yiddish class and says the more she uses the language, the more it comes back. This could partly be her attempt to find her first home, as she cannot travel to Romania, or maybe it is a need to do her part in reviving the Jewish community.

Frieda can no longer physically return to her home in Romania as it was demolished, but she reconnects with her culture through language. As Frieda claims, it is like riding a bicycle. This part of her was not erased and has continued to live within her since childhood; however, Yiddish now carries an added layer of anguish as she cannot fully connect to the role the language had in her life prior to the Holocaust. As part of the Nazi plan, every aspect of Jewish life and Judaism was to be terminated, including language. Valiant efforts were made to keep Yiddish alive throughout the Holocaust, including classes in the Warsaw Ghetto and Theresienstadt. For Frieda, Yiddish is one of the languages of home—her first home and the one where she feels she belonged. This connection to her homeland, her family, and Jews as a whole enables her to continue being a European Jew in America. Additionally, there is a movement occurring for a revival of Yiddish, and Frieda hopes to be part of such an important restoration not only of a language, but also of a people.

While Frieda was still attending high school, Clara received an invitation to a bar mitzvah. Having been a refugee, she did not have a proper dress for the occasion, so Frieda bought a sewing machine on a payment plan of one dollar a week from her wages at a department store. She made her mother a beautiful dress for the event. It was for the son of the Polish boy Clara had hidden in their Romanian home. He was living in Woodbine, New Jersey, not far from their new home in Philadelphia.

It seemed that Frieda left behind a part of herself when her family set sail from Bremerhaven, Germany, toward America. But they were lucky. While in Germany, they contacted a major in the United States Army, who happened to be the director of the displaced persons camp and the son of Frieda's uncle's business partner. He managed to contact Frieda's relatives living in the United States and arrange travel for her family. It was a ten-day journey across the ocean, and Frieda slept for five of those days. When not sleeping, she was often found leaning over the railing, seasick. They arrived on the SS *Marine Flasher* on August 3, 1947.

Stemming from this conversation, Frieda discussed a photograph that had been discovered. It showed her family sitting on the edge of a cattle car. There are a few unidentifiable others in the photo, but the major who arranged their departure is in the middle. Frieda did not know the photo existed until much later in life. Through the Wisconsin Historical Society's website of an interview with the major who facilitated their arrival, she learned of the possibility of photographs. When told that there were photos not available online, she emailed the society to inquire about them. To her surprise, she received five photos. It was a special and rare find, something she is quite proud of. These photographs serve as a physical representation of what Frieda endured and with whom she had survived. When Frieda left Germany for the United States, she had few possessions. She was forced to leave behind material items that might have served as an ongoing connection from before the Holocaust to the present day, but that was not possible.

I asked her if there was a particular reason, she looked at the Wisconsin Historical Society, beyond the interview. She discovered that children who were forced to live in the Romanian ghettos were receiving restitution of 2,500 Euros from the German government if they could provide proof. For Frieda, it was a matter of principle. She requested an application and found it was twelve pages long, with all questions essentially the same but phrased differently. The first challenge Frieda faced was proving she was Jewish. Like the certificate from Popovici, her birth certificate is a lost heirloom. She does not know where it is, if it was destroyed, or how long it has been gone; however, she did have her religious Hebrew marriage certificate.

It was not as simple for Stanley. Frieda asked if he wanted to apply for restitution, but he declined. As Frieda says, he is a busy man. She did as any big sister would do—she filled out the form for him. They heard back from his synagogue that he was probably Jewish, but they could not prove it. In response, Stanley made a circumcision joke, and Frieda turned to Google for answers. This is when she found the interview and the photographs of her family leaving for America. Frieda's endless quest for knowledge was further evident in our search for more documentation. She always wanted to have the ship manifest that listed her family's information, and I found it one evening. I think it was a treasure for both of us. Her desire for a link to Europe is connected to her deep attachment to the Holocaust and her inability to escape its trauma.

Despite being registered on the manifest, the document did not automatically guarantee citizenship for Frieda and her family. During one of her presentations, she jokingly mentioned that she was an illegal alien upon arriving in the United States. This seemed to spark the interest of the upperclassmen, who were concerned she could be deported to Romania. She laughed. This was her way of addressing the political issue of undocumented immigrants. Like many survivors, she advocates for helping those in need and wishes to change how Americans view those often deemed "others."

We discussed the rest of her family and their views. When I asked if any of her children or grandchildren spoke Romanian, she replied, "No, they are American." This divorce from Frieda's past is a method to protect her children from experiencing being outsiders in America, as she had been and still can feel from time to time. I understood what she meant, but I found this to be a uniquely American response. She continued to say she wanted to blend in when she arrived, to mesh with the other kids, as being different was dangerous—dangerous not only on the scale of the Nazis but as any child faces being an outsider in a new school. Frieda did not want this for her children. Her parents felt the immense cultural shock. They never forgot their home, and it was not America. Although they made a life for themselves, they missed where they came from. For both her parents and herself, the inability to return to their homeland stemmed from pain that began during the Holocaust and never stopped aching. This continued absence of homeland, an outcome of Nazi destruction, proved to be an everlasting effect that still impacts Frieda today. It influenced how she raised her children and, in turn, how her children raised their children: devoid of the Romanian language, Romania itself, and other aspects of the culture. This persisted until Frieda began to speak about her Holocaust experience. This void is evidence that Frieda's method of coping is an attempt to move beyond the Holocaust, but the impossibility of doing so has seeped into each generation of her family. With this disconnect from Frieda's first culture, it is apparent that it is an attempt to protect her family from experiencing such traumas as she has. This absence of overt culture in Frieda's life is a separation from her childhood, which can be physically connected to the Holocaust.

Frieda was familiar with having to reestablish herself, but this does not mean she had abandoned the spaces in which she had lived or the person she became because of these relocations. Rather, she took these places with her and collected various aspects of them, such as their cultures and languages, to continue building who she is. It was the journey to America that made her aware of how precious a home is. Clara was the driving force behind their voyage westward. Upon trying to leave Poland, she found a convoy of Greeks headed in the right direction. Once again, Clara managed to change the entire family's citizenship to Greek, and they joined the convoy. Being a child, Frieda does not know how Clara arranged the citizenship changes, but Clara's ability to negotiate saved her family several times. The original plan was to travel with the Greeks to Cyprus and finally arrive in Israel. Stanley recalls how after the group was deloused in Poland, those in charge separated him from the rest of his family. He protested. Having kept the family together for so long, Clara acted and rerouted them to Munich, Germany.

To leave Poland, the family did not have transportation. They walked, but thankfully, they found a truck headed toward their destination. Clara and Stanley sat on the back with many strangers while Frieda and Chaim walked across the border. There were other times during their journey when they managed to find a peasant with a cart and horse. They would take turns resting from walking. Many of these individuals from their journey would become lost to time, shadows of memory. Frieda and her family were leaving behind their second home and divorcing themselves from yet another culture. This pattern adds another layer to the complexity of Frieda's inability to experience a "post-Holocaust." With each move, she lost a potential home and the possibility of stability. In turn, Frieda's life has been structured around having a homelife to prevent such loss from happening again. This prevention symbolizes her inability to escape the emotional and mental hardships she faced during the Holocaust through the physical representation of home.

As they traveled through Czechoslovakia and Austria, Frieda remembers being in Vienna. During their journey, they stayed at displaced persons camps (DP camps), each for brief periods. After finally arriving in Munich, they stayed in the Neu Freimann DP camp for six months and then moved into the city for an additional six months. Their apartment in Munich had four bedrooms and a dining room. Her family utilized the dining room as their new home, while other families lived in the four other rooms. She remembers how each family had to pass through the Weinschenker's room to get to their own spaces. There was rarely a moment of privacy.

Clara maintained their religious practice, and Stanley recalls her pulling blackout curtains over the windows out of fear during Passover Seder. Although the fear existed, she kept her family safe. She did not just provide security for her family; she also expressed her maternal side. Her son remembers being at a trolley in the winter when another woman had a child's sled in hand. His mother traded eight Pall Mall cigarettes for the sled that her children could enjoy.

Other than spending her time with her family, Frieda attended an all-girls school while living in Munich and entered the eighth grade. She was one of three Jewish pupils at the German school. I asked her if she had experienced any antisemitism while attending school and living in Munich. She shook her head, explaining that her classmates seemed to take pity on her and perhaps felt some regret for what happened. Frieda also felt that she was something of a curiosity, as they wanted to know about the few Jewish girls. Even her teachers were kind to her. She took a stenography course and, having never done so before, visited her teacher's home. While working with her teacher, she spoke German just as she had done with her mother. I wondered if this helped her fit in with the Germans, but she was not sure because the two other Jewish girls were also treated kindly. When I asked if she was open about her Judaism, she said yes. They all knew. Each girl attended a religious class, either Catholicism or Protestantism. Frieda chose to sit in on the Catholic class. She sat in the back of the room and worked on homework with the other Jewish girls. It was only during this class that she could feel the antisemitism; it was palpable. They were being taught that Jews killed Christ.

Moving into the city and pursuing an education was largely due to Clara's influence. This was a woman who was often the driving force behind her family's safety, and she was also a clear link between the generations of the family. Whenever anyone in the family spoke of her, it was only with positive sentiments. She provided the maternal support that Frieda lacked. Frieda lost many maternal figures in her life and admits that dealing with children is not always easy for her. It was Edward who wanted a family, while Frieda, I was told, was fearful. I found that Stanley summed these emotions up rather well. He said, in tears, that as a child you are fearful, apprehensive, and think of yourself as not good enough, that everyone is against you, and there is not a way to rationalize it. This was Frieda and Stanley's childhood, and Frieda did not want this for her children. As a mother, Frieda cannot abandon the concept of what motherhood is about—for her, it is survival. This continued consideration of what will help her family survive and what cannot be taken from them if something were to happen is a part of her Holocaust experience. Clara had instilled that education was an important part of life, and Frieda took this lesson and passed it on to her children. This is her way of coping and an attempt to provide what maternal expression she can toward her children. Additionally, Clara often took on maternal roles for her grandchildren when Frieda could not, including being a shoulder to lean on during challenging times, which is understood as a representation of the strong role Clara had to take on throughout Frieda's life.

Frieda did not plan to be a stay-at-home mother and housewife. She has three children—two to replace her parents and one for the Holocaust. Her sons describe their childhoods and that of their sister's differently, as I would have compared to that of my own brother. It was with David that Frieda took classes outside of their home. He also felt that emotions were not generally expressed outwardly, as if emotions were somehow dirty. Although this is true, today it seems the Holocaust has, in a sense, brought them closer. Frieda, as I witnessed, comes alive when talking about her life. This inability to divorce the Holocaust from her current family reflects that she does not have a "post." This closeness was not always present because she could not speak of the Holocaust openly; however, the need, not want, to express her experience to her family highlights how it has shaped her. Yet, I also understand how this could frustrate someone, especially in a parent-child relationship—a relationship that Frieda had not experienced in the traditional sense due to the Holocaust. This is often what she calls her children about, the Holocaust; however, I am told when she drinks, her warm, humorous, and loving personality prevails. Maybe then her guard is let down.

Although this may be true, Frieda taught her children tolerance, a point Mark made during our second conversation. When I speak to Frieda, she is always telling me some tidbit of information she has found, more often than not about the Holocaust. This seemed unique to me as she knows it is my field of interest, but this is also part of who she is. She sends these items to her children and to her brother. In a way, I believe this is part of her coping, but also a way to connect with her loved ones. Frieda wants to share her life story and try to convey a depth of understanding about the Holocaust to her loved ones. She is trying to get them to understand her and why she is the way she is. She does not have a separation from the Holocaust, and as she continues to cope with her Holocaust experience, she attempts to connect with her family. As with any group, there is a desire to pass on knowledge of life. Frieda speaks about her experiences, but she is also self-aware that Holocaust survivors are passing away. She speaks of the desire to have her children pass along her story and talk publicly, but she has never directly asked them to do so. In a sense, this lack of communication is not uncommon.

For David, it was Clara who would tell him about their life in Europe. She was open about their life and struggles during the Holocaust, but for Frieda, this part of her life was not something she wanted her children to be privy to, and this caused a strain on Frieda's relationship with her children. Maybe this is why Frieda was fearful of having children. She could not protect them from her past, as she could not forget who she was and is.

Frieda typically will not speak to groups younger than eighth grade. Her belief is that they cannot truly grasp what she is saying.[14] But can adults truly understand? She argues no, but maybe a bit better than younger children. Not surprisingly, Frieda belongs to a book club. Like her son who had recommended Holocaust books to his child's school, Frieda had suggested Aharon Appelfeld, an Israeli Romanian writer and Holocaust survivor, to add to the book club's list. When Frieda suggested it, the group responded that they had read enough about the Holocaust. Imagine telling a Holocaust survivor that you had enough.

There are, however, groups dedicated to Holocaust survivors and their kin. When I asked Frieda if she ever arranged or attended an event with other survivors, she told me that it did not interest her to join such a group.[15] A few months later, I posted a question to the Bessarabian/Moldavian Jewish Roots group and the Generations of Shoah International (GSI) group on Facebook about how to arrange a cemetery cleanup. Frieda liked the post and then emailed me ideas for people to contact. I wondered if it was easier to be a part of a group where one did not have to always be an active member but could still feel a sense of belonging. Although she now speaks publicly, being active in a group of survivors meant that others would know details that were unspoken in a presentation. These details are unknown to outsiders, and they are not known to her family either. However, there are family stories that I do not imagine any listener of Frieda's story would think to ask about.

As a part of our journey, I shared stories of my family with her, including that of my dog, who I adopted a year before meeting Frieda. I showed her pictures, and she politely seemed unimpressed. I asked her how she felt about animals, particularly dogs—maybe in part because I needed vindication that it was not my animal that she disliked. She told me a story about how her father taught her to fear dogs. When he was growing up, peasants told their dogs to attack Jews, and thus, Frieda associated dogs with hatred. Despite that, she continued with a story that I found entertaining and provided great insight to Frieda and her family dynamic. Her youngest, David, was turning nine and, like many children, begged for a dog. One day Frieda found him sitting with a *yarmulke* on his head in their home. She inquired as to what he was doing, and he said that he was praying for a dog. Frieda began to chuckle at this moment, asking herself, "How could you make an atheist out of the kid?"

Frieda agreed that the next day she would take David to the ASPCA for an inexpensive dog. David and three of his friends arrived from school, anxious to pick out his new dog. Concerned that the ASPCA would be closed, Frieda called and learned they only had thirty minutes before the facility closed for the day. David was adamant that they would make it in time, as long as his mom picked up the pace. They arrived as the gates were closing, but David convinced them to let him in. They agreed that whatever dog he picked would have to be small. He found a small mutt, and the woman working there said he would not grow and would not shed. Yet, he did grow, and he did shed. Their family dog lived with them for thirteen years, including the years David was at college. Sadly, he passed away from diabetes, and as Frieda puts it, after his passing, she was shortly thereafter diagnosed with diabetes. With a bit of chuckle, she added, "God punished me." Today, David has a family dog that he says Frieda will pet, but there are times when she becomes uneasy around the animal. Although her relationship with canines has improved, Frieda still struggles with her deep-seated fear that the dog will attack her. This illuminates the struggle that Frieda faces each day, stemming from the antisemitism in Europe and the inability move past the terror. Although Frieda did not show her maternal side often, I think this was a brief glimpse into how she expressed it.

As the maternal figure, Clara said what she thought, especially to her family. There were family vacations where Frieda and her children went out to California to visit Stanley, Chaim, and Clara. As Clara aged, she began to experience painful arthritis, and Chaim was having heart issues and wanted to be near his cardiologist, Stanley. While on vacation in Desert Hot Springs for three weeks, Chaim tragically suffered a heart attack and passed away. Frieda wanted her mother to return to Philadelphia, but she refused. Clara wanted to be near her husband's final resting place. She lived in California for eighteen more years until she passed away.

Clara is buried with her husband in California, near where Stanley resides. I asked Frieda how often she sees her brother, and she said usually annually, although it can be difficult because he suffers from arthritis, and sitting on a plane for a long period of time is challenging. She said that the last time he planned to come out, he canceled because of a hip replacement. As Frieda said, "Getting old isn't that fun. Do everything you can while you can." She went on to comment that that was her husband's philosophy on life, as well as her son Mark's. While speaking to Mark, he mentioned that he was more like his dad but looked more like Frieda.

Mark was the middle child, although for nine years he was the baby of his family until David came along. I asked him about his childhood and how he thought having a mom who was a survivor impacted his upbringing. He responded he had a normal childhood, and his mother encouraged him to excel, but to excel in education rather than focus on other childhood dreams like sports. She was a tough mom, something I could still see today in their relationship. Her belief was that if you received a "B," it may as well have been an "F." Edward wanted Mark to join the family business, a hardware store, but Frieda told him to be himself. Mark says that he attributes his success to Frieda. She was the driving force for his motivation, much like Clara was the driving force for Frieda.

I am not sure if her family has phrased it this way, but I believe Mark served as Frieda's motivation for visiting and presenting at schools, as he first broached the subject. Having attended her talks, Mark says that it is amazing to watch her speak to students and that he, too, continues to learn new pieces of her story. I believe that speaking about the Holocaust gave her another sense of purpose. When I asked her if she remembered what it was like when she first began to speak publicly, she said she never gave it a thought, and that after being quiet for so long and generally anxious about speaking, she was glad and relieved. That is why when the museum calls her to talk, she always goes. These talks serve as a continuation, an inability to let her own experiences slip from her mind. She is continuously recalling her trauma and sharing it with those who cannot understand what she continues to endure, both by surviving and by retelling her story. She cannot escape the trauma of the Holocaust; there is no after.

When I heard her say this, it sounded like a coping mechanism. When I asked, she said she was not sure if it was, but that it was an obligation: "You can learn it from a book, but it is not the same as talking to a survivor." I believe this is a motto that many feel is true when speaking of the Holocaust or other traumas. As a part of her trauma, she lives with survivor's guilt, and by carrying the burden of witnessing, she may be able to ease that guilt. Frieda has many anecdotes about the students she has spoken to and with. She shared a story about a school that enrolls students who have previously dropped out and are returning to finish their degrees. The typical student is in their early twenties. After speaking to a class there, she remembers one student who asked many questions and afterward went to the computer room and continued searching for more information.

During the first few interviews, Frieda mentioned a young man with whom she previously worked to produce an article about her life. He was a high schooler from Downington, and at his school, they host a Holocaust symposium annually. To prepare for the event, students are taught about the Holocaust for three months before attending an assembly with survivors. Following the assembly, the students break off into smaller groups to meet the survivors. In recent years, the school constructed a monument honoring those who were murdered during the Holocaust and those who survived. On either side is a willow, chosen because willows bend but do not break. Frieda's final comment about the event was that the teacher who started the program was not Jewish.

I always find this interesting because I am frequently asked if I am Jewish. In fact, very early on, Frieda inquired, and I told her, "no," which seemed to spark her interest. This is a conversation that I have had many times, and I admitted to her that the more I answer it, the less I think it is significant to the conversation. Although she understood what I meant, she went on to tell me about a college graduate who attended one of her lectures. Frieda mentioned that the places she inhabited were occupied by both the Soviets and the Nazis; in response, the student asked what the difference was between the two groups. Frieda said she could not believe it—here was an educated young woman who did not know who the Soviets were and who the Nazis were. Tragically, as Frieda states, this could be due to the limited mandatory Holocaust education throughout the United States. Frieda was a woman who fought for her education, learned new languages, and was frequently the outsider, but still obtained as much knowledge as she could. Frieda went to college and earned her degree. Yet, there are many people who do not care to be informed, in Frieda's mind. She is concerned that the farther away we are from certain history, the less people care. Instead, you find revisionists who care only about distorting history. Frieda was faced head-on with revisionists from the Committee for Open Debate on the Holocaust (CODOH).[16] While on the elevator of her building, her neighbor commented that she heard Frieda was an interesting person, but Frieda was not sure why, so she Googled herself.

What she found was not what she expected. There was a conference hosted by Holocaust revisionists who had published a list of Holocaust survivors, including the likes of Frieda and Elie Wiesel, stating that these individuals had not presented since the 1990s, which is not accurate. The group claimed that those who did share their stories were only doing so to gain fame and fortune. Frieda questioned where her fortune was. It is groups like CODOH that Frieda hopes will be combated with knowledge gained from survivors and their descendants. This phenomenon of revisionists, or denialists, contributes to the complexities of using the term "post-Holocaust." With groups like CODOH, certain individuals are attempting to annihilate the Holocaust as a whole, including survivorship. If historians permit the idea of "post-Holocaust," they are opening a gateway for these groups to claim that the Holocaust was not nearly as traumatic as it truly was.

REFLECTIONS

The enduring impact of the Holocaust in Frieda's life demonstrates that survivor experiences transcend traditional historical boundaries. Far from being confined to the years 1933 to 1945, Frieda's Holocaust narrative centers on the aftermath—1945 and beyond—when she began processing the trauma that would define her identity. Her commitment to education through testimony reflects not just a desire to preserve memory, but to a way to transform personal suffering into collective understanding.

The concept of displacement provides a powerful lens through which to view Frieda's experience. Despite officially shedding the "displaced person" status, she remains emotionally tethered to her Romanian origins—a connection that underscores how displacement functions as both a literal and psychological state for survivors. Her fragmented education, lack of consistent friendships, and absence of a stable home reveal the profound disruptions that extend far beyond the chronological end of historical events—a non-event.

To truly comprehend what constitutes a "Holocaust experience," historians must challenge the limitations of terms like "post-Holocaust," which artificially separate past from present. Survivorship itself presents ongoing challenges that demand our attention. Frieda's testimony illuminates how the Holocaust continues to unfold across generations, suggesting that our historical frameworks must evolve to encompass both emotional truth and chronological fact—recognizing that for survivors, history is not simply remembered, but continuously lived.

2
WRITING HISTORY WITHOUT HINDSIGHT
THE IMPOSSIBLE TASK OF LIVING WITHOUT THE HOLOCAUST THROUGH THE EYES OF DIARISTS

> *"For them, the world was now fundamentally different, different in its suppositions as well as in the material circumstances to which they were daily subjected. In and through their diaries, they responded to the staggering psychical and physical changes. They reoriented themselves vis-à-vis the past and replotted their part in the future. And the diaries they created turned out to be not a separate and particular cultural response, but an integral part of other cultural responses—literary, theological, historical, familial—to Nazi persecution."*
> —ALEXANDRA GARBARINI, *NUMBERED DAYS: DIARIES AND THE HOLOCAUST*

Diaries serve as witnesses to historical events and provide insight without the hindsight typically found in memoirs or testimonies. These written artifacts take many formats and serve multiple purposes: they can be letters to loved ones, companions during periods of deep loneliness, or means of preserving one's voice beyond death. For this research, the analyzed diaries have been translated into English from various languages. Notably, not all diaries were intended for public consumption, which is often reflected in the writer's methodological choices.

While the Holocaust is traditionally viewed as ending in 1945, this chapter—following the philosophical framework established throughout this volume—considers diaries written from 1945 and onward to also fall under the category of a Holocaust diary. As trauma theorist Cathy Caruth argues in *Unclaimed Experience: Trauma, Narrative, and History*, trauma disrupts linear temporality, creating what the author terms "belatedness" in narrative experience (17).

Through these diaries, historians encounter chronology rather than memory, though this does not mean that the writers experience time linearly. As Holocaust scholar Lawrence Langer notes in *Holocaust Testimonies: The Ruins of Memory*, survivors often experience "durational time" rather than chronological time, where past trauma constantly interrupts the present. Many writers reflect that their chronology was interrupted or fundamentally altered by their experiences of trauma.

This chapter examines the act of writing in terms of the diary's various roles that it fulfills for the diarist and as a symbol of resistance. Drawing on Dominick LaCapra's concept of "writing trauma" from *Writing History, Writing Trauma*, we analyze how the everyday act of diary-writing helped individuals process their uncertain lives. Rather than following a linear timeline, this chapter is organized thematically to highlight the complexity of temporal experience in diaries. Although entries are often chronologically marked, writers frequently record multiple days in one session, demonstrating what trauma theorist Dori Laub calls "temporal collapse" in *Testimony: Cries of Witnessing in Literature, Psychoanalysis, and History*. This approach reveals various writers' experiences of the same events, contributing to our understanding of the macro and micro historical perspectives. How can diaries help historians develop a deeper understanding of history vis-à-vis the multiplicity of stories they contain? These diaries, and more importantly the diarists, provide emotionally complex accounts of the Holocaust that transcend traditional historical documentation. Drawing on Marianne Hirsch's concept of "postmemory" from *The Generation of Postmemory*, these texts transmit trauma across generations through their intimate documentation of lived experience. Thus, Holocaust diaries should be classified as historical documents, as they provide both contemporaneous information and insight into the emotional implications of events.

The chapter also analyzes writers who emphasize age—their own or others'—specifically addressing the loss or cessation of childhood and how this disruption of temporal constructs alters an individual's ability to continue life as it once was. This analysis builds on Michael Rothberg's theory of "multidirectional memory," which examines how trauma creates overlapping temporalities and memories. Time constructs were maintained through documentation of significant dates and events, including religious holidays, personal holidays (birthdays, anniversaries), and wartime events.[17] These dates often acquired additional meanings for diarists, both emotional and physical, fundamentally altering their experience of time.

As Geoffrey H. Hartman argues in *The Longest Shadow: In the Aftermath of the Holocaust*, trauma disrupts not only individual temporality, but collective historical consciousness. When historians impose their own understanding of time rather than engaging with diarists' temporal experiences, they lose crucial dimensions within the narratives. What is lost is the soul's story and the depth of its destruction. As Elie Wiesel wrote, "The ultimate mystery of the Holocaust is that whatever happened took place in the soul" (Wiesel 1985: 239). This dismissal of the soul and its systematic destruction should not be ignored by historians, as it constitutes a fundamental aspect of the Holocaust.

Finally, this chapter examines accounts of suicide, whether of individuals known personally to the diarists or strangers. These suicides reflect the existential disparities that accompanied the Holocaust and the hopelessness faced by Jewish people. While suicide marked the end of an individual's physical existence and personal narrative, diarists' accounts preserve something of the essence of these lost souls. As Shoshana Felman suggests in *Testimony: Crises of Witnessing*, the act of witnessing through writing creates a form of survival that extends beyond physical death. These suicide cases form an essential part of Holocaust history and reflect humanity's transformation. These victims must be remembered alongside those who were directly murdered by the Nazis.

What, then, could the term "post-Holocaust" mean? Each section addresses how the Holocaust cannot end for the writer or their subjects, and how the erasure of the "before" precludes the possibility of a future or a "post-Holocaust." As Ernst van Alphen argues in *Caught by History: Holocaust Effects in Contemporary Art, Literature, and Theory,* trauma disrupts the possibility of narrative closure. Additionally, we analyze how the termination of life through murder at the hands of the Nazis fundamentally ruptures the possibility of a "post-Holocaust." This builds on James E. Young's concept of "received history," which examines how traumatic events continue to shape both individual and collective memory across generations.

THE ACT OF WRITING

To examine time and the concept of "post-Holocaust" in Holocaust diaries, we must consider Alexandra Garbarini's pivotal work, *Numbered Days: Diary Writing and the Holocaust.* For Jewish Holocaust victims, diary writing "'emerged from a deeply rooted Jewish literary tradition of bearing witness to tragedy as a means of transcending it" (Garbarini 3). This act of testimony, as Laub argues, represents both a confrontation with trauma and an attempt to integrate it into consciousness. Garbarini further explains that "In Judaism, history is invested with meaning, for it is in history that God's relationship to the Jewish people is revealed" (41). These dual perspectives—one referencing a future witness burdened by the Holocaust, the other seeking connection to a past relationship with God that the Holocaust may have rendered impossible—exemplify what Caruth calls the "double telling" of trauma, where past and future collapse into an eternal present (Caruth 7).[18]

This temporal tension reflects diarists' dual function: preserving what was while maintaining hope for what could be. Yet neither perspective can escape the Holocaust's shadow, even following 1945. As Garbarini accurately claims, "genocide transformed the function of diary writing" as Jews confronted unprecedented horrors that remain incomprehensible to those who have not experienced them, a theme throughout these chapters (130). This incomprehensibility aligns with what Langer terms "deep memory"—the raw, unassimilated experience of trauma that resists narrative integration.

For some writers, the diary served as a confidant, someone to listen without judgment, as David Patterson suggests in *Along the Edge of Annihilation: The Collapse and Recovery of Life in the Holocaust Diary* (Patterson 1999: 41). This function becomes crucial when considering what Robert Jay Lifton calls "psychic numbing" in *Death in Life: Survivors of Hiroshima*—the psychological defense mechanism triggered by exposure to massive trauma. The diary provided space for writers to process their evolving identities amid genocide's physical, mental, and emotional devastation: "It is a means of capturing a trace of presence by seeking a trace of significance in the midst of a time that is draining into the void" (Patterson 17). Through maintaining a diary, diarists attempted to preserve time itself, which Patterson argues constitutes the measure of humanity (85).

Chaim Kaplan's compulsion to write, "Record! Perhaps I am the only one engaged in this work, and that strengthens and encourages me" (Kaplan 144), exemplifies what Felman and Laub describe as the "imperative to tell" in trauma testimony. Kaplan's concern for his diary's fate in his final entry—"If my life ends—what will become of my diary?" (400)—transcends mere historical preservation, suggesting what Giorgio Agamben calls "bear witness" in *Remnants of Auschwitz*—the urgent need to testify beyond one's own survival. Through Kaplan's writing, it is apparent that his diary is not merely a witness, but a friend and support system. The demise of his diary is a loss of two futures.

For most diarists, their attempts to maintain temporal continuity ended abruptly with their murders. This rupture exemplifies what Maurice Blanchot terms "the disaster," an event so catastrophic that it destroys the possibility of its own representation. These diarists cannot experience a "post-Holocaust" because their temporal experience has been fundamentally altered by trauma. Drawing on Hirsch's concept of "postmemory," their legacies become inextricably bound to the Holocaust, as evidenced by how Anne Frank's diary has become the paradigmatic Holocaust text, often serving as a problematic point of comparison for other diarists like Rutka Laskier and Petr Ginz. For example, Laskier is referred to as the "Polish Anne Frank," and on the cover of the English translation of Ginz's diary it states, "Recalling the diaries of another teenage victim of the Holocaust, Anne Frank, [Peter Ginz's diaries] reveal a budding Czech literary and artistic genius whose life was cut short by the Nazis." This review contextualizes Ginz's diary in connection with Anne Frank's diary, which other than being child Holocaust diarists, the two authors do not have similar experiences and are not comparable. All this to say that these diarists are not able to escape their direct link to the Holocaust, their diaries, but also, they are now interconnected with one another despite having different experiences and having never met. It is only through the Holocaust that they share a life and a death together, or they share the lack of a "post-Holocaust."

The emotional dimensions of Holocaust diaries deserve careful consideration through the lens of contemporary affect theory and trauma studies. Beyond comparing diarists' experiences, we must examine the emotional toll of both enduring and documenting the Holocaust. This analysis builds on Lucien Febvre's groundbreaking 1941 essay "Sensibility and History: How to Reconstitute the Affective Life of the Past," which argues for studying emotions to prevent historical repetition. As Ruth Leys argues in *From Guilt to Shame: Auschwitz and After*, affect and trauma are inextricably linked in Holocaust testimony, creating what she terms "affective temporality"—where emotional experience shapes temporal perception.

Historians must study the emotions reflected in Holocaust diaries to understand how trauma impacted victims' daily lives and capacity for survival. Ann Cvetkovich's work in *An Archive of Feelings: Trauma, Sexuality, and Lesbian Public Cultures* provides a framework for understanding how trauma archives—including diaries—preserve not just events, but emotional experiences that might otherwise remain invisible to history. By studying the affective dimensions of historical events, we develop what LaCapra calls "empathic unsettlement"—a form of historical understanding that acknowledges both the specificity of trauma and its resistance to full comprehension.

Some diarists explicitly aimed to document emotions, aligning with what Lauren Berlant terms "intimate publics"—spaces where personal feelings become historical testimony. Others attempted to produce objective historical records by suppressing emotional content. However, as trauma theorist Bessel van der Kolk argues in *The Body Keeps the Score: Brain, Mind, and Body in the Healing of Trauma*, trauma inevitably manifests in testimony, even when writers attempt to maintain emotional distance. This aligns with contemporary neuroscience research on trauma's impact on memory and narrative formation.

I argue that attempts to create emotion-free historical records ultimately prove impossible, as humans cannot fully separate emotion from experience, particularly when processing trauma firsthand. As Judith Herman notes in *Trauma and Recovery: The Aftermath of Violence*, trauma disrupts not only the capacity to narrate, but also the ability to maintain emotional boundaries between past and present, observer and participant.

Emanuel Ringelblum's writings exemplify what LaCapra terms the "impossible witness," a historian attempting to maintain scholarly distance while personally experiencing trauma. His initial efforts to document the experiences of others while minimizing his own presence reflects what historian Saul Friedländer calls "the limit of representation" in trauma narratives. For instance, when recording being struck for not saluting a German on September 29, 1940, Ringelblum maintains emotional distance, yet this represents one of his rare personal disclosures. What Young terms "collected memory" emerges in Ringelblum's documentation of the ghetto's collective mood rather than his individual experience.

However, this scholarly distance gradually erodes as trauma intensifies. Ringelblum's increasing use of "we" rather than maintaining objectivity demonstrates what trauma theorist Kai Erikson calls "collective trauma," the gradual breakdown of communal bonds under extreme duress. The moment his careful documentation breaks down entirely comes when confronting children crying alone in the streets because they are orphans and starving: "The couple of *groschen* I give them nightly cannot ease my conscience" (Ringelblum 241). This rupture aligns with what Laub identifies as "the collapse of witnessing"—the point at which traumatic reality overwhelms the capacity for objective documentation.

In contrast, Chaim Kaplan's Warsaw Ghetto diary is what Langer calls "tainted memory," the oscillation between hope and despair that characterizes traumatic testimony. Kaplan's March 10, 1940, entry, "The gigantic catastrophe which has descended on Polish Jewry has no parallel, even in the darkest periods of Jewish history" (Kaplan 129) demonstrates what Rothberg terms "traumatic realism"—the struggle to represent unprecedented historical trauma.

Kaplan's evolving perspective on historical analogy illustrates what Hartman calls "the dialectic of trauma"—the tension between comparing and acknowledging the incomparability of catastrophic events. His initial attempt to find historical parallels—"We are returning to the Middle Ages. The Jews created another world for themselves in the past, living in it forgot the troubles around them, allowed no one from the outside to come in. As for parallels: The present expulsion is one of the worst in Jewish history, because in the past there were always cities of refuge" (82)—gives way to recognition of the Holocaust's uniqueness: "History does not repeat itself. Especially now, now that we stand at the crossroads, witnessing the death pangs of an old world and the birth pangs of a new" (300). This shift exemplifies what Caruth calls "unclaimed experience," the gradual recognition of trauma's unprecedented nature.

The diary serves not only as a confidant, but also as an act of defiance or resistance. In his chapter titled "Repression, Ghettoization, and Protest" in *The Holocaust in Bohemia and Moravia*, Wolf Gruner examines understudied forms of resistance, particularly individual acts of defiance that scholars have often overlooked in favor of collective resistance. Gruner effectively demonstrates how to study both individual and collective resistance simultaneously. He uses Ginz's diary alongside examples of collective resistance, presenting both forms without diminishing either's significance. A reader focusing solely on the Ginz diary sections would still grasp Gruner's core concepts, missing only specific examples of collective action.

Ginz's diary writing represents individual resistance against imminent death, distinct from collective acts Gruner describes, such as Jews refusing restricted shopping hours or providing dirty laundry instead of clean furs when demanded (Gruner 281). Through these parallel examples, Gruner establishes that individual diary writing carries equal importance to collective resistance. However, Gruner stops short of framing diary writing itself as a potential collective act of resistance. We can strengthen Gruner's analysis using James C. Scott's concept of "hidden transcripts"—resistance forms that happen below official notice. When combined with Michel de Certeau's "everyday resistance" and Zoë Waxman's "testimonial practices," we can understand diary-writing as an act that preserves both individual and collective memory against deliberate erasure.

The comparison between Ginz's individual resistance through writing and collective acts like the Oneg Shabbat archive demonstrates what Hirsch terms "connective histories"—the way individual and collective memories interweave to create comprehensive historical understanding. The Oneg Shabbat archive exemplifies what Pierre Nora calls "*lieux de mémoire*" (sites of memory)—deliberate attempts to preserve cultural memory against destruction.

As Sam Kassow stated in a lecture during a 2021 educator workshop, "they turned pens into effective weapons." Unlike bombs or guns, these textual weapons did not have immediate impact on their targets; rather, they were long-term instruments of memory, the effects of which would strike years later. The Oneg Shabbat archive highlights this delayed impact, beginning with the discovery of milk jugs containing documents in 1950. "*Lieux de mémoire*" takes on particular poignancy here, as these buried archives became physical sites of remembrance.

Each act of writing, whether in hiding, a ghetto, a concentration camp, or elsewhere, posed a mortal danger to the writer, their family, and their surrounding community. This defiant resistance can be understood through what Scott terms "weapons of the weak," seemingly small acts that constitute significant opposition to power. For many who sensed their impending doom, writing became what Langer calls "testimonial life," a means of ensuring their existence would outlive their physical death. Although not all diarists consciously wrote to resist the Nazis or their fate, the act of writing itself, regardless of intention, amounts to "everyday resistance." This resistance operated on multiple levels—against evil and against time itself.

When examining resistance through writing, we must distinguish between collective efforts like the Oneg Shabbat archive and individual acts of private diary-keeping. As Garbarini notes, "Diaries may have constituted a form of individual and collective resistance, but that does not mean the process of writing a diary necessarily conferred on an author a sense of relief or that it was an effective means of preserving selfhood. The power of diary writing should not be overstated" (8). However, I argue that the term "author" implies an intent to publish that wasn't universally present. Furthermore, while writers may not have all experienced relief or successful self-preservation through writing, the power of diary writing cannot be overstated. These testimonial acts provide "empathic unsettlement"—a unique window into the Holocaust unmediated by hindsight. The raw emotions documented in these pages constitute what Felman terms "the crisis of witnessing"—testimony that cannot be replicated. As Patterson argues in *Along the Edge of Annihilation: The Collapse and Recovery of Life in the Holocaust Diary*, the act of diary writing during the Shoah transcended mere defiance or resistance, becoming testimony to the very possibility of bearing witness.

TIME CONSTRUCTS

While diaries are traditionally understood as chronological records creating linear pathways through experience, this framework becomes problematic when examining Holocaust diaries. As Caruth argues, trauma disrupts temporal linearity, creating what she calls "a break in the mind's experience of time." Historians cannot verify when diarists actually recorded their dated entries, destabilizing what Nora terms "calendar time"—the official chronology of events. Moreover, adhering strictly to chronological analysis of diaries imposes what Langer calls "chronological privilege"—a rigid framework that fails to capture how events resonated with their witnesses. For instance, when a diarist records both a rumor of another ghetto's liquidation and news of their family's impending deportation, the temporal proximity of the deportation might dominate their immediate writing.

Significantly, diaries differ from memoirs in their relationship to memory and temporality. As Michael Bernard-Donals argues in *An Introduction to Holocaust Studies*, diary entries represent what he terms "traumatic immediacy"—writing unmediated by foreknowledge of future events. This contemporaneous nature of diary writing, free from what Young calls "retrospective testimony," challenges traditional historical emphasis on chronological narrative.

Lang's observation that historians operate within conceptual limitations—analytical, chronological, and topical (84–89)—highlights what

Friedländer terms the "limits of representation" in Holocaust historiography. These constraints compel historians to impose artificial narrative structures—beginnings, middles, and endings—onto experiences that, for diarists living through the Holocaust, existed in what Agamben calls "suspended time"—a temporal space where conventional chronology loses its meaning. As Garbarini accurately articulates,

> They contended that the sense of resolution, or closure, created at the conclusion of a historical narrative contradicted the excess of suffering of the victims, their experiences of chaos and disorder, and ultimately the silence of their deaths. By concluding a history of the Holocaust with either the chronological end point of Allied victory and the liberation of the camps of the rhetorical tying together of loose ends by answering the questions laid out at the beginning of one's study, the historian suggested a movement from catastrophe and the unknown to redemption and the establishment of the stable truth. (12–13)

Historical closure remains inadequate for Holocaust victims and others whose identities were fundamentally altered by their experiences. As LaCapra argues, historical "working through" does not necessarily correspond to psychological or emotional resolution. Such imposed endings provide what he terms "narrative closer," while failing to address emotional, financial, physical, and psychological wounds.[19]

Consider Leyb Goldin's Warsaw Ghetto diary, where time becomes reconceptualized through the prisms of death, food, and humanity. His documentation of waiting for soup personifies what Johannes Fabian calls "body time," the way physical needs reshape temporal experience. Goldin measures time through hunger, reducing the wait by an hour because standing in line means having already started the process and smelled the nutrition (Roskies 2019: 116). This hourly countdown, as Lifton might argue, represents what he terms "death time," the consciousness of mortality reshaping temporal experience. Goldin's focus on hours rather than days or weeks reflects what Blanchot calls "the time of absence," existence measured against imminent extinction:

> Time—and time. Now it stretches like rubber, and then—it's gone, like a dream, like smoke. Right now, of course, it's stretched out horribly, horribly; it's really enough to kill you. The war has been going on for a full two years, and you've eaten nothing but soup for some four months, and those few months are thousands and thousands of times longer for you than the whole of the previous twenty months—no, longer than your whole life until now. From yesterday's soup to today's is an eternity, and I can't imagine that I'll be able to survive another twenty-four hours of this overpowering hunger. But these four months are no more than a dark, empty nightmare. Try to salvage something from them, remember something in particular—it's impossible. (121)

Goldin's words illuminate how time was reconceptualized in the ghetto and more broadly throughout the Holocaust, transcending historians' finite periodization. I argue that, though perhaps unintentionally, the temporal distortion he describes in relation to starvation extends beyond the 1945 liberation period that historians traditionally mark as the Holocaust's end. His measurement of time through soup becomes both timekeeper and daily focal point, revealing a devastating reduction of human existence to animal survival. Despite maintaining a diary, he references food in nearly every passage to mark daily events. This forced measurement of time through starvation rather than human relation represents not only physical death, but the death of the soul—a Nazi strategy to strip Jews of their humanity.

Time's cruelty manifests differently in his contemplation of mortality: "But it's possible that tomorrow or even today I'll give up the ghost. The heart is a sneak—you never can tell. Maybe I'm lying here for the last time and feeling so sluggish for the last time." (120). While initially appearing as resignation to impending death, a deeper reading suggests potential release from the Holocaust-altered time and suffering—an acknowledgment of the ghostly existence he had already become.

Chaim Kaplan writes of existence amid pervasive fear and destabilizing rumors: "It is hard to live in a time when you are not sure of tomorrow, and there is no greater torture than waiting. It is the torture of those condemned to death" (Kaplan 203). He notes that even when good news evokes doubt rather than hope, ghetto inhabitants recognize that relief can only be temporary. Like Goldin, Kaplan lives day-by-day or hour-by-hour, finding futility in hoping for an uncertain tomorrow. His temporal perception shifts from anticipating tomorrow to dreading it, haunted by questions of survival and future horrors.

When historians create a finite period for the Holocaust and suffering more broadly, we must consider experiences from their perspective. Must there be a "stable truth," and what implications does this have for the concept of "post-Holocaust?" I argue that history needs to have a stable truth—if it did, historical study would be unnecessary. However, as scholars, we have a responsibility to recognize that we are still living history and cannot ignore how our studies affect others. By imposing neat chronological endings, we delegitimize ongoing suffering and potentially overlook valuable scholarship.

Drawing on Edith Wyschogrod's concept of the "heterological historian" from her book *Saints and Postmodernism: Revisioning Moral Philosophy*, we must emphasize historians' responsibility to those whose voices have been silenced or erased from history. In this context, historians' erasure occurs through declaring the Holocaust complete after 1945, disregarding continuing suffering. Wyschogrod is not alone in critiquing historians' approach to trauma and history.

Lucien Dreyfus argued in his Holocaust diary that history should belong to the arts rather than sciences. He provocatively claims that historians took pleasure in rewriting history for their own musing, asserting that they considered "truth" least of all and that only contemporaries could legitimately write about history (Garbarini 39). In essence, he contended that without living through the Holocaust, one could not judge history without distorting it. While Dreyfus's criticism of historians' tendency to adapt to new findings has merit, his claim that most reputable historians rewrite history for personal amusement goes too far. Nevertheless, historians' hindsight provides both advantages and potential limitations in researching events. Diarists writing contemporaneously maintain a more immediate emotional connection and understanding of unfolding events.

Patterson argues that "truth" resides within Holocaust diary pages, explicitly challenging Young's approach in *Writing and Rewriting the*

Holocaust, which treats Holocaust diaries merely as historical documents (Patterson 1999: IX). Young claims diarists' proximity to events precludes authoritative perspective (Young 25). I counter that historians' distance from the emotional dimensions of events necessitates such evidence. Patterson questions Young's position by examining readers' motives—while Young assumes readers seek only "historical facts," Patterson suggests they may be more invested in what he calls "the diarist's life of the soul" (Patterson 1999: 9).

When considering the writer's soul, we must examine what the Holocaust destroyed, particularly time itself and the possibility of a future—losses that preclude any true "post-Holocaust" existence. Patterson argues that the Holocaust diary's audience includes the dead, as the diary serves as testimony for the future (24). This begs the crucial question: if the dead constitute part of the audience, does this erase the possibility of a "post-Holocaust?" I argue yes, precisely because the dead must remain part of the audience, the Holocaust will outlive its victims, making a "post-Holocaust" period impossible.

Returning to the diarist's position, the writer attempts to escape time while simultaneously trying to recover irretrievable events through writing. As Patterson observes, "the Holocaust diarist does not advance; she merely wanders and waits and wanders. Already knee-deep in the rubble of any hope for tomorrow, she does not inscribe her diary in time; rather, she takes up an effort each day to inscribe time into her diary" (Patterson 1999: 71). The diarist does more than merely document historical moments—the individual attempts to express how the Holocaust fundamentally altered time itself. In essence, the diary fills a void in this liminal space where conventional human understanding of time and its sanctity has been ruptured. Patterson continues:

> With this erasure of the what next, the is and the was are obliterated. The abolition of time into nonexistence places the Holocaust diary and its measure of time into a singular category. In the Holocaust diary the measure of time is not a tracking of the days of a life; rather, it rises in a struggle to retrieve time, and with it the traces of a life. Briefly stated,

the measure time in the Holocaust diary entails the recovery of a past reconnected to a present made meaningful by a future. (71)

If time is obliterated, as Patterson argues, we lose our ability to situate ourselves within the world's framework, destroying our relationship to the other—a rupture that cannot be reconciled. This irreconcilable break in temporal experience precludes the possibility of a "post-Holocaust."

Cultural anthropologist Michel-Rolph Trouillot argues in *Silencing the Past: Power and the Production of History* that historical narratives present unequal voices, reinforcing power structures that harbor silences—typically the voices of the oppressed rather than the oppressor. Simply put, history typically privileges the victor while erasing the defeated. While some narratives are slowly shifting, dominant voices still predominate historical discourse. However, in genocide, the concept of "winners" becomes problematic—survivors continue to bear their trauma, while perpetrators fail to achieve their goals of annihilation. Additionally, perpetrators may face justice, though rarely. While these represent only two groups within genocide's framework, they are proof of Trouillot's concern with historical voice and power.

When examining diarists through Trouillot's lens, we see them providing voice to the murdered, though some diarists belonged to the perpetrating collective and wrote for different motivations—a topic warranting separate study. Considering Trouillot's argument about history's silences alongside Dreyfus's assertion that only those who lived through events should write about them, we can understand Dreyfus's concerns as potentially stemming from historically perpetuated silences imposed by historians. This suggests historians bear both responsibility and capability to bring marginalized voices forward. This might explain why diarists continued writing despite risks to themselves and others.

The diarists thus assume the role of silence-breaker, ensuring their voices reach historians and the public—defying Nazi intentions of erasure. However, these voices remain eternally bound to Holocaust victim or survivor identity. Without the possibility of separating from this identity, they cannot achieve a "post-Holocaust" existence.

THE MEANING OF CHILDREN

In Jewish tradition, children are understood to be the future, and without the future what becomes of a civilization, a culture, and hope? As the *Zohar* claims, "the world is upheld only by the merit of the 'breath' of little schoolchildren who have not yet tasted sin ... the breath of the little ones becomes 'voice,' and spreads throughout the whole universe, so that they become the guardians of the world" (3: 121). It is this breath that the Nazis sought to smother, and to prevent from forming words, and if these children are not given the opportunity to raise their voices, they cannot uphold their futures or the future of the world.

This section examines how the murder of Jewish children foreclosed any possibility of what Young terms "post-memorial future." Children themselves recognized their precarious position, producing what LaCapra calls "testimonial witness" through their diaries. It is evident that the children understood the horrors of the Nazi regime and wrote diaries to stand witness for their final years in lieu of themselves. Adult diarists frequently returned to children in what Agamben terms "paradigmatic figures" of humanity's depths. Through these dual perspectives—children's self-documentation and adults' observation—readers encounter "the crisis of witnessing" in its most profound form: the destruction of futurity itself. It is through these two routes that the reader may begin to comprehend the loss of a people, the loss of a future, and the continuation of suffering.

Adam Czerniaków, head of the Warsaw Ghetto's *Judenrat*, emerges as what Laub terms a "witness to witnessing." His logbook-diary hybrid represents what historian Friedländer calls "integrated history," administrative record fused with personal testimony.[20] Throughout his writings, Czerniaków repeatedly expresses what Lifton calls "symbolic immortality," the drive to protect children as bearers of cultural continuity.

One of Czerniaków's primary objectives was maintaining children's education, which can be understood through multiple theoretical lenses—what Maurice Halbwachs terms "collective memory preservation"; what van Alphen calls "futurity work," maintaining hope for Judaism's continuation; and what Hartman describes as "humanitarian witness," documenting human dignity and catastrophe. Czerniaków's first statements about the schools were written on September 21, 1939, only twenty-one days after the Nazi invasion of Poland. He mentions the "hit" that struck the school where his wife taught (Czerniaków 76). His words express how it was a great blow to both him and his wife. From there, his commentary continues to express the sadness that Jewish schools were not permitted to operate. On June 4, 1940, registration of schoolchildren began for a Polish school rather than a Jewish school (157). By September 24, 1940, Czerniaków wrote that they had been permitted to instruct children once again, necessitating the creation of the School Commission. This constant back-and-forth about whether schools would be officially permitted continued throughout the existence of the Warsaw Ghetto. While the Nazis aimed to destroy not only Jews but anything Jewish, including education of future generations, the education of Jewish youth could not have been deemed such an imminent threat by the time of the Warsaw Ghetto Uprising, as the Final Solution had already been established at the Wannsee Conference.[21]

Mary Berg, born Miriam Wattenberg, was barely sixteen years old when she was first imprisoned in the Warsaw Ghetto. She wrote a diary-memoir, which she completed after fleeing Europe in 1944. Berg became one of the children who benefited from Czerniaków's protective stance toward children. She was classified as a member of the privileged youth because her mother was an American citizen. This status would lead to her immediate family's release and eventual arrival in the United States. Her physical escape from the Holocaust makes her diary-memoir particularly interesting, as most diarists did not survive. Her voyage to the United States did not end her link to the Holocaust, as evidenced by her inability to know what happened to her friends and her need to complete her diary.

As part of this privileged group, Berg maintained a written record of the "luxuries" she was afforded, even while confined within the ghetto walls. In early 1941, she enrolled in a graphic arts course that she claimed provided an escape from the ghetto's horrors. The atmosphere proved pleasant despite the visibly starved bodies of those taking part in the course. Her education provided her with a reprieve, and she was not alone in this. Other students who were not as privileged as Berg would receive bread rations from collections gathered by their peers.

Her course was not the only one offered to the youth of the ghetto. She also participated in a poster contest for children and won first prize. Her prize included a monetary gift of two hundred *złotys*, presented by Czerniaków, who gave a brief speech (123). Such monetary prizes offered hope for survival, not only to the winning children, but to their families as well. This particular attention to children from Czerniaków was not unique to those who wrote diaries, though we must consider his comparative power within the ghetto to act and assist the youth. Through the lens of trauma theory, as articulated by Caruth, this focus on children represents both a response to collective trauma and an attempt to preserve future memory. On a personal note, Czerniaków was separated from his own son, a topic he reflects on sporadically throughout his diary. I argue it was not a primary point of focus as his diary was not a traditional diary rather more a logbook, as noted earlier.

Czerniaków's diary demonstrates what Laub identifies as simultaneous witnessing and experiencing of trauma. Early in the diary, he focuses on education and occasionally the orphanages, but by 1941, his entries shift primarily to recording starvation and death among the children in the ghetto. By May 8, 1941, "bread cost 12 *złotys* [per kilogram loaf] and watery milk 4–4.5 *złotys* per liter. Children starving to death" (232). In what can be understood through Langer's concept of "choiceless choices," Czerniaków responded to the horror of watching children starve by establishing a kitchen for children whose parents were working in camps (259).

The rupture of normal temporal existence, which LaCapra identifies as a characteristic of massive trauma, is evident in Czerniaków's increasingly urgent attempts to save children. He met with the Provisioning Authority to secure fats and sugars for 2,700 schoolchildren (318). By April 20, 1942, he ordered raids on stores with "luxury foodstuffs. Sardines, chocolate, bacon fat, cakes, etc., were confiscated. The cakes were distributed among the children in the streets. The rest will be given to the orphanages" (345). A month later, he ordered another requisition of luxury foods, this time from restaurants for distribution to orphans (358). He stated, "The most tragic dilemma is the problem of children in orphanages, etc. I raised this issue—perhaps something can be done" (385).

Drawing on Hartman's work on witness testimony, we can understand these diaries as historical and repositories of trauma. As Patterson wrote,

"Among the children of the Holocaust, as we have seen, the murder of their bodies begins with the undermining of their being; before they are killed, their child*hood* is killed" (Patterson 1999: 200). As a teenaged diarist, Rutka Laskier wrote, "I am writing this as if nothing has happened. As if I were in an army experienced in cruelty. But I'm young, I'm 14, and I haven't seen much in my life, and I'm already so indifferent. Now I am terrified when I see 'uniforms.' I'm turning into an animal waiting to die. One can lose one's mind thinking about this" (Laskier 30).

This temporal distortion was echoed in Berg's diary: "Yesterday was the Day of Atonement, and today is my birthday. I feel very old, despite the fact that I am only nineteen" (Berg 236). Time had become distorted, with these "children" experiencing more death than life and more hardships than many adults had in their lives. As Berg tragically wrote, "The number of our friends is growing smaller and smaller" (Berg 219).

Sarah Fishkin, a Jewish Polish seventeen-year-old diarist, wrote on June 25, 1941, "All thoughts of staying alive become shrouded in great sadness. I feel in my heart the desire to perish together with my family, to end my young life beside my parents." (Holliday 337). This reveals the destruction of the fundamental assumptions about safety and continuity that normally enable children to develop, according to Herman. For a child to reflect on life only through the lens of sorrow rather than joy, and to express a desire for death, reveal the anti-world in which she existed. Fishkin could not maintain hope in life, nor redeem her lost childhood, which had been replaced by endless sorrow. Through her diary, the reader learns that Fishkin, like other child diarists, understood that everyone, regardless of age, would meet the same fate. While this universal end is true in times of peace, Fishkin conveyed something more profound: they would all meet this end by force. Additionally, Fishkin and the other children faced a complete absence of future, unable to orient their lives toward a future self—a key aspect of childhood. Through this loss of future orientation, their youth was effectively obliterated:

> It is difficult to believe that the good times are gone, that our moments of joy, the hours of studying and enjoying ourselves are past, that I must give up forever my thoughts of future goals and the fantasies I hoped to

see realized. I would never have believed that it would all disappear so soon, be cut down, burned out, orphaned in so short a time. Emptiness and desolation, saddened aching hearts, are our present constant companions. There seems to be no future for the Jewish population. (338)

Breaking down her words, Fishkin first focuses on the activities that she once experienced as a child—having fun and going to school. These pastimes traditionally orient themselves toward a future, one that Fishkin, along with other children of the Holocaust, would never live to experience. Through "durational time," she acknowledges the absence of a future for the Jewish population, including herself, meaning she cannot and will not experience a "post-Holocaust": "No human heart can remain untouched and unpained by all this. It is beyond human endurance to see so much trouble and so much suffering experienced. It is painful to see people tortured by people until life is ended" (338). Her observation aligns with what Laub identifies as the collapse of witnessing—even survivors, as Fishkin poignantly writes, would not emerge untouched by the Holocaust and all that they have suffered.

The account of an unnamed teenaged diarist in the Łódź Ghetto demonstrates his role as the caretaker to his younger sister. In what he considers a moment of weakness, he steals his sister's bread after consuming his own portion three days before the next distribution (Holliday 397). His subsequent guilt-ridden confession reveals an innocence lost: "We are so tired of 'life.' I was talking with my little sister of twelve and she told me: 'I am very tired of this life. A quick death would be a relief for us'" (400). His emphasis on "life" exemplifies what LaCapra terms "founding trauma"—they could no longer live as young people should. Both siblings had lost their capacity to enjoy life, with his sister preferring death to their current existence. Their childhoods ended abruptly with the Holocaust, and their futures were likely terminated prematurely by the Nazis, leaving no space for a "post-Holocaust."

Dawid Sierakowiak, a teenager in the Łódź Ghetto, wrote, "A student from the same grade as ours died from hunger and exhaustion yesterday. As a result of his terrible appearance, he was allowed to eat as much soup in school as he wanted, but it didn't help him much; he's the third victim in the class" (Sierakowiak 90). The theme of children's deaths permeates his diary: "The statistics show an unbelievable increase in the number of children and young people sick from tuberculosis here, and the hearse is as busy as ever" (96).

As their peers disappeared or died, these children began to distance themselves from their age groups. This served as a defense mechanism, particularly as the Nazis deemed children unfit for work: "The Germans are demanding all the children up to age ten, the elderly over sixty-five, and all other sick, swollen invalids, people unable to work, and those without employment. The panic in the city is incredible" (215). By tearing away their innocence and declaring them useless, the Nazis declared the Jewish future pointless. The children were forced into becoming adults to be useful to the Reich. Laskier witnessed, "These children are the most predominant symbol of the gray ghetto. The parents have been deported, and the children were left abandoned to their destiny, to go stray in the streets. The people's faces express sadness and worry" (58). Her use of "these" children indicates psychic numbing, as she distances herself not only because of her privileged status, but also through her inability to accept what she is witnessing. Sierakowiak's clinical notation states that, "Eighty infants, all frozen to death, were supposedly brought to Łódź from Koluszki today. They were the children of deported Jews" (72) is an example of Herman's "traumatic dissociation." Although Berg, Laskier, and Sierakowiak were children themselves, their consistent references to "other children" without self-inclusion suggests they could no longer identify with childhood itself. Whether they survived or not, the impossibility of reclaiming their childhoods provides evidence that they could not and would not experience a "post-Holocaust."

HOLIDAYS AS A FRAMEWORK OF TIME

This section examines two perspectives on calendar dates through the lens of the victims of the Holocaust. The first considers religious holidays, including Passover, Rosh Hashanahh, and Yom Kippur, and the second, personal holidays, including birthdays and wedding anniversaries.

"Durational time" is evident in how the Nazis were known for their particular cruelty during Jewish holidays within both the ghetto and *konzentrationslager* (KL) system, as documented in numerous diaries. Young diarists especially noted their birthdays and their transformed meanings, demonstrating "founding trauma." These dates function beyond mere temporal markers; they represent an attempt to maintain connections to the past while serving as a reminder of the impossible future. The empty chairs at birthday celebrations or uncertainty about a loved one's fate haunts survivors.

The diary of Hannah Szenes (Senesh) demonstrates Laub's impossibility of witnessing. On September 23, 1939, this Jewish Hungarian teenager wrote of arriving in Palestine alone, her mother remaining in Hungary and her brother in France. Her Yom Kippur entry reveals survivor guilt. Yom Kippur is considered the highest of holidays and the most solemn day of the year in Judaism, and Szenes spent it dreaming of the Holy Land. The "day of repentance" encourages introspection, prayer, and atonement, with the hope of entering the new year having been forgiven for past transgressions. Szenes felt the twinge of guilt as she had left Hungary and was in Palestine, leaving her mother alone in a dangerous world. In observance of Yom Kippur, Jews fast at sundown until nightfall the next day. The end of the fast is often concluded with a feast called "break-fast," where family and friends gather to reconnect, an act that Szenes could not fulfill.

Szenes expresses her loneliness: "I made an accounting of what I had left behind, and what I had found here, and I didn't know whether the move would prove worthwhile" (Holliday 319). Her growing apprehension as communication with family becomes restricted demonstrates "traumatic disruption" of normal familial bonds. Although her diary does not bluntly express that her connection from such a young age to Zionism stemmed from what was happening in Europe, she was aware of the war that had engulfed her world.

On June 29, 1940, Szenes writes that her brother can no longer communicate with his family because of the establishment of the Vichy government (220).[22] It is at this point that her words turn to apprehension and fear because of the known and unknown. Her mother is still able to communicate and writes a concerned letter fearing that her daughter may be worse off than she is, but Hannah feels guilty for having the safety she is experiencing in Palestine (327).

By Rosh Hashanahh, September 21, 1941, Szenes experiences a disruption of traditional religious time compounded by living away from her mother for two years and her brother for three. The holiday's emphasis on divine judgment and future promise becomes complicated by her separation from family. One more year passed, and she wrote that she had received a letter from her mother. In the letter, her mother tries to protect her, but Hannah understands the fear that her mother attempts to mask. From her mother's letters, Hannah experienced further pangs of survivor's guilt: "Sometimes I feel a need to recite the Yom Kippur confession: I have sinned, I have robbed, I have lied, I have offended—all these sins combined, and all against one person. I'm so overwhelmed with this need for her at times, and with the constant fear that I'll never see her again. I wonder, can I bear it?" (329). This entry reveals what Leys called "guilt without fault"—the psychological burden of survival. What then could this mean for Szenes's repentance and future? Despite the distance from Europe, the Nazis were able to tear apart at the seams of Szenes's Judaism.

On June 12, 1943, Szenes enlisted in the British Army, and by January 1944 she headed to Europe to fight, her form of repentance. As a member of the volunteer paratroopers with the British Army, Szenes was captured by the Hungarian Arrow Cross; despite being tortured for weeks, she did not betray her sources. The Arrow Cross apprehended her mother, Katherine, as a way to threaten Szenes, but she did not betray her people. Eventually, Katherine was released; however, her daughter remained in the custody of her torturers. Katherine went to great lengths to try to find her daughter legal assistance, but Hannah had been labeled a spy.[23] Tragically, Katherine was not able to save her daughter, and ultimately Hannah was murdered by firing squad. She became a hero and a martyr for her people.

Katherine survived the Holocaust and continued to keep daughter's memory alive (Tydor Baumel 1). What then does this mean for Szenes's "post-Holocaust" or her mother's? Her mother moved to Palestine, just as her daughter had done in 1943. Katherine organized Hannah's remains to be buried in the military cemetery on Mount Herzl in

Jerusalem. That same year, a kibbutz was established named in memory of her daughter, "Yad Hannah" (Tydor Baumel 1). These commemorations meant that Katherine could not and would not abandon the memory of her daughter or the Holocaust. Additionally, these dates became anniversaries directly associated with Katherine's loss stemming from the Holocaust. With the use of Szenes's diary, it is evident that both daughter and mother will forever be connected to the Holocaust. It is through her diary that Katherine held onto her daughter and learned more about her life in Palestine.

The diary of Yitskhok Rudashevski, a fourteen-year-old Lithuanian boy in the Vilna Ghetto, documented Jewish holidays and the impossibility of maintaining traditional observances under Nazi persecution. In his September 12 Rosh Hashanahh entry, he avoided commenting on his family's celebration (Holliday 157). The New Year is typically celebrated by the sounding of the shofar, prayer, and partaking in festive foods and sweets; however, as a prisoner of the Vilna Ghetto, the Jews could not risk observing the holiday, as being caught meant death. This shows what LaCapra's "empathic unsettlement"—the recognition of extraordinary circumstances have transformed the ordinary: "poverty has been scrubbed away. Formerly this would not have made an impression on me" (Holliday 158).

Eight days later, Rudashevski writes of Yom Kippur, the holiest of holidays in the Jewish religion. Rudashevski reflects on the somber feeling in the ghetto and introspects his relationship with Yom Kippur. As Rudashevski agonizes,

> A sad mood suffuses the ghetto. People have such a sad High Holy Day feeling. I am as far from religion now as before the ghetto. Nevertheless, this holiday drenched in blood and sorrow which is solemnized in the ghetto, now penetrates my heart. In the evening I felt so sad at heart. People sit at home and weep. They remind themselves of the past. . . . Drenching each other with their tears as they embrace, they wish each other a Happy New Year. . . . I run out into the street and there it is also the same: sorrow flows over the little streets, the ghetto is drenched in tears. (160)

Although Rudashevski admits he was not particularly religious before his imprisonment in the Vilna Ghetto, he confesses that this particular day weighs heavily on his heart because of the lives lost. He writes of those forced to spend their holiest day mourning the murdered and yearning for an irrecoverable past. The blood and tears that mark the date cannot be erased from the holiday, as these individuals will never again take their place at the table.

Dawid Sierakowiak also reflected on holiday experiences as a way to understand his present conditions: "Our holiday starvation will be identical to what we experience every other day of the week" (Sierakowiak 77). This poignant statement proves that Jews were deprived of any ability to observe their religious holidays and traditions. The Nazis relished every opportunity for the Jews to starve, and never allowed a moment to break the fast, a meal traditionally shared with family and friends.

This torturous starvation would tear apart Dawid's family: "Tremendous anxiety pervaded our household because before the holidays Father took a bit of bread away from me" (151). He hoped his mother would defend her children, but she was dying just as their father was. Dawid's parents would die not long after this moment that fractured his family. Left to fend for himself and his younger sister, who would also tragically succumb to starvation, Dawid's experience exemplified how the Holocaust's annihilation of families removed the possibility of a "post-Holocaust" future.

Marg Berg also wrote about her connection with Jewish holidays. With varying emotions, she wrote about the Day of Atonement on September 23, 1939, when the Nazis began "an intensive bombardment of the Jewish district" (Berg 6). Berg observed that the Germans deliberately selected Jewish holidays to inflict their worst torments on the Jewish people. The assault was not only physical, but psychological, emotional, and spiritual. The depths to which the Nazis were willing to attack Jews and Judaism proved their aim was not simply to annihilate the people, but everything that made them Jews.

Two years later, on September 20, 1941, Berg recorded her apprehension about the upcoming Rosh Hashanahh, noting growing fear that the Nazis planned a savage attack on the Warsaw Ghetto for the New Year: "Alas, our apprehensions before the holidays were justified. Only yesterday, on the eve of Rosh Hashanah, the Germans summoned the community representatives with Engineer Czerniaków at their head and demanded that they deliver at once five thousand men for the labor camps" (87–88).

Each year, Berg marked the holiday season with remarks about the Nazis' strict adherence to the Jewish calendar. On October 1, 1941, before sunset, when the Kol Nidre prayers were taking place, an announcement ordered residents on the right of Sienna Street and other areas to relocate before October 5 (96).[24] Less than a year later, the Nazis blockaded Ostrowska and Wolynska streets on Yom Kippur, forcing 380 out of 2,500 policemen to maintain the area while deporting the remaining 2,120 policemen and their families (181). Those who were forced to work on their holiest day were, to say the least, spiritually tortured.

Chaim Kaplan corroborated Berg's account of Nazi destruction during holidays. On December 15, 1941, he wrote that the first day of Hanukkah "has been turned into a day of mourning. The courtyard of the prison on Dzielna Street was turned into a slaughterhouse today" (Kaplan 283). Hanukkah serves to mark the deliverance of the Jews from oppression under the Syrian Greeks in the second century BCE. Seemingly, this holiday being celebrated in the Warsaw Ghetto is ironic as the Jews were once again being oppressed for their existence. Despite this, some Jews continued to observe Hanukkah in secret to maintain their identities.

Kaplan described the carnage of the shooting that occurred in the courtyard on Hanukkah. Two days later, Kaplan noted the absence of Hanukkah candles and the total blackout throughout the ghetto. He reflected on how beggars were ignored despite the holiday's philanthropic traditions. On the eighth night, the *Judenrat* organized a festival to mark the opening of the school, deliberately avoiding acknowledgment of the holiday due to the Nazi threats (285). These altered observances and the inability to respect the traditions of Judaism made it impossible for Jews to maintain their identities, both in the moment and in any potential future, permanently marking Hanukkah with the impact of Nazi persecution.

In his diary, Rudashevski also marks his birthday. On December 10 he writes,

> It dawned on me that today is my birthday. Today I became 15 years old. You hardly realize how time flies. It, the time, runs ahead unnoticed and presently we realize, as I did today, for example, and discover that days and months go by, that the ghetto is not a painful, squirming moment of a dream which constantly disappears, but is a large swamp in which we lose our days and weeks. (Holliday 172)

His statement carries dual significance. First, he comments on his personal sense of time in relation to his birthday, and second, he reflects on the collective time experience of those in the ghetto. Notably, he only mentions his birthday in passing, suggesting he received no traditional celebration for this important date. Birthdays lose their significance for those who know they will not survive, as these dates merely mark days closer to their demise. The second aspect of his writing reveals how time in the ghetto was not merely a terrible memory or passing moment, but rather a void that consumed time itself, and with it, humanity. This consumption means those who lived in the ghetto could never escape its lasting impact, making a "post-Holocaust" existence impossible. Adam Czerniaków marked his twenty-eighth wedding anniversary with his wife by noting the absence of his son, Jas, whose fate remained unknown to them (Czerniaków 256). He intermittently wrote of their shared concerns about their son in Lvov, having no knowledge of his fate since the Nazi invasion. Their wedding anniversary became yet another reminder of their son's absence—what should have been a day of celebration instead marks the void of both celebration and son.

The Nazis' brutal marking of Jewish holidays in the ghettos created inescapable trauma. These days, which should have been times of celebration and religious observance, were transformed by the Nazis into periods of fear and dread. For Holocaust survivors, these dates would become anniversaries of deportation and murder. The empty chairs at holiday tables could never again be filled by loved ones, but instead became occupied by haunting memories of their murders.

SUICIDE: THE LAST ACT

As diarists documented their struggle to survive, they recorded others' suicides. The term "choose" is inadequate here, the concept of "choiceless choices" better describes their situation. The inhabitants of the ghettos, camps, and other areas throughout Europe were aware of the horrors they faced and the slow deaths awaiting them. What then does this mean for a "post-Holocaust"? The diary entries often provide the only memorial to these individuals. Readers lack the backgrounds of these individuals and who they were before or during the Holocaust, what Caruth calls an "unclaimed experience." Suicide crossed demographic boundaries, seemingly stemming from what Lifton identified as the desire to maintain human dignity in death rather than endure unimaginable suffering. This annihilation of the possibility of a future through suicide represents a fundamental fracture in temporal continuity. By "choosing" death in the present, these individuals rendered any "post-Holocaust" existence impossible for themselves. Their temporal existence becomes permanently trapped within the Holocaust framework, creating what might be termed a "terminal present," where future time is foreclosed entirely.

Czerniaków's suicide, following his refusal to provide deportation lists to the Nazis, highlights Laub's "collapse of witnessing." His final diary entry records a conversation with SS Herman Worthoff about the deportation of Jews from the Warsaw Ghetto, before noting that 4,000 men were "ready to go [for deportation]," with 5,000 still needed (Czerniaków 385). His suicide note reveals the "crisis of testimony": "They are demanding that I kill the children of my people with my own hands. There is nothing for me to do but to die" (Urynowicz 1). His suicide speaks to the impossibility of a "post-Holocaust," as fulfilling the request to provide 9,000 Jews would have killed a part of his soul. Czerniaków's suicide represents a moment where moral time collapses, and where the normal progression of ethical decision-making encountered an unresolvable paradox. His choice of suicide, rather than facilitating deportations for the Nazis, reveals how the Holocaust created temporal ruptures where continuation itself became morally untenable. His final diary entry creates a permanent suspension in time, where his existence is forever defined by this moment of impossible choice.

Czerniaków is often hailed a hero by historians for his suicide, rather than handing over Jews from the Warsaw Ghetto. This was unlike his counterpart Chaim Rumkowski, who was notorious for supplying the Nazis with children and elderly deported from the Łódz Ghetto. Raul Hilberg, in his groundbreaking book *Perpetrators, Victims, Bystanders*, is one of the first historians to pit these two against one another, painting Czerniaków in a positive manner, while Rumkowski is seen as an evildoer. That is not to say that Hilberg was not critical of Czerniaków's role in the *Judenrat*, but wrote of him as a moral figure. Patterson, not as harshly critical, states that "Similarly, Czerniaków's suicide is not a rejection of life; it is a refusal to take part in the extermination of life" (Patterson 1999: 48).

Emanuel Ringelblum viewed Czerniaków negatively because of his assimilated background, which led Ringelblum to conclude that he could not deeply identify with those imprisoned in the ghetto. This criticism of Czerniaków reflects Hartman's "witness testimony"—the complex relationship between observation and judgment. Ringelblum's statement that "Suicide of Czerniaków—too late, a sign of weakness—should have called resistance—a weak man" (Henry 151) demonstrates what Leys argues is tension between empathy and critical witnessing. When considering Gruner's argument from earlier in the chapter, Czerniaków's act of suicide is defined as an act of defiance or resistance, as he did not comply with the Nazi's request; however, Ringelblum would argue that this "sign of weakness" was not resistance, but rather giving in to what the Nazis wanted—another Jew dead. Ringelblum's argument, although not devoid of some truth, seems to dismiss the human aspect of Czerniaków's suicide or, in other words, the emotional toll, much like what historians are taught to do when studying history. Interestingly, it does bring into question Ringelblum's own emotions while writing his diary and his inability to not judge Czerniaków's suicide.

The conflicting interpretations of Czerniaków's suicide by Ringelblum and others reveal how the Holocaust created what might be called "fractured moral time," a disruption where normal ethical frameworks for understanding human actions became inadequate. These contested readings of his final act demonstrate how the Holocaust continues to resist integration into a cohesive historical narrative. This temporal instability further undermines the possibility of a true "post-Holocaust," as the moral meaning of events remains perpetually suspended in contested interpretation.

Berg's wrote of Czerniaków's suicide by stating that he displayed "great courage and energy" leading up to his final hours, despite the heavy burden that was weighing upon him (Berg 167). Even beyond the walls of the Warsaw Ghetto, the news traveled about Czerniaków's suicide. On July 27, Dawid Sierakowiak briefly noted that the chairman had committed suicide and proceeded to state that those in the Warsaw Ghetto had not suffered as those in the Łódź Ghetto (Sierkowiak 200). As the head of the *Judenrat*, Czerniaków would have been known by most, if not everyone, in the ghetto. These recordings of Czerniaków's suicide reveals how quickly such news spread throughout the ghetto, showing what Laub terms "the imperative to tell." Berg's observation that Czerniaków displayed "great courage and energy" contrasts with Ringelblum's harsher assessment, demonstrating what Hartman calls "conflicting testimonies" (Berg 167). This spread of information conveys Halbwach's "social frameworks of memory"—how traumatic events are communicated and remembered within communities.

In addition to writing about Czerniaków's suicide, Berg wrote about the suicides of those who were born Christian and whose parents were Jewish, and who were thereby deemed Jewish under the Nuremberg Race Laws. Berg believed that these children suffered doubly because they lost their identities, and this was reflected in the number of suicides that occurred within the group, which she noted is higher than that of the Jewish youth (Berg 113).[25]

The case of Tadek's suicide following his father's collaboration and subsequent murder explains the direct impact suicide had on Berg. Tadek was a friend who admired Berg in a romantic way. Tadek's father had colluded with the enemy and was murdered by the underground for his actions. Having been close to his father, Tadek took his own life the following day. Berg wrote about Tadek's father's murder and then noted, "Tadek could never bear this disgrace; he must have felt that he would never be able to wipe the stain from his name" (Berg 234). But was it the stain of his father's actions or the loss of his father that he could not bear? Either way, Tadek's early demise prevented him from ever living his life beyond the context of the Holocaust.

Prior to committing suicide, Czerniaków wrote about the suicides committed by those in the Warsaw Ghetto both in the abstract and specific. He wrote, "The number of suicides among the Jews has been greatly increasing during the last months. Not so long ago Freider and his wife took poison. Yesterday it was Ludwik Bergson's and his wife's turn" (205). He wrote a detailed observation about a "27-year-old section leader in the Battalion [who] committed suicide by taking poison, the reason being the resettlement and a beating that he received at a bridge while returning from work" (212). He managed to inscribe these individuals' names or at least their final moments into his diary for the future; however, this means that these individuals are only remembered as victims of the Holocaust who committed suicide as a means to end their suffering and, in turn, their legacies cannot permit a 'post-Holocaust' because of the way in which they are memorialized.

Interestingly, there were those who wrote that suicide did not happen or was not as predominant as anticipated, but suicides were still recorded. Leyb Goldin, a member of the Oneg Shabbat, wrote of a man named Friedman who had died. The paragraph that he dedicates to Friedman can be read like an internal dialogue. First, he acknowledged Friedman's death, but then pondered how it was that he had died. Was it starvation? Had his throat been cut? Friedman continued, "Maybe he took his own life? Yes... no. People don't take their own lives nowadays. Suicide is something from the good old days. ... But hunger is a bestial, a wild, a rawly primitive—yes, a bestial thing. If you're hungry, you cease to be human; you become a beast. And beasts know nothing of suicide" (Roskies 118). If the reader looked at this at a surface level, it might be read that Goldin believed that suicide was not a part of the narrative of the Holocaust; however, we must look at this in depth to understand that he is not making that claim.

In reference to starvation, it is true that Friedman was starving while in the Warsaw Ghetto, but what does it mean to wonder if the man had his throat cut? Was it a literal cut or was Goldin referring to the Nazis who forced them to their deaths? He ends the diary entry by saying that people did not have the luxury of taking their own lives because they were no longer humans. They were starving and were turned into beasts. I believe that he was arguing that starvation is the real reason, in this case, that an individual may commit suicide, because they were already dying and suicide would allow them to avoid a slow, painful, and ultimately inevitable death. The beast was the hunger, and death was the only way to silence the beast that consumes its prey. Goldin argued it was not a choice because starvation was forced upon them. It was not a broken heart or the loss of a home that led people to *choose* to take their life. They ultimately were stripped of their humanhood, their freedom, and their free will to make the choice to commit suicide. It is worth noting that in Hebrew there is no exact translation for the English word "suicide." *Ibed atzmo* is a phrase used in its place, meaning "to lose oneself," which can refer to losing one's essence rather than one's physical being. Additionally, the phrase *ibed atzmo ladaat* could be utilized, meaning "lose knowledge of oneself." These translations, in the context of the Holocaust, make it apparent that individuals were forced into the suicide as the Nazis continuously attempted to annihilate the essence of the Jew.

These examples, although just a fraction of what was written regarding suicide in Holocaust diaries, reflect the inability for those impacted by the Holocaust to escape what they experienced. For the majority of those referenced in this section, it was the only way they are remembered, which is in the context of the Holocaust and the context of their deaths. Additionally, for the writers who transcribed the names of the deaths of another, they are forever impacted by the witnessing of a suicide. This means that both the person who committed suicide and the writer are unable to escape the influence of the Holocaust on their lives or their deaths, and tragically cannot experience a "post-Holocaust."

This dual temporal imprisonment—of both victims and witnesses—creates a testimonial loop where diarists become perpetually bound to the Holocaust through their role as chroniclers. By documenting these suicides, writers like Berg, Ringelblum, and Czerniaków themselves become temporally trapped in their witnessing capacity, unable to establish narrative identities beyond their Holocaust experiences. Their own temporal existence becomes inseparable from the "unclaimed experience" of trauma. The Holocaust did not merely occur within time—it fundamentally shattered temporal continuity itself, creating wounds in individuals that resist integration into historical narratives.

CONCLUSION

For Holocaust diarists, the possibility of escaping was an impossibility. They etched themselves into the history of the Holocaust via their pens along with the names of those they inscribed on their pages. Diarists risked their lives and the lives of others to write down their experiences because they knew that it could not be expressed in any other manner. They were resisting their own fates at the hands of the Nazis and surviving through their words. Although their words live on while many of them were murdered, it is evident that diarists are linked to their Holocaust experiences, eternalized in their diaries and forever linked to the Holocaust. Through time constructs historians must learn that the before, during, and after will create limitations that are not fruitful to all modes of scholarship, and can alter how we understand victims and survivors. How we experience time, as those who have not experienced genocide firsthand, is different from how a diarist who lived through time, and thereby how we read diaries should be altered to understand from their perspective, a perspective of inhumane conditions and ultimately, genocide. If we begin to view history from the perspective of those experiencing it, we will begin to understand that a "post-Holocaust" cannot occur.

When we think of children and holidays that we celebrate, these are often happy thoughts that may bring a smile to our faces; however, in the context of genocide, they are some of the most devastating periods. Children have lost their innocence and their ability to be children, including experiencing the joy of holidays, including their birthdays, which brings them closer to their deaths. They are not given the opportunity to become adults in a natural capacity, and these souls are not able to disconnect from the Holocaust. These children will never grow old, build their own families, have a career, hold their own children, or die from natural causes.

In relationship to dying from natural causes, we must consider the final act of suicide. This last moment of trying to maintain humanity in a time when being yourself would get you killed, suicide was the final way to have free will. From the perspective of the historian reading diaries, these individuals who commit suicide are forever a part of the history of the Holocaust. Their names, if known, are forever linked to those who hoped that death was better than the "lives" they were suffering through. This means that the way in which these individuals are remembered is often through their deaths rather than the lives they lived, because that is the only information available about them. Their memories are forever linked to the Holocaust and there is no way to untangle this connection without losing a part of their identities. In turn, they, along with each group and individual mentioned in this chapter, are forever associated with the Holocaust, and for some that is the only method in which they are remembered—otherwise there would be no record of their existence. A "post-Holocaust" is an unobtainable time construct for those who were part of the Holocaust.

3

THE CONTINUATION OF TRAUMA THROUGH TRANSCRIBING

FIRST-GENERATION SURVIVORS' MEMOIRS

> *"Even if I wrote on nothing else, it would never be enough, even if all the survivors did nothing but write about their experiences, it would still not be enough."*
> —ELIE WIESEL, *ALL RIVERS RUN TO THE SEA*

Memoirs enable historians and the public to access both emotional and historical representation of events, including the Holocaust. In this chapter, a *memoir* is defined as writing authored by or transcribed in collaboration with a Holocaust survivor about their Holocaust experience. Unlike diaries, which capture the immediacy of events as they unfold, memoirs involve retrospective reflection across temporal distance. This temporal gap, however, does not diminish the ongoing trauma associated with these experiences; in fact, it often reveals how past trauma continues to fold into present existence. It is crucial to recognize that not all survivors choose to document their trauma, and those who do may omit details due to guilt, suppressed memories, or considerations of readability. These memoirs provide invaluable perspectives otherwise inaccessible to non-survivors, offering a window into how traumatic time operates differently from chronological time.

While historians broadly accept memoirs' value, traditional methodology requires fact-checking and editing survivors' accounts rather than relying solely on their testimonies, creating a temporal hierarchy that privileges documented chronology over experiential time. Auschwitz survivor Charlotte Delbo addresses this tension in her memoir *Auschwitz and After*, "Today, I am not sure that what I wrote is true, I am certain it is truthful" (Delbo 1). Her statement acknowledges that while specific data may not always be precise, her narrative remains authentic across time's passage. This highlights the problematic dichotomy historians face between "historical truth" or "facts" and testimonial evidence, where different temporal frameworks compete. As Laub argues, historians' preexisting historical knowledge, which is organized chronologically, can impede their ability to truly listen to survivors, preventing access to crucial testimonial information that follows trauma's temporal logic (Felman and Laub 63–64). This chapter proposes that historians should consider survivors' testimony as its own valid historical category with distinct temporal significance, rather than dismissing it when it fails to align with documented chronological facts.

Memory itself does not function chronologically. Howard Eichenbaum's biological research demonstrates that while the hippocampus works to orient memories spatiotemporally, it can sometimes mismatch information, leading to nonlinear transmission of memory (Eichenbaum 81). Memory itself does not function chronologically. Thus, human recollection operates through associative streams of thought, potentially moving from 1943 to 1941 and then to 1989 in a single testimonial moment. When trauma that survivors encounter in the present triggers memories connected to the Holocaust, they simultaneously experience past memories while remaining in the present—a temporal collapse where different moments coexist. The present and the past are not discrete temporal categories but are interlinked, as these memories fundamentally shape the present self. These memoirs represent an ongoing temporal engagement with Holocaust trauma rather than its conclusion. As Elie Wiesel noted, "Worse: they [survivors] feared being inadequate to the task, betraying a unique experience by burying it in worn-out phrases and images. They were afraid of saying what must not be said" (Wiesel 2011: 8). The act of writing and recall itself constitutes a reimmersion in Holocaust trauma, creating a recursive temporal loop rather than a linear progression.

While writing can retraumatize, collapsing the temporal distance between past and present, it can also serve as a coping mechanism and tool for processing traumatic experiences across time. James W. Pennebaker and Sandra Kliher Beall argue that "Confronting the event, then, should help the individual categorize the experience into a meaningful framework" (Pennebaker and Kliher Beall 274). Their research, though not specifically focused on genocide survivors, demonstrates that trauma survivors who engage in writing can reorganize their temporal experience both individually and socially. Written testimony allows information transmission without requiring direct interpersonal confrontation, creating a temporal bridge between past experience and present understanding. Public engagement with survivor experiences increased significantly after the 1960s Eichmann trial, which globally broadcast Holocaust testimonials and demonstrated how the trauma of the 1940s remained temporally present in the 1960s—revealing the ongoing nature of survivor trauma. Like Eichmann trial witnesses, memoir writers fulfill a vital witnessing role that transcends conventional temporal boundaries. Many survivors write not only their own stories, but also bear witness to others' trauma under Nazi persecution, extending their temporal reach beyond personal experience. Memoirists often represent the final temporal link to those murdered, creating an inescapable connection to experiences that might otherwise be lost to time.

As survivor numbers decrease, maintaining temporal connection with Holocaust narratives becomes more challenging. However, teaching history as an ongoing temporal influence rather than a discrete past event might bridge this gap. For instance, the phrase "Never Again," while commonly associated with the Holocaust, potentially creates problematic temporal distance from genocide as a continuing possibility across time. While many Holocaust scholars—including Lucy Dawidowicz, Emil Fackenheim, Saul Friedländer, Daniel Goldhagen, Steven Katz, and Deborah Lipstadt—warn against comparative approaches, examining memoirs from different genocides may enhance understanding of genocide's fundamental nature across different temporal contexts. While each genocide's methods and rationales differ, making each uniquely horrific, survivors share the ongoing temporal experience of trauma regardless of the specific genocide's techniques or historical moment.

This enduring trauma manifests not just in memory, but in physical pain, tangible events, and visible emotions, as survivors cannot fully escape the temporal reach of their experiences. This chapter will examine "after," the impossibility of temporal return, witness-bearing and guilt across time, suicide as temporal rupture, analyzing how each relates to the problematic term "post-Holocaust." For Holocaust survivors, no true "post-Holocaust" exists, as such terminology negates the temporal continuity of trauma, imposing an artificial chronological boundary on an experience that refuses temporal containment.

AFTER?

Time links humans through structured interactions, meetings, and social connections. Without temporal anchoring, human connection dissolves. As Wiesel describes, his displacement from normal temporal constructs—obligations, schedules, social accountability—marked his forced departure from humanity itself.: "He longer had obligations, no clocks to keep him in check, no need to pretend to stay busy, no sleep schedule, and no one to ask where he had been. It was just him. He was isolated" (Wiesel 2011: 116). This temporal displacement exemplifies Halbwachs' "collective memory"—the way social groups construct and maintain temporal frameworks that enable shared experience and meaning-making.

Twenty-five years after his forced departure from Sighet, Wiesel returned to his childhood hometown, now haunted by Nazi atrocities, searching for a buried timepiece—his first and last gift from his murdered parents. The watch, which his father buried to keep from Nazi confiscation, becomes a powerful symbol of temporal rupture in trauma theory. When uncovered, the timepiece was damaged—time had not preserved but rather accelerated its decay. This physical deterioration mirrors what trauma theorists describe as the disruption of linear temporality in survivor experience. The watch's stopped time metaphorically represents the "unclaimed experience." Furthermore, the act of burial and retrieval links to Nora's *"lieux de mémoire"*—physical locations and objects that serve as anchors for collective remembrance.

For Wiesel, as for many survivors, time became fundamentally disrupted. His childhood was not merely interrupted but irrevocably stolen. His decision to rebury the watch mirrors that of his father's act in 1944. This act of reburial illustrates what Hoffman terms "after memory"—the way subsequent generations inherit and process traumatic histories. Yet, as Wiesel poignantly questions, "After? Did you say: after? Meaning what?" (57). This rejection of "after" aligns with trauma theory's understanding of how catastrophic events resist integration into normal temporal frameworks. It also exemplifies what van Alphen describes as the "failed experience" of trauma—events that resist narrative integration and temporal placement.

Wiesel's questioning extends beyond time to God, reflecting what Langer terms the "divided self" of Holocaust survivors—a splitting between pre-trauma and post-trauma identity. His theological struggle emerges directly from his experiences in Auschwitz-Birkenau, Buna, and Buchenwald. His questions—about continuation, divine silence, and future possibility—represent what LaCapra describes as the "acting out" of trauma, where past experience continues to haunt the present. This spiritual crisis also demonstrates what Rachel Falconer identities as "temporal haunting"—the way traumatic past events continue to intrude upon and shape present experience.

The account of the young *pipel*'s execution demonstrates what scholars of trauma term "witness trauma."[26] Wiesel responds to the question, "'For God's sake, where is God?'" with "'Where He is? There is where—hanging from these gallows'" (Wiesel 2006: 65). He articulates the "collapse of witnessing": "No, the tragedy of the survivors did not end with the liberation of the camps" (Wiesel 1995: 145). This observation aligns with contemporary trauma theory's understanding of the ongoing nature of catastrophic experience. As Wiesel notes, "For the camp, survivor life is a battle not only for the dead but also against them. Locked in the grip of the dead, he fears that by freeing himself, he is abandoning them. Hence the near-impossibility of loving, or of believing in humanity" (298–299).

This description highlights what Leys terms the "temporal delay" of trauma—its tendency to persist beyond the original event. It also demonstrates what Primo Levi called the "grey zone"—the moral and psychological complexity of survival in relation to those who perished.

Otto Dov Kulka's *Landscapes of the Metropolis of Death* provides a different perspective on traumatic temporality. His return to Auschwitz-Birkenau and Theresienstadt after thirty-three years demonstrates "multidirectional memory." This concept is further developed through what Alison Landsberg terms "prosthetic memory"—the way contemporary individuals incorporate traumatic histories they did not personally experience. Dov Kulka's observation that while physically "Auschwitz had been buried," the place's emotional reality persisted, which illustrates what Hartman terms the "intellectual witness"—the scholar who must navigate both personal trauma and academic analysis (Dov Kulka 7).

Dov Kulka's nonlinear narrative structure, beginning with "A Prologue that Could Also Be an Epilogue," exemplifies what trauma theorists call temporal disruption. His metaphor of water's fluidity connected to "the current of time that passes the Metropolis of Death" (56) aligns with contemporary understanding of trauma's resistance to chronological narration. This temporal fluidity, particularly in his account of his mother's death, demonstrates the "crisis of witnessing." The water metaphor is also connected to what Young identifies as "received history"—the way traumatic events are processed and transmitted through metaphorical and symbolic frameworks.

The fluid temporality in both Wiesel's and Dov Kulka's narratives demonstrates what Andreas Huyssen calls "present pasts"—the way traumatic histories continue to shape contemporary experience and understanding. Their works contribute to what Aleida Assmann terms "cultural memory"—the way societies maintain and transmit knowledge of traumatic events across generations through various forms of representation and commemoration.

It is not until the end of his recollections that Dov Kulka informs the reader why he decided to return to Auschwitz-Birkenau. As he stood at the Temple Mount, "Not immediately, I left the Temple Mount, physically, but in my consciousness returned to Auschwitz. It must have been then that I arrived at the decision to return there and wander through the desolation, amid the polarity in which of course I always feel the heaving presence of life and death there, the machinery of that dreadful history which is no more" (74). Here, in one of the holiest places on earth, he found himself drifting to Auschwitz, the one place he can never escape. When he visits Auschwitz-Birkenau, he wanders through various familiar places, recollecting, "So much for the trip to two places in which I had really been, two buildings that I entered back then, in which I lived back then, in which I absorbed, which have remained with me" (9). His statement seems an attempt to remind himself that it was "back then" as opposed to present—the reminder that there is nothing to be scared of. He points this out throughout his book, that it is no longer as it once was, but to whose benefit is to point this out?: "From here, the way to the third place was unavoidable, the place where I seemingly lived and remained always, from that day to this, and I am held captive there as a life prisoner, bound and fettered with chains that cannot be undone" (9). It would seem that the reminder that he was physically safe at Auschwitz-Birkenau was necessary to continue on his journey, as being physically present could only add another layer to the nightmare that never ended.

There are moments when he reflects upon his time in the camps and attempts to recall specific details, seemingly insignificant ones like what they sat on: "Try as I might, I could not remember whether there were benches or a dirt floor. When I tried to visualize benches, what suddenly came to mind were the benches in the dining hall of the kibbutz in Israel, and I understood that it was not from there" (19). This intermingling of memories and place is linked to the continuation of time and trauma, an inescapable part of who he is as a Holocaust survivor. Rather than visualizing what might have been present in the camp, thinking about the kibbutz aligns with cognitive behavioral therapy (CBT) principles as an effective coping mechanism. Psychologist Elena Oumano wrote an article pertaining to coping with phobias, specifically public speaking. Although these two situations do not equate, the coping mechanisms are meant to be reactions to "*interpretations* of a situation" rather than a "*situation*" much like Dov Kulka is processing. It is not the situation itself, but his interpretation of the site and experience (Oumano 6). A part of the process of CBT is visualization along with journaling, as Dov Kulka does, possibly subconsciously, but nonetheless as an attempt to avoid the trauma of the space (7).

Otto Dov Kulka is not alone in his continuation of suffering. Charlotte Delbo wrote in her memoir, *Auschwitz and After*, about the difficulties of the return: "none of us will return" (Delbo 113). In a literal sense, she began her memoir addressing who arrived at Auschwitz and how they do not leave. She wrote that each person brings along what and who they cherish most—children. They will not return because, as she says, "It is a one-way street" (7). It is a street where people disappear; never to return. Some will go through the process of being tattooed, a permanent mark that would never permit an "after." Of course, there are those who have attempted to remove the number that was unwillingly needled into their arms, but it is then replaced with a different type of scar. The physical being takes on other scars that last. Delbo speaks of time and aging: she sees a young boy walking with a blanket covering his head, only to discover that it is a woman who has been reduced to a frail skeleton (26). Time, as reflected in Holocaust memoirs, is not as historians portray it in Auschwitz. Children are old, hunger ravages all bodies, lice and disease take their toll and continue to affect survivors. Delbo later states that they left the camps only to carry the symptoms of the diseases they had survived.

Wiesel and Delbo write about the Holocaust as a continuation of their lives, an event that changed them, but nonetheless represented an interruption of life. Marceline Loridan-Ivens was also a survivor who experienced this interruption. She was a French Jewess who ultimately was imprisoned at Birkenau while her father was at Auschwitz. It is through this connection that Loridan-Ivens finds the desire to continue—a connection of the heart that was only kilometers away, yet often seemed like a whole planet apart. Her "papa" did not survive Auschwitz, but Loridan-Ivens returned to her mother and two siblings in France. Her mother and siblings had not been taken to concentration camps and had remained at home while their father and sister were tortured to the point of no return. When she arrived home, she found that her family could not possibly understand what the concentration and extermination camps were. To cope with the camps and being an outsider in her own family, Loridan-Ivens declared that May 10 would be her birthdate (Loridan-Ivens 61). This date was the day that the Russians liberated her from Theresienstadt after marching there from Auschwitz. What does this mean for her past and future? With her declaration of birthdate, Loridan-Ivens effectively erased any sense of the "past" or "after." She was attempting to annihilate a part of who she was and remove the trauma of being a survivor; however, through the rest of her memoir, despite her efforts, it proves impossible to not carry the guilt and responsibility of survival.

Although those who wrote these memoirs survived the Holocaust, they are haunted by what they saw, what they did, and the daily struggle of survival. They, along with other survivors who wrote memoirs, provide the insight that the idea of "post-Holocaust" is a flawed term. When any individual lives through a traumatic experience, it is not removed from their memory, but rather it is ingrained forever. The trauma of the Holocaust molded new people. For survivors, especially those who made their life's work upholding the message of remembrance stemming from the Holocaust, there is no such concept as "post-Holocaust." It is a continuation of time following the experience, and although the circumstances have changed, the mentality, the emotions, and the conditioning have not. Due to this continuation of time, the Holocaust is not a "was," but an "is." There is a danger in placing the trauma only in the past, which implies that survivors no longer live with the trauma of the Holocaust. The Holocaust has become a part of the survivors: a future would indicate a separation from the event rather than living with the event each day.

THE UNFULFILLING DREAM OF THE RETURN HOME

"My dream stands in front of me, still warm, and although awake I am still full of its anguish: and then I remember that it is not a haphazard dream, but that I have dreamed it not once but many times since I arrived here, with hardly any variations of environment or details. I am not quite awake and I remember that I have recounted it to Alberto and that he confided to me, to my amazement, that it is also his dream and the dream of many others, perhaps of everyone." (Levi 60)

The dream that Primo Levi recounts is one of returning to humanity and rejoining society as a human being. More specifically, he dreams of his sister, a friend, and others gathered to listen to him recount his trauma. But as he describes the horrors, he finds that they do not—or perhaps cannot—comprehend what he is saying. He recognizes the indifference in his sister's face as she leaves, causing him a deep sense of loss (60). In this dream, Levi imagines returning home to his family who would understand the horrors he has lived through. The desire to return meant that survivors could still hold onto the idea of a future, something to aspire to. It also meant they dreamed of the "before," before the Holocaust—a time that no longer was attainable. Yet, when survivors were no longer physical prisoners of the Nazis, they found that their dream would never become reality and, in turn, the future that they had hoped for could not exist. Therefore, those who had physically left the camps discovered they were still captives of the anguish inflicted by the Nazis. The horrors of surviving the Holocaust did not simply end with the liberation of the camps. Tragically, this reality was far from the response that survivors received when they attempted to return to their previous homes. Their dreams had become nightmares, forever haunting them.[27]

Throughout Europe, rebuilding had begun, both architecturally and emotionally, but where did those who had been imprisoned in the camps belong? Large cities, such as Minsk, Rotterdam, and Warsaw, were almost leveled from bombings, endured food shortages, and other ramifications from the war that had struck Europe. As survivors began their pilgrimages home, they found that not only was it physically changed, but additionally, the citizens did not welcome more mouths to feed. They especially did not welcome the Jews, who prior to the outbreak of World War II were being attacked for simply being born into the covenant of Judaism. Each national context contributed to the situation that survivors faced upon return.

The Vichy government in France was guilty of condemning Jews to death. One raid carried out by the French police in the German-occupied zone was conducted in Paris on July 16 and 17, 1942—the Vel d'hiv roundup. Twelve thousand Jews were sent to Drancy, including four thousand Jewish children who were not even requested by the Gestapo. This raid was not formally acknowledged by the French government until

1995, which speaks to France's mindset regarding the Holocaust. Charlotte Delbo, a French Gentile from Bordeaux, returned to a liberated Paris. After France's liberation on August 25, 1944, the country faced the task of rebuilding economically, politically, and socially. Roughly 1.8 million French citizens were displaced in the prior years and needed aid, including repatriation from other areas of Europe. Due to the complexity of France's history of filling both collaborator and victim roles, the nation was divided on the next course of action. The destruction of France ran deeper than the physical devastation, although physical it had been: statistics showed that one of every twenty buildings had been destroyed and one in five had sustained damage—part of the monumental task of rebuilding a nation (Fogg 283–284).

Delbo noted, "I was no longer open to imagination, or explanation. This is the part of me that died in Auschwitz. This is what turned me into a ghost" (Delbo 239). It was unbelievable even to those who lived through it. What kind of life could a human have who had experienced more death than life? She knew while in the camp that a part of her had died: "Deep within me was a terrible indifference, the kind of indifference that comes from a heart reduced to ashes" (117). She had survived, but at what cost?: "But what's the good of knowing when you no longer know how to live?" (239). She could no longer read a book or immerse herself in anything because what was the point? Her experiences were beyond books.

Delbo describes the desire she feels to die, but not as a prisoner—as a human: "I wish to die but not to be carried on the small stretcher" (Delbo 67). This statement epitomizes "founding trauma." Her struggle to return to France and the world crystallizes around this fundamental disruption. Death had become more common than life, and she no longer wanted to be a part of what Langer calls the "anti-world" of Auschwitz. Yet how could anyone return to a world where life was valued when death had become so normalized? As Delbo stated, "none of us will return" (113). A deceptively simple statement that embodies Caruth's "impossible history" of trauma, where survival itself becomes a crisis.

The impossibility of return for Delbo represents a rupture in "collective memory." What meaning could life possibly have beyond Auschwitz, an anti-world that possessed no limiting principle? When placed in a rehabilitation center, Delbo encounters another survivor, Gilberte, who asks where she is from. Her response—"Auschwitz"—rather than naming her hometown in France (243). Did Auschwitz become her new origin point? Though she was imprisoned for less than a year, a fraction of her life, the time in Auschwitz is what Rothberg calls "traumatic realism," where traumatic experiences warp temporal perception, making brief periods feel eternal.

This temporal disruption illustrates what Agamben describes as the "state of exception" becoming normalized. If there is nothing before Auschwitz, there can be no "after." Delbo has eliminated her "before," and as Laub suggests, without a preserved pre-trauma self, there can be no post-trauma integration. The erasure of "before" prevents the possibility of an "after," creating what Eva Hoffman calls "paradoxical time," where past trauma continuously intrudes into the present.

When Delbo physically rejoins French society, she describes an ongoing internal interrogation—questioning whether each person she meets would have given her water (254). This represents what Leys terms "trauma's aftermath," where survival behaviors persist beyond their original context. Although physically free, she cannot escape what Levi calls the "grey zone" of moral ambiguity that characterized camp existence. Her struggle extends beyond individual experience to what Felman calls "testimonial objects"—the absent witnesses who could validate her experience but are forever lost: "I pretend to be like everyone else . . . but have no hold on life" (260). This statement embodies what Lifton identities as the "death imprint," the permanent psychological marking that survival of mass death leaves on the psyche.

This persistent alienation exemplifies "social death"—a profound disconnection from normal human relations that persists after physical survival. Delbo's testimony thus illustrates how the Holocaust created not just physical victims but what Jean Améry calls "minds in mourning"—survivors who must perpetually negotiate between their traumatic past and an uncomprehending present.

Delbo, like many survivors, writes of dreaming about freedom, only to find emptiness upon "achieving" it. Life could never return to its pre-Holocaust state, and the experience of the camps proved impossible to forget: "That's the difference; time does not pass over me, over us. It doesn't erase anything, doesn't undo it. I'm not alive. I died in Auschwitz but no one knows it" (267). This temporal stasis exemplifies what Halbwachs terms "collective memory rupture." Her strongest connection remained with the dead: "It seems to me I'm not alive. Since all are dead, it seems impossible I shouldn't be also. All dead. Mounette, Viva, Sylviane, Rosie, all the others, all the others" (257). Even on her return flight to France, she seeks the presence of the dead, questioning her belonging in a world that offers no answers (236).

The dead became her closest companions, the only ones who could understand her experience. While survivors worked to preserve the memory of the dead through names and dates, Delbo's relationship with memory transcends mere documentation (149). She remained trapped not in physical space but in what Caruth calls the "wound of consciousness"—the persistent trauma that defies temporal boundaries:

> I'm not alive. I'm imprisoned in memories and repetition. I sleep badly but insomnia does not weigh on me. At night I have the right not to be alive. I have the right not to pretend. I join the others then. I am among them, one of them.... I don't believe in life after death. I don't believe they exist in a beyond where I join them at night. No. I see them again in their agony, as they were before dying, as they remained within me. (261)

This represents the only possible "after"—death itself—because beyond the Holocaust lay not temporal progression but of "durational time." The haunting losses witnessed by Delbo and other survivors created "founding trauma," comprehensible only to those who shared the experience.

Her attempts to maintain connections became exercises in loss: "Presently, I am no longer alive.... Nothing can fill the abyss between other people and myself, between myself and myself" (259). This internal splitting exemplifies "psychic numbing." Even her return home revealed temporal discontinuity—her mother had died and her father had remarried (271). Life had continued beyond the camps, creating what Hirsch calls "postmemory gaps." For Jewish survivors, the impossibility of return carried additional dimensions. Unlike other Nazi victims,

Jews systematically lost all trace of their homes—both material possessions and family connections. This systematic erasure demonstrates Agamben's "bare life"—existence stripped of social and cultural meaning. The common saying "home is where the heart is" became a cruel reminder of "received history."

Isabella Leitner's experience as a Hungarian Jewish survivor demonstrates this multiplied alienation; her prewar experiences of antisemitism—"I cannot count the times I was called a 'dirty Jew' while strolling down Main Street, Hungary" (Leitner 24)—illustrates "multidirectional memory," where different forms of violence intersect and reinforce each other. The Arrow Cross Party's willing participation in Jewish persecution exemplifies what Christopher Browning terms "ordinary men" becoming perpetrators. Leitner's declaration "I shall not return" (27–28) represents what Laub identifies as "preemptive trauma"—the anticipation of further violence that precludes the possibility of return. Her immigration to America with two sisters demonstrates what scholars term "survivor diaspora," yet she remained trapped in what Leys calls "trauma time": "I don't know how people live. I know only how they die'" (99).

Her relationship with motherhood reveals what Hoffman terms "paradoxical inheritance." When contemplating telling her mother about her pregnancy, she thinks: "I stood in front of the crematorium, and now there is another heart beating within that very body that was condemned to ashes" (104). Her second son becoming "the voice of the six million" (106) exemplifies what Nadine Fresco calls "phantom pain," the transmission of trauma across generations.

The situation in Poland further complicated the possibility of return. As Jonathan Huener notes, Poland's position as both victim and site of Nazi death camps created what he terms "contested memory" (35). Simon Wiesenthal's observation that "Poland was a cemetery" (83) exemplifies "testimonial objects," that is, physical spaces that bear witness to trauma.

The postwar violence against returning Jews, such as the Kielce pogrom where forty-two survivors were murdered (Gross 92–93), demonstrates what Jan Gross terms "postwar antisemitism," revealing the continuation of what survivors had fled. This persistent violence rendered the concept of "after" impossible, creating what scholars call "continuous trauma"—where the end of the Holocaust did not mean the end of persecution. For these survivors, the dream of return became what Jean Améry terms "irreconcilable memory," a nightmare that continued to haunt them. The persistence of antisemitic ideology across national boundaries ensured that what Primo Levi calls the "grey zone" extended beyond liberation, effectively eliminating any possibility of a true "after."

ATTEMPT TO RETURN HOME

As survivors returned home after the Holocaust, they encountered what Caruth calls a "double wound," or initial trauma of their experiences and the secondary trauma of finding their prewar concepts of "home" irretrievably altered. For many, the idealized dreams of returning to loved ones, warm food, and familiar possessions collided harshly with reality. While some found surviving family members, nearly all faced devastating losses, and even those whose physical homes remained standing often discovered them occupied by others, with no legal recourse for reclaiming these tangible connections to their past lives.

Marceline Loridan-Ivens's return to France, was haunted by the absence of her "papa"; he was the only one who could truly understand her suffering (Loridan-Ivens 27). Her mother, who had not been deported, exhibited what trauma theorists identify as defensive avoidance, dismissing Marceline's attempts to share her experiences as dramatic (33).[28] Her mother's insistence that "You have to forget," (39) reveals both her own trauma response and what LaCapra calls an "acting out"—a compulsive repetition of traumatic memory that paradoxically tries to repress it.

Marceline's response, "I wasn't running away from ghosts, quite the contrary, I was chasing after them, after you. Who else could I share anything with?" (35)—demonstrates Laub's description of survivor's need to tell their story as a way to survive. Her disconnection from family members who had not shared her experiences creates "collective memory" fractures, where shared frameworks of understanding break down. Her wish "to be treated like an orphan" (36) speaks to the profound rupture in familial relations that trauma creates.

Livia Bitton-Jackon's reflection on liberation—"We will be freed—to do what? To face a world in which little children were gassed with their mothers. To face the world in which this was possible. My God. My God. I have just been robbed of my freedom" (Bitton-Jackson 177)—reflects Langer's "durational time," where trauma of the Holocaust creates a permanent temporal rupture. Her question," Can anyone understand the pain of the uprooted? This was my home once, my town, my country. Without it I am not whole. Yet, it is no longer mine.... It is not my home anymore" speaks to what Eva Hoffman calls "exile consciousness"—a permanent state of displacement that persists even after physical return (206). The gathering of thirty-six survivors in Bitton-Jackson's hometown, where "We do not speak about the past. Neither do we talk about the present: It simply does not exist" (209), demonstrates Felman's "testimony's crisis." Their silence about both past and present reveals what psychoanalyst Donald Winnicott might call a "false self" adaptation—a protective mechanism that allows survival but prevents authentic engagement with reality.

Mel Mermelstein's careful specification that suffering did not end "in Buchenwald" illuminates what Hartman terms the "survivor's paradox"—the simultaneous need to testify to trauma while acknowledging its ultimate incomprehensibility. His assertion that "liberation and freedom were meaningless" (219) to Buchenwald inmates demonstrates "psychic numbering." Mermelstein makes the declaration that "misery, torture, starvation and death" were over with regard to the concentration camp, but that does not mean that it was not still occurring, just not in the same locale. This is at the heart of the trauma and the experiences of survivors. The misery felt, which could stem from physical torture that happened in a concentration camp or from a disease contracted; the torture, of nightmares or the never knowing what happened to loved ones; the starvation, whether it be physical or the starvation of the soul that can no longer turn to God because of what they experienced; or the death, which happened during liberation or the suicides or the dying of survivors as they grow older.

Lucy Lipiner, author of *Lusia's Long Journey Home: A Young Girl's Memoir of Surviving the Holocaust*, was a child during the Holocaust whose immediate family fled from Poland to the East when the Nazis invaded. Lipiner recollects in her memoir her family's journey through Ukraine, Soviet Russia, Siberia, and lastly to Tajikistan. Although she had managed to escape physical harm, the emotional toll was damaging: "Their loud 'discussions' were about the possibility of returning home" (Lipiner 45). Despite Lipiner's young age at the time, she understood that home was no longer a possibility and that they would remain homeless and stateless for years to come: "I think she [mother] didn't understand that life as we remembered it before September 1 was gone forever" (45). This disillusionment of home was possibly the only shred of hope that Lucy's mother had. Her mother had left behind four siblings and dozens of cousins, nieces, and nephews.

Eventually they attempted to return to Poland by taking a train ride from Tajikistan to Poland, lasting for six weeks. Once again, they left behind friends, a shelter, and relative safety in search of their home. But on arrival, "Something was terribly wrong in the country we had so longed to return to" (141). It was at this moment of return that Lucy learned about the horrors of the Holocaust, the camps, the ghettos, and antisemitism. As more information was gathered, her family attempted to find relatives in Poland, only there were none to find. They were murdered (142). This grim discovery led to her family's decision to leave Poland and find a new place to call home. Her father declared, "We have to leave. We cannot remain in this country. This land is drenched in the blood of our people" (142). For him, the country had already been disconnected from the sense of home and had become a place of loss and murder. Other than his wife and children, though his family no longer lived in their home country, they would forever be a part of the land.

Lipiner's childhood experience of displacement and her evolving concept of home illustrates what attachment theory John Bowlby terms "separation anxiety" complicated by historical trauma. Her ultimate realization that home meant "wherever home happened to be … near Mama and Papa" (152)—the process of rebuilding attachment and meaning after traumatic rupture. Lipiner wrote, "It had been almost ten years since I had experienced a real home. What would it be like to have a home with more than one room? I couldn't even imagine that" (174). After her stay at the orphanage, she and her sister were reunited with her parents at another displaced person's camp where they waited for clearance to be sent to New York City. America would be their new home. They arrived on August 23, 1949, in a foreign land, with only a few bags of belongings, without speaking the language and only knowing those in their family (better than others who arrived with no possessions and, more importantly, no one to build a new home with).

Each survivor's return "home" represented a unique confrontation with loss, yet a common thread emerged: the discovery that "home" had become an impossible memory, existing only in the traumatic space between remembrance and absence. These memories were inextricably linked to the profound emptiness within physical spaces—not just the absence of loved ones, but the complete erasure of their material presence. The post-Holocaust Jewish diaspora from Europe revealed more than simple displacement; it demonstrated how the very concept of homeland had been irreparably fractured for many survivors, who could no longer conceive of their countries of origin as places of belonging.

While many Jews chose to leave Europe, the decision to stay or depart was far more complex than a simple choice. Practical barriers to emigration were substantial: potential emigrants needed to secure sponsorship, gather sufficient funds for travel, and, in the case of destinations like the United States, pass stringent mental and physical health examinations. These requirements created a cruel paradox—survivors needed to demonstrate both sufficient trauma to qualify for refugee status and sufficient wellness to be deemed "acceptable" immigrants.

The Nazis' systematic program of dehumanization had deliberately severed connections not only to life but to memory itself. By destroying photographs, confiscating personal belongings, and eliminating all tangible traces of Jewish existence, they attempted to erase not just lives, but the evidence that these lives had ever been lived. The burden of memory thus fell to survivors, who became unwilling archives of lost worlds—carrying within them not just their own trauma, but the responsibility to remember those who had no one else left to remember them.

The ultimate irony emerged when reparations became available: survivors were required to prove, through psychological evaluation, the impact of experiences that were, by their very nature, beyond the scope of ordinary psychological assessment. This bureaucratic requirement forced survivors to translate their ineffable trauma into clinical terms, potentially retraumatizing them through the very process meant to acknowledge their suffering. The demand for psychological proof of trauma revealed a fundamental misunderstanding of how catastrophic experiences resist categorization within standard diagnostic frameworks.

BEARING WITNESS AND THE BURDEN OF SURVIVOR'S GUILT

The evolution of Holocaust survivor testimony reflects complex intersections between memory, identity, and historical witness, all occurring within a fractured temporality that defies conventional chronology. Annette Wieviorka's assertion that the Eichmann trial marked a turning point in survivors' social identity requires nuanced examination, particularly as it imposes a linear historical framework onto an experience that refuses such temporal ordering. While she correctly identifies the trial as a moment when survivors assumed a more public role of bearing witness, her argument understates the significant testimonial work already occurring within survivor communities between 1945 and 1961—work that existed not as "pre-Eichmann" testimony, but as expressions inhabiting their own temporal reality. The trial did not initiate survivor testimony so much as it transformed its social reception and cultural meaning, revealing how collective memory itself operates outside linear time, with recognition often occurring asynchronously to the testimonial act itself.

Wieviorka's observation that "with the Eichmann trial, the witness became an embodiment of memory, attesting to the past and to the continuing presence of the past" (88) reveals a crucial temporal paradox in Holocaust testimony. Rather than marking a clear delineation between past and present, survivor testimony demonstrates the impossibility of temporal boundaries in trauma. The body of the survivor becomes a site where multiple temporalities converge simultaneously—the past exists not as memory but as an ongoing reality that continually erupts into what others perceive as the present. The very concept of "post-Holocaust" becomes problematic, as survivors' experiences resist containment within traditional historical periodization. They exist in what Maurice Blanchot might call "the time of the disaster"—a time that is neither past nor present, but perpetually occurring, defying the very grammar of historical discourse.

The theoretical framework proposed by Felman and Laub in *Testimony: Crisis of Witnessing in Literature, Psychoanalysis, and History*, which characterizes the Holocaust as an "event without witnesses," requires critical reassessment through this lens of temporal disruption. Their assertion, echoed by Agamben's concept of the "complete witnesses" being those who perished, inadvertently creates a hierarchy of testimony that privileges death over survival while simultaneously imposing a sequential logic—before/after, witness/posthumous—onto an experience that fundamentally ruptures such temporal distinctions. This framework, while attempting to honor those who perished, risks minimizing the vital witness of those who survived through various means—in ghettos, in hiding, or through flight—whose testimonies exist in what Eva Hoffman calls the "accordion of time," where past and present perpetually fold into one another. Their experiences, though different from those who perished in camps, constitute essential testimony to the full scope of Nazi persecution, occurring across a temporal continuum that refuses neat historical demarcation.

Writing serves multiple functions in Holocaust testimony, extending witness beyond direct experience while simultaneously disrupting normative temporality. Survivors' accounts frequently memorialize not only their own experiences, but also those of others they encountered—fellow prisoners, helpers, and even distant observers—creating what Mikhail Bakhtin might call a "chronotope" where multiple temporal experiences converge in a single narrative space. This expansion of testimony through writing demonstrates how survivor narratives attempt to construct meaning from tragedy while simultaneously preserving memory of both survivors and victims, collapsing the temporal distance between those who lived and those who died. Yehiel De-Nur took the stand at the Eichmann trial to bear witness on behalf of those who could not. His collapse on the witness stand, followed by his literary work under the name Ka-Tzetnik 135633, demonstrates how testimony occurs across multiple modes of expression while simultaneously existing outside conventional time—his testimony was neither completed nor interrupted, but exists in a state of perpetual emergence. His insistence on using his camp number rather than his name reflects "durational time"—the persistent presence of camp experience in survivor consciousness, where identity itself becomes unmoored from linear biography. De-Nur's writing, "The nameless ones! It's them. Them! All those anonymous ones! Write their name: K. Tzetnik!" (Ka-Tzetnik 135633: 16), reveals how survivor's guilt becomes intertwined with the obligation to testify in a temporal mode. His inability to separate himself from the "nameless" demonstrates what LaCapra calls "empathic unsettlement," the ethical necessity of maintaining connection with trauma while acknowledging its ultimate irrepresentability, creating what Paul Ricoeur might call a "third time" that exists between phenomenological experience and cosmic chronology.

De-Nur was not alone in his need to write and bear witness stemming from survivor's guilt, itself an expression of temporal disjunction where one lives simultaneously in the time of survival and the time of those who did not survive. Otto Dov Kulka, as mentioned previously, is a Holocaust survivor who chose to become a Holocaust scholar. That, in and of itself, is an undeniably fierce way to commemorate all those that were murdered and could be linked to survivor's guilt; however, for the purpose of argument, we will focus on his memoir. His distinctive narrative style, particularly his use of dissociative language, illustrates the "collapse of witnessing" as well as the collapse of temporality itself—his scholarly and memorial work exists simultaneously, with neither taking precedence over the other in a chronological sense. His description of "circling as a moth circles a flame" reveals both the compulsion to return to traumatic memory and the impossibility of direct confrontation, suggesting a spiral temporality that Giorgio Agamben might call "kairological time"—time experienced not as linear progression but as intensity and recursive return.

> I say that I was bound and remained bound, or fettered by chains, but that is because I was never there, because my foot never stepped into those courtyards, inside those buildings. I circled them as a moth circles a flame, knowing that falling into it was inevitable, yet I kept on circling

outside, willingly or unwillingly-it was not up to me—all my friends, the butterflies, not all of them, but almost all of them, were there and did not come out of there. (Dov Kulka 9)

However, it is not that he was not physically there, but that he did not go where the majority of prisoners went, to death. This creates a temporal schism in his experience, where his survival places him simultaneously inside and outside the defining temporal event of Auschwitz—mass extermination. He wrote, "Thus the immutable law remained for me and thus did I remain caught up within it, which was actually what I discovered when I returned decades later. In that return, with the completion of the last act, which I had not been 'privileged' to experience—the act of descending into the ruins that survived, at least to those of the gas chamber of the crematorium" (40). His use of "decades later" collapses the temporal distance, suggesting not a chronological return but an ontological one—a completion of a suspended moment that had remained perpetually present despite the passage of calendar time. As he witnessed an unimaginable number be murdered, he remained—occupying what Giorgio Agamben might call "the time of the remnant," a suspended temporal state that is neither fully inside nor outside the event itself. Much like De-Nur, who wrote about the constant abandonment, Dov Kulka felt that he did not suffer as much as other prisoners because he survived, creating a paradoxical temporal position where his continuing existence in linear time became a form of exclusion from what Jean Améry called the "moral time" of the camps.

Franci Rabinek Epstein's memoir demonstrates how survivor testimony negotiates multiple temporal and psychological spaces, existing in what Marianne Hirsch calls "heterotemporal" reality. Her shift to third-person narrative when describing Auschwitz, referring to herself as "A-4116," exemplifies Caruth's "crisis of representation"—the challenge of narrating experiences that resist traditional narrative forms while simultaneously marking a temporal split where the camp prisoner and the postwar narrator exist in parallel rather than sequential timeframes. Upon liberation, Epstein finds herself watching a newsreel at a movie theater. She is with a soldier who has become a confidant and as they watched it became clear that it was footage of the liberation of Bergen-Belsen: "I watched in total detachment, incredulous about what I was seeing. 'My God, that's you and Kitty!' Exclaimed Jason, with very uncharacteristic excitement" (181). This moment crystallizes the temporal fracture in survivor experience—she exists simultaneously as the person in the footage and as someone watching that person, unable to reconcile these two temporal positions that conventional chronology would place in sequence. Her detachment from her own situation and inability to cope can be linked not only to PTSD, but also to survivor's guilt in that she was the only one left and there was the proof—a visual documentation that paradoxically both confirms and makes unreal her own historical experience. She grappled with navigating friendships with those who had been close to her before the Holocaust, who were now imprisoned alongside her in Auschwitz: "Old friends very often proved to be impossible to get along with in the suffocating new environment, while strangers became friends for life" (55). This is due not simply to the change that trauma inflicted on her as a victim, but to the way trauma dislocates individuals from shared temporal experience, placing them in what Lawrence Langer calls "durational time," where relationships can no longer be sustained by referencing a common temporal past.

Upon her return to Prague, she questioned, "But was it really home? Here I was with three lovely people I had met ten minutes before, who fussed over food as if they had to make up for all the undernourishment we had suffered for three years in one meal, in a tiny three-room apartment that they were ready and happy to share with us" (193). The survivor's guilt of being unable to link these people and this space with home weighed upon her conscience, revealing how trauma disrupts not just psychological but temporal continuity—the home she returns to exists in a different temporal reality than the one she left, despite their physical sameness. On a broader scale, she considers Prague her home, a place that had not been bombed and appeared the same as when she was deported, but it was not the same home she recollected (193). This uncanny disjunction reveals what Ernst Bloch would call "non-synchronicity"—the coexistence of multiple temporal realities in a single space. To cope with her guilt and sense of abandonment, she bought a puppy who she named Tommy after a puppy that was killed in a hunting accident. The first Tommy had provided a distraction from the Nazis, and his replacement was intended to do the same. This attempted repetition represents what Freud called "the compulsion to repeat"—not simply psychological coping, but an attempt to establish temporal continuity across an unbridgeable rupture. Very quickly, Epstein discovers that she has become overly attached to the puppy and gifts it to her boss's child (206). Her reaction is twofold: one, she is attempting to hold onto to something from before, but finds it too difficult because she will not continue living if she is constantly holding onto the past (the puppy), and two, it may be too difficult to try to remember what once was and can never be again. In giving away the puppy, she acknowledges what Walter Benjamin might call "the time of now," or the recognition that genuine historical continuity is impossible after catastrophic temporal rupture.

The complex intersection of survivor's guilt and the imperative to bear witness emerges powerfully in Holocaust testimonies. Olga Lengyel's guilt of survival began the moment she arrived at the camp. These are the first lines of her memoir:

> *Mea culpa*, my fault, *mea maxima culpa*! I cannot acquit myself of the charge I am, in part, responsible for the destruction of my own parents and of my two young sons. The world understands that I could not have known, but in my heart the terrible feeling persists that I could have, I might have, saved them. (Lengyel 11)

Lengyel's account of the selection process reveals how survival itself became a source of unbearable guilt—her attempt to save her children by sending them with her parents, an action based on incomplete knowledge, transformed into a lifelong burden of self-recrimination that exists outside normal temporal progression. Her recollection of "'Mama, Mama!' that will ring in [her] ears forever" (23) demonstrates what Caruth terms the "crying wound," or a voice that speaks beyond conscious knowledge, belonging simultaneously to her children and to all children lost in the Holocaust. The phrase "will ring in my ears forever" collapses all future time into a continuous present of trauma.

The moral complexity of survival in extremis emerges starkly in Lengyel's work in the medical block. The infanticide performed to save mothers' lives represents "choiceless choices" that exist outside normal temporal and moral frameworks. Along with the women she worked with, she made the decision of how to deal with newborn babies and their mothers. Life was a crime and, if discovered, both baby and mother would suffer the consequences, death. The women of the infirmary made the life-saving decision to kill the babies, to save the mothers. They would often lie to a mother and say that the baby was stillborn and not permit them to see the baby. Yet in that process, "the Germans succeeded in making murderers of even us. To this day the picture of those murdered babies haunts me" (114). This revelation shows how the Nazi system forced survivors to participate in actions that would generate additional layers of trauma and guilt while simultaneously collapsing conventional temporal boundaries. The murdered babies exist not in the past, but in a perpetual present that "haunts me to this day." Her use of present tense, "haunts," reveals how these events refuse historical containment.

The imperative to witness, as articulated by Lengyel's fellow prisoner—"You have no right to throw away your life" (80)—transforms individual survival into collective obligation that transcends normal temporal boundaries. This transformation of personal trauma into testimonial duty reflects what Felman terms the "biographical commission," or the obligation to live in order to tell or what Paul Celan calls "meridian time," a temporal reality where survivors live simultaneously for themselves and for those who cannot speak. Her life was no longer her own, but the life of all those she had seen who suffered, for which someday she would be called to bear witness on their behalf. As L. (her friend) said, "We must observe everything that goes on here. Later we shall write down everything we've seen" (81). L. establishes witnessing as both a survival strategy and a moral imperative. This is a profound temporal inversion, where future testimony structures present experience.

Shlomo Venezia experience in the *Sonderkommando* at Birkenau highlights the "grey zone." The *Sonderkommando* were groups of prisoners in the Nazi extermination camps who were forced to dispose of the bodies of the murdered. Venezia witnessed thousands of last moments, occupying what Emmanuel Levinas calls "the time of the Other": "Since he was at the heart of that machine designed to pulverize human lives, Shlomo Venezia is one of the few survivors able to bear witness to the 'absolute' victims, those drowned amid the multitude of forgotten faces not saved by chance and an exceptional fate" (Venezia: Prasquier Note). Much like other survivors wrote, you cannot escape the experience, the burden of surviving the Holocaust:. "Everything takes me back to the camp. Nobody ever really gets out of the Crematorium" (15). This statement reveals not merely psychological trauma but temporal entrapment. Although Venezia survived the *Sonderkommando*, a part of him was left in the ashes.

He was asked if he feels "the need to bear witness," to which he responded in the affirmative and added it is difficult because it must be done properly and in detail. For example, he went to schools to share his story, but students were not aware of the Holocaust, and this made his burden heavier. To bear witness is not simply retelling a story; he says that it "exacts a huge sacrifice. It reawakens a nagging pain that never leaves me.... I call it 'the survivors' disease'" (154). Regardless of this pain, Venezia bears witness, perhaps because if he didn't, the disease would spread. Venezia's survivor's disease could be equated to survivor's guilt. It is what drives him to bear witness as a sense of responsibility, but also a burden for surviving while he watched so many perish at the hands of the Nazis. It is an inescapable feeling that as he says, "It's a disease that gnaws away at us from within and destroys any feeling of joy" (154).

He notes, "Life. Since then, I've never had a normal life" (155). Venezia married and had children, but he never shared his experience with them. He knew he would never be a normal father, and his wife had to balance that aspect of their marriage. He bears witness to strangers to unload his survivor's guilt, yet he cannot express the pain to his family. By sharing his story with children, Venezia is preventing future generations from forgetting all those souls that were erased from the physical world. As he expressed, he has an obligation to remember because he survived. It is also his attempt to prevent the burden from being passed on to his family. Although the burden is shared subconsciously (a matter that will be addressed through the analysis of intergenerational memoirs), he attempts to separate his suffering from his family. This could be that he saw many families enter the gas chambers and suffer as they suffocated or as he watched members of the *Sonderkommando* find their own family members within the tangled corpses. The psychological compartmentalization reveals a temporal compartmentalization as well.

Wiesel's declaration that "With its full burden of distress, shame and horror, the experience the survivor draws from it makes of him a privileged person: a witness" reveals the profound paradox at the heart of Holocaust testimony (Wiesel 2011: 179). His shocking assertion that he would not have preferred to experience the Holocaust from afar demonstrates how the survivor-witness position, despite its horrific origins, creates a unique form of authenticity, a connection. This authenticity, however, comes at a devastating psychological cost—the burden of having survived while others perished solely for being Jewish. The dual nature of witnessing as both privilege and burden manifests in Wiesel's writing through a complex temporal structure. His statement, "Here again, I could spend my life retelling that story" about his father's death, which reveals how certain traumatic moments resist integration into normal temporal experience (Wiesel 1995: 92). The death of his father represents not just a personal loss, but a rupture in time itself—a moment that demands endless retelling precisely because it can never be fully narrated or understood.

This temporal rupture is particularly evident in Wiesel's description of being unable to mourn at the time of his father's death. The absence of immediate mourning transforms into a lifelong process of grief, manifesting through the recurring presence of his father's death in all his writings. Each retelling represents both an attempt at mourning and a testimony to the impossibility of adequate mourning under such circumstances. The haunting detail of his father's final moments—"His last word had been my name. He called out to me and I had not answered" (Wiesel 2006: 112)—encapsulates the complex guilt of survival. Wiesel's inability to respond to his father's call becomes a metaphor for the survivor's impossible position—caught between the obligation to witness and the inability to adequately respond to the dying. His subsequent observation about not shedding tears, followed by the jarring exclamation "Free at last!," reveals the psychological complexity of survival (112). The question of what kind of freedom this represents—whether freedom from the burden of care, from witness, or from the last living connection to his pre-Holocaust life—remains deliberately ambiguous, suggesting the impossibility of resolving the contradictions inherent in survival. Through this passage, Wiesel demonstrates how the act of bearing witness becomes both a privilege that gives meaning to survival and a burden that makes that survival almost unbearable. The testimonial act itself becomes a form of ongoing mourning, never complete and never adequate, yet necessary as both memorial and warning.

The imperative to document his father's final moments extends beyond personal memorial to become an act of resistance against historical erasure. Wiesel's awareness that without his testimony, his father's death "would have been lost like millions of other stories from the Holocaust" reveals how individual witness serves collective memory. Yet this testimonial act occurs within what he acknowledges as an impossible position. This paradox—the necessity of bearing witness despite language's inadequacy—defines the survivor-writer's struggle. Wiesel's insistence that "Still, the story had to be told. In spite of all risks, all possible misunderstandings. It needed to be told for the sake of our children" (Wiesel 2011: 11) reveals how testimony transcends individual memory to become an intergenerational obligation. This transmission serves dual purposes: preserving memory of the dead while counteracting the Nazi attempt to erase Jewish existence from history

The figure of Moshe the Beadle in Wiesel's work emerges as an archetypal witness-messenger, embodying both the urgency and futility of early Holocaust testimony. His return from among the dead to warn the living, met with disbelief, prefigures the fundamental challenge of Holocaust testimony: "Therein lies the dilemma of the storyteller who sees himself essentially as a witness, the drama of the messenger unable to deliver his message: how is one to speak of it, how is one not to speak of it?" (16). This dilemma reveals what Langer calls the "ruins of memory"—the gap between traumatic experience and its communication. Wiesel's engagement with Midrashic tradition—"Whoever sees himself as a severed branch becomes other" (178)—provides a theological framework for understanding witness as both burden and necessity. The metaphor of the severed branch suggests that isolation from collective memory leads to a kind of spiritual death, while the assertion that "Time is a link, your 'I' a sum total" establishes memory as a form of connection across generations. This understanding of memory as connective tissue between past and future transforms individual testimony into collective responsibility.

The dual nature of memory as both burden and necessity emerges in Wiesel's question "What does it mean to remember? It is to live in more than one world, to prevent the past from fading and to call upon the future to illuminate it" (1995: 150). This conceptualization of memory as multitemporal existence suggests what Halbwachs terms "collective memory frameworks," or the social structures through which traumatic memory is preserved and transmitted. Wiesel's assertion that memory is "the only possession a survivor has" (1995: 336) transforms remembrance from personal burden to sacred trust. His ultimate declaration that "To be a Jew today, therefore, means: to testify. To bear witness to what is, and to what is no longer" (2011: 184) establishes witness as central to "post-Holocaust" Jewish identity. This fusion of religious and historical obligation creates what might be termed a "theology of witness," where bearing testimony becomes both religious duty and historical necessity.

SUICIDE: THE ONLY POST

Suicide must be considered as a distinct trajectory within Holocaust experiences and memory. While cultural and religious frameworks often cast suicide as a morally negative or selfish choice, this perspective warrants reexamination in the context of unprecedented trauma. Even our terminology—the phrase "committed suicide"—carries stigmatizing connotations, implying criminality, as suicide has historically been classified as a crime, including within Jewish tradition. The Holocaust inflicted unimaginable suffering, and suicide represented one response to that trauma. In the camps, as documented in survivor memoirs, there were *Muselmänner* who deliberately walked into electrified barbed wire to end their suffering, individuals who hanged themselves in the barracks, and those who intentionally defied their captors knowing it would result in death. Given the circumstances of genocidal violence, how can we evaluate these choices through conventional moral frameworks? While precise statistics on Holocaust-related suicides—both within the camps and beyond—remain impossible to compile, certain individuals who died by suicide or wrote about contemplating it have been preserved in historical records. Their names and stories, when documented, offer crucial insights into this dimension of Holocaust experience and memory. The cessation of direct persecution did not end the suffering. Survivors carried multiple layers of trauma, unprecedented in both scale and nature—trauma for which contemporary psychological frameworks and therapeutic approaches were largely inadequate. Rather than speaking of "healing" or "working through" such trauma, which suggests a naive possibility of resolution, it is more accurate to acknowledge the ongoing nature of Holocaust trauma and its transmission across generations.

For Jean Améry (born as Hans Mayer), who changed his name after liberation, suicide represents neither a negative action nor a subject for psychology analysis. Améry, a Holocaust survivor who wrote extensively about trauma's layered nature, ended his own life in 1978. He preferred the term "voluntary death." While reading his work with this biographical knowledge creates an inevitable lens, his philosophical position on suicide emerges clearly: he views it as a legitimate choice at certain moments. He notes, "Whoever was tortured, stays tortured" (Améry 1980: 34). The physical torture he endured under the Nazis transformed into an inescapable psychological torment: "There was nothing left to come his way except bodily pain and loneliness: what we call a future was blocked. And so he turned to a nonfuture, which would have meant a life entirely enveloped in death. In death, into something clear, into death itself" (Améry 1999: 6). Though Améry wrote these words about another's suicide, they mirror his own experience. His writings reveal the persistence of his suffering and its inescapability. When questioned about collective guilt among German youth, he noted his inability to respond with the confidence of a "future-oriented person." The capacity to envision a future of maintaining hope eluded him. For Améry, the Nazis embodied and epitomized torture (Améry 1980:76). Torture transcends physical assault to become an ontological violation—an attack on one's entire being. Once torture eliminates the future, there can be no "after."

Améry's discussion of the perpetrator's future-oriented perspective can be understood through Caruth's framework of trauma as a "wound of the mind," where the traumatic experience refuses linear temporality. As Caruth argues, trauma manifests as a temporal disruption where past experiences intrude into the present, much like Améry's description of torture: "It still is not over. Twenty-two years later I am still dangling over the ground by dislocated arms, panting, and accusing myself" (36).

The concept of embodied memory, as theorized by Halbwachs, becomes particularly relevant when examining Améry's physical manifestation of trauma. His assertion that he "is" still dangling, rather than merely remembering the experience, aligns with contemporary trauma theory's understanding of how the body holds and expresses traumatic memory. This somatic dimension of trauma challenges traditional psychological approaches that separate mind and body in trauma processing.

Améry argued, "Only those who have entered into the darkness can have a say in this matter. They'll unearth nothing that appears useful in the light outside" (10). He later explains that he can write about suicide because he can empathize and is introspective (25). Améry lived in a world where suicide was not an abstract concept: it held a strong potentiality, and eventually, his own suffering ended with suicide.

> For what it comes to for them is the total and unmistakable singularity of their situation, the situation vécue, (lived situation) that can never be completely communicated, so that therefore every time someone dies by his or her own hand or even just tries to die, a veil falls that no one can lift again, which in the best of cases can only be illuminated sharply enough for the eye to recognize as a fleeting image. (Améry 1999: 8)

When Améry discusses the impossibility of communicating the "situation *vécue*," his observation parallels with LaCapra's concept of "empathic unsettlement," the recognition that certain traumatic experiences resist full representation or understanding by those who have not experienced the trauma directly. This theoretical framework helps explain the void in language that Améry identifies regarding both suicide and Holocaust experiences.

The divergent perspectives of Viktor Frankl and Jean Améry on suicide and survival illuminate crucial aspects of trauma theory and Holocaust memory studies. Their contrasting approaches to survival and meaning-making demonstrate what LaCapra terms the difference between "acting out" and "working through" trauma. Frankl's emphasis on finding meaning represents an attempt at "working through," while Améry's position aligns more closely with the concept of "acting out"—a repeated confrontation with the traumatic past that resists integration.

The tension between Frankl's insistence of meaning and Améry's rejection of psychological frameworks can be understood through Caruth's concept of trauma as "unclaimed experience." Améry's assertion that suicide "breaks with the logic of life and therefore also with psychology" aligns with Caruth's understanding of trauma as that which exceeds normal mental processing and categorization (Améry 1999: 18). His rejection of psychology points to the "collapse of witnessing."

Améry's description of memory as "Absolute time, absolute since body and mind now know that no further deceptive repetitions will be organized, compresses itself on two levels. Memory, arrested in time, the memory of past times in the present" (88) resonates with Halbwach's theory of collective memory, particularly in how traumatic memory exists outside normal temporal frameworks. His experience of being perpetually suspended "by dislocated arms" demonstrates what van der Kolk terms "the body keeps the score," or the way trauma manifests in somatic memory that defies conventional psychological categorization.

The concept of "post-Holocaust" experience that Améry rejects can be analyzed through Rothberg's theory of "traumatic realism." Améry's insistence that all his experiences remained linked, including his eventual suicide, challenges linear narratives of survival and recovery. This perspective aligns with what Hoffman terms "paradoxical legacy," the way trauma continues to shape experience even in supposed aftermath.

The apparent contradiction between Frankl's and Améry's positions on suicide reflects a broader tension in Holocaust studies between "received history" and individual testimony. While Frankl attempts to construct what Young would term "redemptive narrative," Améry's position represents what Langer calls "tainted memory"—memory that resists redemptive interpretation. When Améry describes suicide as a "nonway, because it was leading nowhere," he articulates what Lifton terms "psychic closing off," a response to what cannot be integrated into normal experience. This connects to what Hartman describes as the "intellectual witness," or those whose testimony carries the weight of both bearing witness and acknowledging the impossibility of full representation.

The tension between their perspectives illuminates a central paradox in Holocaust testimony: the simultaneous imperative to find meaning and the recognition that conventional frameworks of meaning may be inadequate to the task. This paradox is what Felman and Laub term the "crisis of witnessing"—the fundamental challenge of representing and working through trauma that exceeds normal categories of understanding.

Another survivor who wrote about suicide was Marceline Loridan-Ivens. Her experience in Birkenau, where she witnessed both murder and suicide (arguably all murder), demonstrates Langer's "choiceless choices." The concept of suicide within the camps represents Agamben term "the state of exception," where normal ethical considerations become suspended under extreme circumstances.

The temporal disruption in her narrative becomes evident when she challenges readers: "But I'm talking to you about a time you never knew. Imagine the world after Auschwitz, when the wish to live replaces the wish to die" (84). This paradoxical shift from survival imperative to suicidal ideation after liberation aligns with what Lifton identifies as "death guilt." Her haunting question, "How then can one cope with trauma, with the Holocaust?" resonates with what Caruth describes as a fundamental rupture in the continuity of experience.

Loridan-Ivens's description of her own suicide attempts reveals the persistence of trauma: "In an attempt to 'obliterate' like her father, Loridan-Ivens tried to drown herself in the Seine" (61–62). This act of attempted self-erasure demonstrates what LaCapra terms "acting out," a repeated confrontation with traumatic memory that resists integration into normal experience. Not long after her attempt, she contracted tuberculosis and was sent to a sanatorium to recover. This only solidified that she was a burden to her family and attempted to commit suicide for a second time (61–62).

The intergenerational transmission of trauma within her family exemplifies what Rachel Yehuda terms "biological inheritance of trauma." Her brother Michel's deterioration is particularly telling of the transmission of trauma: "He was sick from the camps without ever having been there. When he got to be the age you were when you disappeared, he took some pills and alcohol, this time enough so he wouldn't wake up again. We only broke down his door and found his body inside a full month later" (67). His eventual suicide, described starkly as "this time enough so he wouldn't wake up again" (67), demonstrates the persistence of what LaCapra terms "transferential relations to the past." Before his untimely death, he would call her and "leave her threatening messages, posing as an SS officer." This appropriation of the perpetrator's voice illustrates what Nicolas Abraham and Maria Torok call the "phantom"—the way trauma can be transmitted across generations through what remains unspeakable.

Loridan-Ivens captures the disorientation of survival in vivid terms: "It was like a blinding light after months in the darkness, it was too intense, people wanted everything to seem like a fresh start, they wanted to tear my memories from me" (64). This passage aligns with what Laub describes as the "collapse of witnessing," or the fundamental difficulty of reintegrating into a world that cannot comprehend the survivor's experience. Her resistance to societal pressure to forget is further emphasized when she notes that "they thought they were being rational, in harmony with passing time, the wheel that turns, but they were mad, and not just the Jews—everyone! The war was over, but it was eating all of us up inside" (64).

The devastating impact on family systems becomes clear through her sister Henriette's fate. Henriette committed suicide at sixty years old in the same fashion that Michel had: "She also died from the camps without ever having been there" (67). Her family suffered, first the loss of their father, the loss of who Marceline was, Michel, their mother, and finally Henriette. This profound observation exemplifies what Maria Yellow Horse Brave Heart identifies as "historical trauma response." The family's collective suffering is further emphasized in Loridan-Ivens's lament, "Because there was no family without you [father]" (69), illustrating what family systems theorist Monica McGoldrick terms "ghost in the family system." Her raw questioning—"Why was I incapable of living once I'd returned to the world?"—demonstrates the "crisis of witnessing." The impossibility of return is captured in her observation that her family "could not return to what they once were, there were pieces to their puzzle that would forever be missing." This permanent rupture aligns with "durational time," where trauma creates an insurmountable break in temporal experience.

Loridan-Ivens's memoir thus reveals how Holocaust trauma operates not just on individual survivors, but on entire family systems. Her powerful statement that they "wanted to tear my memories from me" (64) encapsulates what Hartman terms the "intellectual witness," the obligation to remember despite social pressure to forget. Through her testimony, we see the inadequacy of conventional psychological frameworks for understanding the long-term impacts of severe trauma, particularly when that trauma affects multiple generations through both direct and indirect exposure.

The testimonies of Dr. Miklos Nyiszli and Filip Müller illuminate what Agamben terms the "grey zone" of moral complexity within the concentration camp system. Nyiszli's position as a doctor for the *Sonderkommando* exemplifies "choiceless choices," where traditional ethical frameworks become inadequate for understanding survival decisions.[29] His paradoxical role of preventing suicides while recognizing their moral validity demonstrates what Primo Levi describes as the "extreme situation" where conventional moral categories breakdown.

Nyiszli's observation that "At Auschwitz it was never a question of whether you would live or die, but merely a question of time, of when you would die" (91) aligns with Caruth's identifies as temporal disruption in traumatic experience. The certainty of death created what Lifton terms a "death environment," where suicide became, paradoxically, an assertion of agency within a system designed to deny all human autonomy.

The account of the Greek Jewish prisoner who attempted suicide after witnessing his family's murder illustrates as the "collapse of witnessing." Nyiszli's professional obligation to prevent suicide while privately acknowledging its legitimacy demonstrates what psychiatrist Herman terms "dialectic of trauma," or the tension between knowing and not knowing, between professional duty and moral understanding. His conclusion that the man's death "would have been moral and devoid of the physical and mental anguish" (108) represents what van der Kolk identifies as the rational recognition of irrational circumstances.

Nyiszli's forced participation in Dr. Mengele's research, marked by his clinical observation about "vast possibilities for research" (56), demonstrates what Friedländer terms "deep memory"—the way trauma can be simultaneously remembered and distanced through professional language. His final declaration that he would "never lift a scalpel again" (222) represents "working through" of trauma through professional renunciation.

Filip Müller's testimony provides a different perspective on *Sonderkommando* trauma. While Müller was a member of the *Sonderkommando* in Birkenau for three years, he witnessed murder on an unimaginable scale. He witnessed the murders of families, lone children, his own relatives, and could do nothing to stop this with the exception of suicide. His question "what sort of life it would be for me in the unlikely event of my getting out of the camp alive" (111) exemplifies "durational time," where trauma creates a permanent rupture between past and future. His contemplation of his irreplaceable losses, culminating in his suicide attempt, demonstrates "survivor's guilt."

The pivotal moment when Müller joins others in the gas chamber "to die an anonymous death" represents "collective memory" in its most extreme form. The intervention of the women who convince him to live, particularly the symbolic passing of the locket, demonstrates what Felman calls the "testimony of survival," or the obligation to bear witness even in the face of overwhelming despair.

Müller's transformation regarding stealing food from the dead, marked by his eventual "eating bread while his hands are covered in blood and feces," illustrates what psychiatrist Henry Krystal terms "massive psychic trauma"—the fundamental alteration of basic human responses. His recognition that "the person that Müller was would never be again" aligns with what Laub identifies as the "second Holocaust"—the ongoing impact of survival itself.

The final observation about writers who committed suicide, including Primo Levi, Tadeusz Borowski, and Paul Celan, demonstrates "intellectual witness"—those who bore testimony through writing but ultimately succumbed to what Améry describes as the inescapable weight of traumatic memory. Their fates illuminate what Caruth identifies as the "paradox of survival," where living itself becomes a form of ongoing traumatic experience. These testimonies reveal how the *Sonderkommando* experience represents an extreme case of what trauma theorists term "limit experiences," or situations that challenge our basic frameworks for understanding human behavior and survival. The accounts of both Nyiszli and Müller demonstrate how conventional psychological and moral frameworks prove inadequate for comprehending the depth of trauma experienced by those forced to witness and participate in the mechanics of mass murder.

CONCLUSION

The testimonies examined in this analysis demonstrate how Holocaust trauma fundamentally disrupts traditional temporal frameworks, challenging the very notion of "post-Holocaust" as a meaningful category. Through the lens of what Caruth terms "unclaimed experience," we can understand how trauma resists integration into normal temporal and narrative structures, persisting instead as what LaCapra calls "acting out"—a repeated confrontation with experiences that refuse to become past.

The diverse perspectives presented through these testimonies, from Améry's philosophical rejection of psychological frameworks to Loridan-Ivens's account of intergenerational trauma, and from Nyiszli's medical ethical dilemmas to Müller's *Sonderkommando* experiences, illuminate what Langer terms "durational time," where trauma creates not a past event but an ongoing present. The act of bearing witness through memoir writing itself represents what Felman and Laub identify as the "crisis of witnessing," where the very attempt to articulate trauma reveals its resistance to full representation.

The persistence of trauma across generations, evident in the experiences of survivors' families, demonstrates what Yehuda terms the "biological inheritance of trauma." This transmission of trauma challenges conventional therapeutic narratives of recovery and closure, suggesting instead what Maria Yellow Horse Brave Heart identifies as "historical trauma response," the way trauma continues to shape individual and collective experience across time and generations.

These testimonies compel us to reconceptualize how we approach genocide survivors and their experiences. Rather than imposing artificial temporal boundaries through terms like "post-Holocaust," we must recognize what Halbwachs terms "collective memory"—the way traumatic experience continues to shape present reality. This understanding requires a fundamental shift in both scholarly and public discourse, acknowledging what Hartman calls the "intellectual witness," or ongoing obligation to bear witness to experiences that resist closure or resolution.

The inadequacy of the term "post-Holocaust" becomes evident when we consider what Lifton terms "death guilt," the persistent psychological burden of survival itself. This analysis suggests that we need new frameworks for understanding how genocide continues to shape both individual and collective experience long after the historical event has ended. Rather than seeking closure or resolution, we must develop what LaCapra terms "empathic unsettlement"—a way of engaging with traumatic testimony that acknowledges its ongoing nature while respecting its fundamental resistance to complete understanding.

This research thus contributes to a broader reconceptualization of how we approach genocide studies, trauma theory, and survivor testimony. By recognizing the ongoing nature of traumatic experience, we can better support survivors while honoring their diverse perspectives and experiences. The challenge for scholars and the public alike is to develop frameworks that acknowledge what Hoffman terms the "paradoxical legacy" of genocide—its simultaneous resistance to full representation and its demand to be witnessed and understood.

4

RETHINKING THE "POST" IN "POST-HOLOCAUST"

TRAUMA IN GENERATIONAL SURVIVORS' MEMOIRS

With the aging and inevitable passing of Holocaust survivors, we must look to subsequent generations to bear witness and record their stories. The succeeding familial generations of the Holocaust are referred to as second-, third-, and fourth-generation survivors in most scholarship. They exhibit signs of trauma stemming from their parents or grandparents, providing evidence that a "post-Holocaust" cannot exist for these individuals.[30] Those in close proximity to survivors are impacted not only by events linked to the Holocaust that they experience firsthand, but also events they have not directly experienced.[31] For these descendants, the Holocaust is not a historical event that ended in 1945, but an ongoing lived reality that shapes their identity, relationships, and worldview. It must be noted that those labeled "second-generation" or "third-generation" individuals represent a continuation of the "first" generation rather than separate groupings. These designations are based solely on birth chronology. Additionally, the subsequent generations experience trauma of their own as intergenerational survivors.

Dina Wardi termed this group "memorial candles," as these are the individuals who have taken on the task of remembering their family's history despite its burden. Each "memorial candle" straddles what Wardi calls a "double reality" (Wardi 108). They simultaneously create their own present and future while remaining connected to their parents' and grandparents' past. This temporal duality overlooks the direct trauma that the second—and third-generation individuals experience:

their nightmares, mental health issues, and familial struggles stemming from the Holocaust. Wardi eventually acknowledges these individuals' trauma, by emphasizing their additional layer of borrowed memories in their psyches (Wardi 194). Wardi notes that "memorial candles" are predominantly females, a pattern reflected in this chapter. Daniel Heller suggests this gender disparity may relate to *halacha*, which establishes that a mother's Jewish identity determines her child's Jewish identity. Thus, daughters ensure the preservation of both family history and Jewish heritage. The "memorial candles" discussed in this chapter primarily reflect experiences with their mothers, despite some having two survivor parents. The Nazis, understanding *halacha*, specifically targeted mothers as they represented the continuation of Jewish lineage. By attempting to eliminate mothers, they sought to prevent the future existence of Jews and Judaism.

Regarding terminology for inherited memory, several scholars have proposed different concepts. Ellen Fine's "absent memory" describes the creation of memories based on others' recollections (Fine 78). However, this term minimizes the trauma later generations endure through their interacts with Holocaust survivors. Froma Zeitlin's "vicarious witnessing" suggests later generations echo their parents' memories, considering these echoes inherently defective (Zeitlin 8). This framework fails to acknowledge later generations' direct experiences with the Holocaust's impact, including witnessing their parent's nightmares and coping with the absence of extended family. Other scholars have contributed terms such as Gabriele Schwab's "haunting legacy" and Eva Hoffman's "postgeneration." Marianne Hirsch, a second-generation survivor herself, coined the term "postmemory," which she defines as:

> To grow up with overwhelming inherited memories, to be dominated by narratives that precede one's birth or one's consciousness, is to risk having one's own life stories displaced, even evacuated, by our ancestors. It is to be shaped, however indirectly, by traumatic fragments of events that still defy narrative reconstruction and exceed comprehension. These events happened in the past, but their effects continue into the present. (Hirsch 5)

She argues that the "post" in "postmemory" transcends mere temporality, allowing for the ongoing impact of the Holocaust (5). While Hirsch's definition validates the intergenerational trauma experienced from 1945 onward, the term "post" problematically suggests finality rather than acknowledging the continuously evolving nature of traumatic memory transmission across generations. The prefix "post" implies a temporal break—an after—that fundamentally misrepresents how Holocaust memory operates within families. For descendants of survivors, the Holocaust is not something that happened before they were born, but something that continues to happen in their daily lives, manifesting in psychological, behavioral, and even physiological patterns. Furthermore, since all memory is inherently "post," this raises a crucial theoretical question: how does a second—or third-generation survivor's memory fundamentally differ from that of a direct survivor? The concept of temporal disruption is central to understanding why a "post-Holocaust" period remains impossible for survivors and their descendants. Traditional historiography relies on clear chronological boundaries, with events neatly categorized into "before," "during," and "after." However, for Holocaust survivors and their descendants, time operates differently. As Huyssen argues, "The temporal status of any act of memory is always the present and not, as some naive epistemology might have it, the past itself" (Huyssen 3). This present-tense quality of traumatic memory disrupts linear temporality, creating what Caruth calls "a history that is essentially not over" (Caruth 62).

Raul Hilberg posits a dichotomy between memory and history. Dominick LaCapra, working with the concept of "truths," argues that historiography cannot be reliably linked to such "truths" as empirical evidence (LaCapra 1). He contends that "truths" create a subject-object binary, leading to questions of subjectivity and objectivity. This framework problematically assumes historians can achieve objectivity (4–5). This raises particular complications for Holocaust scholars who are themselves survivors. While LaCapra advocates for empathic unsettlement—maintaining critical distance while attempting to understand the other's position—this becomes particularly complex for second—and third-generation individuals who experience the Holocaust's impact directly through their familial relationships (30).

Some descendants choose writing as a medium of traumatic expression. These texts, which I term "second-generation memoirs" or "third-generation memoirs," fall into two distinct categories. The first comprises works where children or grandchildren document their family member's Holocaust narrative, though the author's presence inevitably manifests through stylistic choices.[32] The second category intentionally interweaves the survivor's story with the author's own narrative of inherited trauma. Hoffman, in her second-generation memoir *After Such Knowledge*, distinguishes between survivors writing "from memory" and subsequent generations writing "about memory" (188). However, this distinction becomes problematic when applied to the second category of memoirs, including her own work. Her framework potentially diminishes the agency of subsequent generations in experiencing their own Holocaust-related trauma. This could stem from her personal relationship to her parents' survival narrative and her family's losses. It's more accurate to conceptualize the suffering of subsequent generations not as lesser, but as qualitatively different, shaped by postmemorial transmission.

These memoirs serve dual purposes: preserving Holocaust testimony for future generations and providing a therapeutic medium for processing inherited trauma. Writers including Hoffman, Hirsch, and Wanderer Cohen identify writing as a crucial mechanism for working through intergenerational trauma. This chapter analyzes these memoirs through several theoretical lenses: temporal frameworks, the construction of generational survivor identity, pilgrimages to sites of memory, bearing witness, and the transference of trauma across generations.

STYLE OF TIME WITHIN GENERATIONAL MEMOIRS

Unique to second—and third-generations' memoirs is their nonlinear temporal approach, contrasting with survivors' chronological narratives. While survivors typically structure their accounts around documented historical events, later generations interweave their experiences with their ancestors, demonstrating how Holocaust trauma fundamentally disrupts linear temporality. This disruption represents not merely a stylistic choice, but reflects the lived experience of time for descendants of survivors—where past events from before their birth intrude into present consciousness. However, characterizing this as mere "intertwining" creates an artificial separation, suggesting two distinct timelines that occasionally intersect. The reality is far more complex: descendants' identities are inextricably linked to their survivor ancestors—their narratives cannot exist independently. Rather than intersecting parallel stories, these narratives present a singular, transgenerational experience of trauma where later generations process both inherited trauma and the trauma of witnessing their loved ones' suffering.

Though some later-generation authors maintain chronological structures, most adopt nonlinear approaches reflecting their processed understanding of inherited trauma. Their narratives resist the concept of "post-Holocaust," as the Holocaust's impact remains actively present rather than historically distant. This analysis focuses on memoirs incorporating authors' personal narratives rather than purely documentary accounts.

Mirla Geclewicz Raz's *The Birds Sang Eulogies: A Memoir* exemplifies this approach through its multivoiced narrative structure. Using typographical distinctions and clear attribution, Geclewicz Raz weaves together the perspectives on survivorship across three generations. The shared trauma responses between second—and third-generation individuals, despite their different relationships to the survivor, demonstrate the persistence of transgenerational trauma as one story of a family of survivors. To achieve this distinction Geclewicz Raz uses different typefaces to represent different voices in her family's story. For example, when her mother speaks, the words appear in italics. This visual technique helps readers navigate between different time periods and perspectives while emphasizing how these voices and experiences blend into one family narrative.

Helen Epstein's work, initially structured as scholarly interviews with second-generation survivors, transforms into what Laub calls "testimonial dialogues."[33] Though she begins with academic intentions connected to her psychological research, the shared experience of inherited trauma dissolves the boundary between researcher and subject. Her methodological shift from formal interviews to conversations exemplifies what LaCapra terms "empathic unsettlement." The text demonstrates what Hirsch calls "postmemorial working through" when Epstein notes, "his story merged with the stories each of us had heard at home, so much that the feelings he described became our own" (Epstein 1988: 24). Her use of present-tense narration reflects what scholars term "traumatic temporality," where past trauma maintains psychological immediacy in the present, affecting each participant differently, yet creating shared patterns of experience.

Sarah Segal's *An Heiress of Holocaust: How My Family Survived the Holocaust and the Lasting Effects on My Life* employs what might be termed "encapsulating narrative structure." By framing her parents' testimony within her own experience and concluding with her life in Israel, she creates what Young calls "collected memory"—a complex interweaving of historical documentation and inherited trauma. Her shifting narrative voice between personal testimony and historical analysis demonstrates what Halbwachs terms the intersection of "collective memory" and individual experience. The alternation between conversational and academic tones reflects the dual nature of second-generation testimony: both inherited memory and scholarly witness.

Barbara Ruth Bluman's *I Have My Mother's Eyes* exemplifies what Nadine Fresco terms "absent memory" through its multilayered temporal structure. Her interweaving of terminal illness narrative with her mother's Holocaust testimony creates what Hartman calls "witnesses by adoption." The memoir's completion by her daughter adds what Marianne Hirsch terms "postmemorial succession"—the transmission of trauma across three generations. Bluman's nonlinear approach on the macro level, contrasted with chronological chapter structures, reflects what scholars term "traumatic temporality." The title itself functions as what Hirsch calls a "memorial object," simultaneously representing physical inheritance and metaphorical transmission of traumatic memory. Her rejection of "post-Holocaust" periodization aligns with "founding trauma," where historical events maintain active presence in family systems. The physiological connection suggested by the title demonstrates what Nicolas Abraham and Maria Torok term "transgenerational phantom"—the embodied transmission of trauma across generations.

STRADDLING GENERATIONS: JOSEPH POLAK

Joseph Polak's memoir *After the Holocaust the Bells Still Ring* demonstrates the complexity of what Hirsch terms "points of memory." Polak survived Westerbork and Bergen-Belsen, and he was just three years old when the war ended. In essence, he writes that his story is unbelievable because if anyone should not have survived, it was an infant. As one of the Holocaust's youngest survivors, his position bridges multiple categories: the "1.5 generation" (Suleiman), "*Kriegskinder*" (children of war), and "*Nachgeborenen*" (those born after). For example, when describing his early experiences, he writes: "I don't think I ever grew up. Almost to the present, I find myself fully comfortable only among young people, not adults, not even adults younger than me" (136). This liminal status challenges traditional categorizations of Holocaust memory and survival.

Polak's earliest and most devastating memory was the "Lost Train" to Troebitz from Bergen-Belsen, which served as a defining moment that exemplified Langer's concept of "durational time." He described it as "also my worst memory of these years" (83), marking the traumatic separation from his mother and the beginning of his orphaned existence. This moment crystallized his deepest fear: believing his mother was dead and wondering who would care for him.

He found himself at *Joods tehuis* recovery home with other Holocaust survivors. Polak astutely observed that residents were "not there to recover from physical illnesses," but rather from "the Holocaust itself, from which ... there is neither recovery nor escape" (104). His understanding of trauma as an "incurable life-long disease" that can be "passed onto future generations, a contagion" aligns remarkably with contemporary epigenetic trauma studies. As he powerfully conceptualizes it, these individuals were not simply in the Holocaust; rather, the Holocaust is in them, an incurable disease that continues to plague them. These individuals are the only ones who can testify to his suffering and bear witness to the Holocaust.

At *Joods tehuis*, Polak formed a profound relationship with Haya, a peer who uniquely represented what Maurice Halbwachs terms "collective memory," the shared traumatic experience that creates lasting bonds between survivors. When she departed suddenly without warning, it reinforced what Laub calls "the second wound," the trauma of abandonment that follows initial survival. "I searched for her the morning after they left and could not find her" (Polak 106) he recalled, capturing the renewed sense of loss and abandonment. Their reunion in the United States six decades later demonstrated the concept of "durational time," where traumatic memory exists in an eternal present. Polak wrote with remarkable emotional immediacy: "I am still able to come close to tears and experience how deeply I grieved for her when I searched for her the morning after they left and could not find her" (106). The preservation of this emotional intensity across decades reveals trauma's ability to collapse temporal distance.

What makes Haya's case particularly significant is her status as the only person from this period whom Polak remembers independently, without relying on what he calls "the accounts of others" (108). This direct memory, preserved across decades, exemplifies what Hirsch calls a "point of memory," where personal recollection intersects with larger historical trauma. The profound impact of their brief connection illustrates "unclaimed experience," where trauma creates bonds that resist temporal logic. Their eventual reunion demonstrates trauma's ability to collapse temporal distance, creating "empathic unsettlement," where past and present emotional experiences become indistinguishable, as evidenced when Polak writes he can still "experience how deeply I grieved for her" (106). Yet Polak's reflection on memory's dependence reveals a deeper anxiety about identity and narrative ownership: "Your story is never really your own, it is always what others tell you it is, you are dependent on them for your biography, and you can never let these authors go for fear that when they are gone, your story will be obliterated" (108). This dependency on others' accounts highlights the fragility of survivor identity and the constant threat of narrative erasure, making Haya's case all the more remarkable as an instance of truly independent recollection.

It wasn't until spring 1946, after a year of rehabilitation, that he was reunited with his mother, which paradoxically became another trauma. He believed, up to this point, that his mother was dead, but she never stopped searching for him. Heartbreakingly, Polak failed to recognize her because "she has gained her figure back" (85). This moment illustrates "traumatic rupture" having known his mother only as a concentration camp victim, Polak's perception of her identity had become inextricably linked to Holocaust trauma, demonstrating what researchers term the "transgenerational phantom."

This persistence is evident in his powerful observation about memory's overwhelming presence: "Memory, these days, at least for us, is not at risk. It is omnipresent. Sometimes it even feels as though it would take over experience. Sometimes we have to fight to continue living in Amsterdam and Boston and Jerusalem instead of in Westerbork, Bergen-Belsen and Troebitz" (73). This struggle between past and present, between traumatic memory and lived experience, captures the ongoing challenge faced by survivors who must actively resist being consumed by their memories while ensuring they are never forgotten.

This struggle exemplifies what LaCapra calls the tension between "acting out" and "working through" trauma. Polak's description of having to actively resist being pulled back into camp memories demonstrates "unclaimed experience"—trauma that resists integration into normal memory. His characterization of this as an "impossible task" reveals "durational time," where past trauma maintains an eternal presence, creating what Polak describes as an "inescapable loop of memory" that prevents survivors from ever fully leaving the Holocaust behind.

Although Polak cannot escape memories of the Holocaust, he acknowledges that his memories of life in the camps were primarily told to him by his mother. In addition to her recollections, he conducts research about the Holocaust to fill in gaps, incorporating excerpts from memoirs written by others who were in the same camps. His inability to remember the trauma from the camps parallels the experience of second-generation survivors, whom he believes should be classified as survivors themselves. He anticipates being one of the last first-generation survivors alive to bear witness and fears people will not trust him as a survivor because his memories are not always firsthand (130). Moreover, he worries that his young age during the Holocaust will cause others to dismiss his testimony, much as adults often discount children's stories.

Though Polak has no memory of his father, who was murdered by the Nazis, he lives his life searching for him while battling night terrors and suffering from rheumatic tremors (86; 130). His suffering remains as present and profound as that of adult survivors. As Polak explains, "It is also to piece one's life together on the basis of the accounts of others. Your story is never really your own, it is always what others tell you it is, you are dependent on them for your biography, and you can never let these authors go for fear that when they are gone, your story will be obliterated" (108). For him, the loss of older Holocaust survivors represents a loss of self, comparable to a child losing a parent who connects them to their past. As he reflects, "I don't think I ever grew up. Almost to the present, I find myself fully comfortable only among young people, not adults, not even adults younger than me. I'm often astonished to find that I am older than some of the grown-ups who continue to frighten me with their social comforts and certainties" (136). Polak perpetually searches for connections to the past, present, and future that remain elusive.

What all this speaks to is the extraordinary unimportance of the year 1945. It marked the end of the war, but hardly the end of the Holocaust. The trauma of the Holocaust, only now being faced, only now being processed, hurtled through the 1950s and perhaps the 1960s. Survivors acted out; certainly, any of the child survivors were next to impossible to parent, wild and unmanageable. And children born into these families—families whom the Holocaust during these years was not a thing of the past but an ongoing reality—I would classify not as children of survivors, but as survivors themselves (110).

This passage articulates the central argument against any notion of a "post-Holocaust." Polak decisively rejects 1945 as a meaningful temporal boundary, challenging conventional historical periodization that would confine the Holocaust to the years 1933–1945. By extending the very definition of survivorship beyond those who directly experienced the historical events to include descendants born after so-called liberation, Polak reconceptualizes the Holocaust not as a historical event with clear temporal boundaries, but as an ongoing psychological reality that continues to claim new victims decades after the so-called liberation. This understanding fundamentally disrupts any attempt to establish a "post-Holocaust" era, as the traumatic effects continue to manifest in new generations.

PILGRIMAGE TO EUROPE: RETRACING TRAUMA

Second-generation survivors often undertake journeys to European Holocaust sites, but these aren't ordinary trips—they represent what scholars call "memory-work." While a typical trip aims for relaxation or pleasure, these journeys serve as pilgrimages—deliberate visits to places of profound meaning where survivors and their descendants engage with traumatic history.

Polak's experiences with such pilgrimages reveal different layers of trauma and memory. His first solo journey to Bergen-Belsen in 1992 shows how institutional validation can intersect with personal memory. When museum staff confirmed his presence on three lists, this documentation provided official proof of his survivor status (108). This moment illustrates how survivors sometimes need external verification of their own lived experiences—a complex dynamic in trauma studies where personal memory meets historical record.

His 1995 pilgrimage demonstrates how memory works across generations. Although Polak had grown up hearing his mother's Holocaust stories, she hadn't spoken about Westerbork. He only discovered its significance to his own history through researching *Joodse Raad* (Jewish Council) records. This reveals how trauma survivors often have gaps in their narratives that later generations must piece together through historical research. When he finally visited Westerbork, he found himself sharing the space with both survivors and Dutch rescuers, showing how sites of trauma can become places of shared meaning for different groups touched by historical events (44). The emotional peak of this pilgrimage came at Bergen-Belsen, where Polak gave a speech describing how the Holocaust remains present in survivors' lives, "lurking" like "the angel of death." His words resonated deeply with another survivor, who approached him afterward to share her own experience. Her confession that she spends Sundays at her local Holocaust memorial rather than with her loving family—"there, somehow, I am in my element; there, believe it or not, is where I feel most at home" (74)—reveals how trauma can permanently alter one's relationship to space and time. These places of memory become more than historical sites; they transform into spaces where survivors feel most connected to their identities and experiences.

This inability to fully leave the sites of trauma behind, even decades later and thousands of miles away, demonstrates "durational time"—where past trauma maintains an active presence in the survivor's daily life, refusing to be confined to history. The American survivor's weekly visits to her local memorial show how the need to connect with these spaces of memory persists, even when the original sites are far away. Through these pilgrimages, we see how Holocaust memory works across generations and geography, creating what scholars call "postmemory"—where children of survivors inherit not just stories, but deep emotional connections to places they may never have been before.

Despite giving a powerful speech about survival, Polak wrestles with profound questions of authenticity and memory. Having survived Bergen-Belsen at age three, he grapples with what scholars call "testimonial anxiety," doubting his legitimacy as a survivor due to his young age during the events. This self-questioning reflects a broader phenomenon among child survivors, who often struggle to reconcile their status as survivors with their limited direct memories.

His attempt to connect with Bergen-Belsen's physical space demonstrates what memory scholars term "site-specific memory activation." However, because the British had burned the camp to prevent disease spread, Polak encounters what Nora calls an "absence of presence"—where the physical traces of trauma have been erased, complicating the process of memory recovery (74). This absence creates a particular challenge for child survivors, who may hope that returning to significant sites will trigger dormant memories.

When Polak reaches Troebitz, the site of his first clear memory, he makes a crucial observation about generational differences among survivors. Child survivors, he notes, possess distinct cultural markers that set them apart: they speak Hebrew instead of Yiddish, and English without accents. Most significantly, they carry what he calls a "lighter touch without the darkness" (76). This observation reveals what trauma theorists term "differential trauma response," how age at the time of trauma shapes both its impact and expression.

His characterization of child survivors as "breezy" compared to adult survivors demonstrates what Suleiman calls the "1.5 generation phenomenon"—where those who experienced the Holocaust as very young children develop distinct coping mechanisms and cultural identities that bridge survivor and postwar generations. This position creates a unique form of postmemory, where the absence of direct traumatic memories combines with the presence of survivor identity to create a complex relationship with the past.

When second—and third-generation survivors undertake pilgrimages to Europe, they are participating in what Feldman calls a "ritual reenactment of survival" (3). These journeys serve a deeper purpose than simple tourism—they represent what memory scholars term "performative testimony," where descendants physically trace their ancestors' paths to understand their trauma and survival.

The motivation for these pilgrimages varies among descendants. Some grow up with the Holocaust as a constant presence in their lives, while others encounter silence around their family's history. As survivors age and pass away, these journeys become increasingly significant—what Hirsch terms "acts of postmemory" or attempts to establish physical connections with stories that might otherwise remain abstract. Think of it as creating a bridge between inherited memory and physical space.

The preparation for these journeys demonstrates what scholars call "memory reconstruction." Descendants often spend considerable time researching, gathering family stories, and piecing together their relatives' wartime movements. This detective work becomes part of what Hoffman calls "the inheritance of trauma"—the active work later generations do to understand their family's past.

Feldman's analysis of Israeli youth trips to Poland provides a framework for understanding all generational survivors' pilgrimages. His observation that these journeys transform participants into "victims, victorious survivors, and finally . . . witnesses of the witnesses" (3) reveals how physical presence at sites of trauma creates what memory scholars call "secondary witnessing." This transformation isn't limited to Israeli youth—it applies to all descendants who undertake these journeys, regardless of their current nationality or residence.

The concept of becoming "witnesses of the witnesses" is particularly significant in understanding how trauma and memory pass between generations. These pilgrimages serve as what Pierre Nora terms "sites of memory transfer," where later generations actively take on the responsibility of carrying forward their family's testimony. By physically retracing their ancestors' paths, descendants participate in what scholars call "embodied memory work," creating their own connection to historical events they did not personally experience. This process establishes what memory theorists call "transgenerational witness," where subsequent generations become active participants in preserving and transmitting Holocaust memory rather than passive inheritors of trauma.

When later generations undertake journeys to Europe, they're engaging in what memory scholars call "temporal pilgrimage," attempting to connect with a moment in time as much as a physical place. These descendants often carry what Hirsch terms "inherited memory images"—mental pictures of prewar and wartime Europe constructed from their parents' or grandparents' stories. When they arrive at these locations, they frequently encounter what memory theorists call "temporal displacement"—the jarring realization that these places have continued to exist and change beyond the moment of trauma their family experienced. This temporal displacement further underscores the impossibility of a "post-Holocaust" period, as descendants discover that their internal psychological landscape, shaped by transmitted trauma, exists in profound tension with the external physical world. The continuing trauma maintains an active presence in their psyches, even as the physical locations have been transformed by time creating disjunction that further entrenches their experience of temporal disruption.

This expectation that time should have remained frozen in European cities reveals something profound about how Holocaust memory is transmitted across generations. When survivors share their stories with children and grandchildren, they often describe locations as they existed during the 1930s and 1940s. These descriptions become fixed points in the descendants' imagination, creating what scholars call "memorial time," where certain places exist perpetually in their wartime state in family memory, even as the physical locations continue to change and develop.

This temporal disconnect provides compelling evidence for what trauma theorists call "continuous traumatic present," where the Holocaust isn't simply a historical event, but an ongoing reality that shapes family identity across generations. When descendants discover that these places have changed, it can create what psychologists term "memorial disruption," a secondary trauma where the inability to physically connect with the past reinforces the sense of loss and displacement.

The impossibility of truly "returning home"—both temporally and physically—demonstrates what scholars call "transgenerational trauma transmission." Just as survivors cannot return to their prewar homes, their descendants inherit this sense of perpetual displacement. This inheritance challenges the very notion of a "post-Holocaust" period, suggesting instead what theorists call "continuous trauma time," where the impact of historical events remains actively present in family systems across generations.

Victor Turner's foundational concept of pilgrimage describes a journey from the familiar to the unfamiliar, where pilgrims enter what he calls a "liminal period"—a transitional state outside normal social structures (Turner 1978: 3). While this basic framework helps us understand the structure of memorial journeys, it requires significant modification when applied to Holocaust memory. The key difference emerges in Turner's assertion that the liminal period reduces anxiety, stress, and guilt. For descendants of Holocaust survivors, these journeys often intensify rather than relieve emotional burdens. When second—and third-generation survivors visit sites of family trauma, they aren't entering neutral "liminal space," but rather what memory scholars call "sites of traumatic inheritance." These locations trigger what Hirsch terms "postmemorial affect"—inherited emotional responses to places of family trauma.

Turner's concept of liminal space transcending ordinary time and social order (Turner 1974: 273) does resonate with Holocaust pilgrimages, but in a distinctly traumatic way. Rather than providing escape from normal structures, these sites force confrontation with what LaCapra calls "founding trauma," events so profound they permanently alter one's relationship to time and space. Most significantly, Turner's elliptical model of pilgrimage—moving from structure to antistructure and back—proves inadequate for Holocaust memorial journeys. His model assumes pilgrims can return to their original state, but as we have seen with survivors (discussed in chapter 3), return becomes impossible after profound trauma. For their descendants, these pilgrimages often create what trauma theorists call "secondary traumatization," where connecting with sites of family trauma fundamentally alters their understanding of self and history.

The psychological impact that Turner's model does not account for what memory scholars term "transgenerational trauma transformation," how engaging with physical sites of family trauma can trigger profound psychological changes that prevent simple "return" to previous states of being. These journeys do not complete an ellipse but rather create what we might call a "trauma spiral," where confronting sites of family trauma leads not back to the starting point, but to a transformed understanding of self and history.

Feldman notes that participants struggle to readjust to daily life after these intense experiences, observing that they find it "difficult to readjust to ongoing daily and school life after their intense experience in a different space, with very different rhythms of time" (230). This difficulty mirrors what trauma theorists call "temporal disruption," where encountering sites of historical trauma alters one's relationship with present time. Just as their surviving relatives could never fully return to prewar normalcy, descendants often find their worldview permanently altered by these encounters with family history.

Hirsch's observation about the "impossibility of return" for those "who were never there earlier" (213) introduces a fascinating paradox in Holocaust memory. She deliberately leaves ambiguous both whose trauma is being encountered and who is attempting to "return." This ambiguity reflects the complex nature of what memory scholars call "inherited trauma," where descendants carry the psychological weight of events they never personally experienced. This brings us to a crucial question about the nature of "return" itself. For survivors, physical return to Europe often proved impossible after liberation—many immigrated and rebuilt lives elsewhere. But Hirsch suggests something deeper: that when descendants visit these sites, they are attempting a different kind of return—not to a physical place they once knew, but to a moment in family history that exists primarily in transmitted memory.

The potential for these visits to traumatize survivors adds another layer of complexity. When descendants visit places their relatives have avoided, it can create what psychologists call "secondary trauma activation," where the younger generation's engagement with historical sites triggers fresh trauma for survivors. This demonstrates how Holocaust memory continues to operate actively across generations, challenging any simple notion of "return" or closure. Understanding this helps us see why these journeys cannot be understood as simple tourist visits or even traditional pilgrimages. They represent what we might call "transgenerational memory work"—attempts to bridge the gap between inherited memory and physical space that often transform both the visitor and their family's relationship to the past.

Mirla Geclewicz Raz, the daughter of two Holocaust survivors, convinced her parents to return to Poland with her. She explains in her second-generation memoir that it took her months to convince them to go (Geclewicz Raz 135). Her family went to the towns where both parents were respectively from and she proclaimed that,

> Suddenly, I felt extremely uncomfortable to be surrounded by Poles. As we walked towards the crowds, I asked my parents to only speak English. The reason was that I was worried that if my parents spoke Polish that somehow the Poles would discern that we were Jewish and would then harm us. Such was my paranoia. Perhaps it was my lack of sleep playing with my emotional state. Perhaps it was knowing how the Jews in Poland had been treated as Polish citizens. I went over to my mom and told her about my fears. She looked at me as if there were something wrong with me and said, "Don't be ridiculous. These people won't hurt you. They're harmless." At that moment, I felt the emotional weight vaporize. Here I was, surrounded by Poles, and my mother said I had nothing to worry about. (138)

This "paranoia" represents a common psychological pattern among children and grandchildren of survivors, particularly in their relationship to spaces where the trauma occurred. This response exemplifies what trauma theorists call "inherited hypervigilance"—a heightened state of anxiety passed down through generations. Geclewicz Raz's experience illustrates a phenomenon of memory that scholars term "temporal stasis" in Holocaust memory transmission. When she undertakes her pilgrimage, she expects to encounter a 1940s Poland because her mental image of the country has been shaped entirely by her family's Holocaust narratives. This expectation demonstrates how traumatic memory can create what we might call "frozen timeframes," where locations become permanently associated with specific historical moments in family memory.

For descendants like Geclewicz Raz, Poland exists primarily as the site of the Holocaust, making the concept of "post-Holocaust" Poland almost impossible to grasp. Her experience shows how inherited trauma can create what memory theorists call "temporal anchoring," where certain places remain perpetually fixed in their moment of historical trauma, regardless of actual changes over time. This fixed temporal perspective reveals something crucial about how Holocaust memory operates across generations. Rather than experiencing these locations as places that have evolved over time, descendants often encounter them through what Hirsch terms "postmemorial vision"—seeing them primarily through the lens of their family's traumatic past. This creates a unique form of historical engagement where the present-day reality of these places must compete with deeply ingrained family memories of trauma.

The experiences at Auschwitz-Birkenau reveal another aspect of inherited Holocaust memory. Geclewicz Raz arrives carrying what we might call "anticipated trauma response," an expectation of emotional breakdown based on her understanding of the site's horror. However, her actual experience—"I was in Auschwitz and was stalwart" (Geclewicz Raz 147)—demonstrates the complex nature of engaging with what scholars term "mediated trauma sites." The difference between her expectation and experience stems from a crucial transformation: what was once an active death camp has become what memory scholars call a "memorial-museum space." The absence of the sensory elements her parents described—the smells, the orchestra's cruel music, the presence of murderers and prisoners—creates what we might term a "memory gap." The site's current state as a memorial cannot fully convey what her parents experienced, yet it exists in her mind as their description of it, frozen in time.

This disconnect between inherited memory and present reality helps us understand how Holocaust trauma travels across generations. Children of survivors often carry what Hirsch calls "postmemory"—a version of these places constructed entirely from their parents' testimonies. When they encounter the actual locations, transformed by time and preservation efforts, it creates a unique form of cognitive dissonance: the sites simultaneously exist as both their parents' descriptions and their present reality. These experiences show us how memorial sites can never fully bridge the gap between historical trauma and present-day remembrance. The very elements that make these sites accessible to visitors—their transformation into organized memorial spaces—also distances them from the raw horror of their historical reality. This paradox is central to understanding how Holocaust memory operates across generations: even as we preserve these sites for memory and education, we inevitably transform them into something different from what survivors experienced.

Lori Klisman Ellis also made a pilgrimage with her mother to Auschwitz-Birkenau. She remarked that "It was still so hard to believe that she, along with my family, was going to retrace the steps in Auschwitz. In my mind, I was thinking who would ever want to go back to the place where they feared for their lives every minute of the day, where there was no food or water, where death emanated all around you" (Klisman Ellis 123). Her mother had told her that she had to go to Auschwitz during this trip because this was the last place that she saw her brother Srulek alive and she had hoped to find closure and say goodbye to him. The staff was able to locate documentation that her brother survived the selection and was eventually transferred to Bergen-Belsen, but after that they did not have any further information that they could provide (123). Now the question was if he had survived the Holocaust. Her family does not have the answer and may never know the truth, much like many other families. This lingering question is one of only many that create this impossibility of a "post-Holocaust." Her mother had made the trip to say goodbye and receive closure, but instead she left with more questions.

When Zilber embarks on her journey without her mother's "blessing," she encounters what trauma theorists call "transgenerational anxiety." Her nervousness about visiting places where her family was murdered reflects how children of survivors often inherit not just memories, but emotional relationships to specific locations. This inherited anxiety demonstrates how trauma can shape geographic relationships across generations, even for places never personally experienced. Interestingly, Zilber's first encounter with Lithuania creates an unexpected sense of familiarity through what we might call "cultural memory transmission." Her recognition of foods like those her mother prepared in America shows how Holocaust survivors maintained cultural connections even in displacement. This familiar comfort, however, exists alongside profound discomfort—notably her inability to enter Polish antique shops because they gave her "the creeps" (124). This reaction demonstrates what scholars call "object trauma," the way seemingly ordinary items can become charged with historical violence when we consider their potential origins in Holocaust theft.

Her documentation process—photographing everything while wondering about her mother's presence—illustrates what Hirsch terms "postmemorial work." Without certainty about specific locations' significance, Zilber attempts to capture everything, demonstrating how children of survivors often feel compelled to preserve potential connections to family history. This uncertainty transforms her journey into what we might call "speculative memory work."

At concentration camp sites, Zilber experiences what memory scholars term "object witnessing." When she wonders if she's looking at "aunt Genya's shoes or my name-sake-grandmother, Eta's, hairbrush" (115), she's engaging in what we might call "familial projection," seeing potential family connections in anonymous artifacts of mass murder. Her discovery that her grandmother and aunt were killed in Birkenau rather than Auschwitz shows how these pilgrimages can also serve as fact-finding missions, filling gaps in family knowledge. The encounters in Chynowie and Mlynek demonstrate what memory scholars call "verification moments." The liberation site sign and the elderly woman's testimony provide what Zilber experiences as physical confirmation of her mother's survival narrative. Her trembling response to the Stutthof sign reveals how inherited trauma can manifest physically in later generations.

Finally, Zilber's failed attempt at property restitution illustrates what scholars term "bureaucratic retraumatization." The lawyer's reference to

1999 as a cutoff date shows how administrative timeframes can conflict with psychological ones—while governments may declare endpoints to Holocaust claims, the loss continues to affect families across generations. This perpetual loss of family possessions demonstrates how the Holocaust refuses temporal containment, creating what we might call "continuous dispossession" that affects subsequent generations.

BEARING WITNESS WITHOUT WITNESSING

The Latin distinction between *testis* (third-party witness) and *superstes* (direct witness) reveals an important complexity in how we think about Holocaust testimony. While English collapses these into a single word, "witness," the distinction helps us understand different forms of bearing witness. But here's what's fascinating: second—and third-generation survivors challenge this binary. They're neither purely third-party observers (*testis*) nor direct witnesses (*superstes*), but occupy what we might call a "inherited witness" position—they carry forward testimony through both direct family experience and historical knowledge.

The Biblical Hebrew concepts of *zakhor* (remembrance) and *shamor* (guardianship) offer a deeper framework for understanding this inherited witness role. These terms show us how Jewish tradition conceptualizes memory as an active, ongoing process that connects past, present, and future. When we apply this to Holocaust memory, we can see how descendants of survivors aren't just preserving stories, but are actively maintaining what we might call a "living testimony." They're both remembering (*zakhor*) their family's experiences and guarding (*shamor*) these memories for future generations.

Felman and Laub's work on testimony adds another crucial layer to our understanding. Their observation that listeners become "co-owners of the traumatic event" helps explain how trauma passes between generations. When children and grandchildren of survivors hear Holocaust testimony, they're not just receiving information—they're experiencing what we might call "transmitted trauma." This challenges their suggestion that listeners maintain separate space from the trauma. For descendants of survivors, the boundary between witness and victim often blurs because the Holocaust shapes their own identity formation. Their concept of the "second holocaust"—where survivors view new catastrophes through the lens of their Holocaust experience—helps explain how trauma travels across generations. When survivors teach their children "lessons" from the camps (don't love, don't tempt fate, don't have family), they're passing on what we might call "survival frameworks" that continue to shape family dynamics long after 1945. This creates what Felman and Laub call "a history of repetition"—where the Holocaust isn't just a past event, but an ongoing reality that shapes each new generation's understanding of the world.

This helps us understand why second—and third-generation survivors see themselves as witnesses who will carry forward testimony after the last survivors pass away. They are not just preserving historical facts, but maintaining what we might call an "active witness chain" that connects past trauma to present responsibility. Their role combines elements of both *testis* and *superstes*, creating a new category of witness that Jewish tradition might recognize as fulfilling both *zakhor* and *shamor*—remembering the past while guarding its significance for the future.

Elizabeth Rosner, a second-generation survivor and author of *Survivor Cafe: The Legacy of Trauma and the Labyrinth of Memory*, claims that she has been witnessing her parents' story since before she could truly comprehend that she was bearing witness (Rosner 4). Her book, although not labeled as a memoir, reflects upon her experience as a second-generation survivor and what it means to her. Rosner's philosophy in relation to bearing witness is: "It's no accident we express it this way: *embodied* history, *bearing* witness... A living presence transmitted in real time, entering the bodies of those who are listening. Something entirely *un*bearable that must, somehow, be borne, and then passed on" (32). Bearing witness, at this point in her life, is viewed as a history that bears down upon her. Much later in her book, in conversation with other second-generation survivors, she realizes that they see it as a badge of honor rather than a burden. For Rosner, she was aware that her parents saw her birth and subsequent life as a way of defeating Hitler and the Nazis (71). In this sense, she and her generation would bear witness to the survival of the Jewish people as a whole. Consequently, this would prevent the "double killing," as Elie Wiesel stated (Wiesel 2006:

xv). The meaning here is that the world cannot deny the Holocaust because there are witnesses ready to stand as testimony to history that can be linked to the trauma of today. Rosner also points out that as a witness, part of her responsibility is to listen to other witnesses.

With this in mind, as Polak and other Holocaust survivors have previously demonstrated, bearing witness is an essential rationale for writing memoirs. However, the question arises: how does an individual who was not present during 1933 to 1945 bear witness? These descendants possess the legacy of trauma, the continuation of trauma, that derives from being a relative of a Holocaust survivor. For these individuals, there is no "post," because their loved ones were forever changed by the Holocaust; consequently, their children or grandchildren never knew them as they were before the trauma. Moreover, for some generational survivors, trauma is inflicted upon them emotionally or physically, causing their own extension of trauma originating from the Holocaust.

Having grown up with survivors, they have witnessed who their loved ones became and have come to understand the Holocaust's influence on them. Therefore, they not only continue to bear witness to the period before their parents became parents, but also to the people their parents became because of the trauma they endured. This perspective is unique to second—and third-generation survivors—they lack tangible memories from before 1945 (unless they make pilgrimages to the sites, and even then, they access only fragments), yet their relatives have passed down their stories to be remembered, making them witnesses. Additionally, they carry the memories of their upbringing with an omnipresent Holocaust.

Melvin Jules Bukiet compiled an anthology of second-generation survivors, including himself. In his introduction, he writes about the inability to escape the Holocaust as survivors told those who had no choice but to listen: their children (Bukiet 13). Second-generation children are thus perpetually aware of the Holocaust, preventing them from ever disconnecting themselves from the horror. Even for those whose parents did not explicitly share their horrors, there were and are impacts from the Holocaust that affected them.

As Bukiet states, "If a chasm opened in the lives of the First Generation, they could nonetheless sigh on the far side and recall the life Before, but for the Second Generation there is no Before. In the beginning was Auschwitz" (13). To address the first part of his statement: those who survived the Holocaust can (sometimes) remember what life was like before—possibly recall family members who were murdered or homes they once lived in. However, for the second-generation individuals, there are no such personal memories.[34] They were born and raised in a world without extended families, without ancestral homes, without heirlooms like wedding rings passed down through generations. If they have no before, they cannot have an after.

Therefore, second-generation survivors must rely on their parent(s) to remember and create these memories—a mutual relationship in which if the mantra "never again" were to have even a small chance of being true (which I argue has already been proven impossible), one must pass on these memories, and the child must disseminate them through tasks such as writing memoirs. This responsibility requires an almost impossible requirement: "It's our job to tell the story, to cry, 'Never Forget!' despite the fact that we can't remember a thing" (16).

Bukiet continues: "'Memory' is the mantra of all the institutions that reckon with the Holocaust, but memory is an inaccurate term. For anyone who wasn't *there*, on either side of the barbed wire, Jew or German, thinking about the Holocaust is really an act of imagination. All we know is how little we know" (16). Bukiet questions what this means for a second-generation's understanding of time and their role in it when "the most important events of your life occurred before you were born?" (18). He concludes by comparing first—and second-generation survivor writing: "Also, a matter of genre, even when the First Generation claim they're writing fiction, their pages usually bestride memoir. They have no need to imagine; we have no option but to imagine" (21). As mentioned in the chapter about first-generation memoirs, while survivors may claim their writings are fiction, how much is truly invented rather than witnessed remains questionable. However, for second-generation survivors, an informed imagination becomes necessary to understand their parents and, by extension, themselves.

Sarah Segal begins her memoir by acknowledging the weight of bearing witness and accepting her position as the "memorial candle." She writes of the obligation to prevent the Holocaust from joining the forgotten horrors of history, committing herself to continue conveying the message of her people (Segal 26–27). This task, however, carries profound burdens. When we consider Wardi's interpretation of a "memorial candle," we can understand Segal's body as represented through the wick, with the flame representing the souls of those remembered. Alternatively, Segal's body might be interpreted as the wax necessary to support both wick and flame against the winds that threaten to extinguish the memory. In this metaphor, the wax gradually diminishes as the flame burns—much as the bearer of testimony sacrifices parts of themselves in the act of remembering. Segal's burden manifests early when her mother is placed in a psychiatric facility. In her mother's absence, she assumes the responsibilities her mother had previously managed, embodying the role of the memorial candle in both practical and symbolic terms.

> Every morning, I breathed Mom's horrors from the Holocaust into my lungs. From my earliest childhood, my life was interwoven with the sights, stories and lessons that I had to draw from my mother's bitter experience. At night, she would return to the 'lager,' beg for her life before the Gentile Chernovsky standing over her, trying to rape her. Her mental illness destabilized me and exacerbated the imbalance in my life. I was an extension of her. Everyone said I looked like her. Yes, I was crazy like her. I hated her, loved her, blamed her and pitied her all at once. (Segal 16)

By bearing witness to her mother's trauma, Segal develops her own trauma. As she conveys it, she begins experiencing nightmares that mirror the stories she had etched into memory in order to carry their history. She felt as if she was becoming the "symbol" of her parents, an extension rather than an individual due to this memorialization (22).

Segal describes a particularly powerful moment of witnessing within her childhood home. Her family gathered around the radio as it broadcast survivors' testimonials during the Eichmann Trial—creating a scene of bearing witness to the witness. Through the airwaves came the voice of Leibl, a close family friend, testifying about his Holocaust experience. His testimony revealed his position as part of the *Sonderkommando* unit at Auschwitz, which Segal describes as "the worst thing imaginable" (164). Segal leaves ambiguous whether this response stems from the common misconception that *Sonderkommando* members betrayed their people, rather than recognizing them as victims who had no choice, or from the newfound awareness of the specific horrors their friend had endured.

Following his court testimony, Leibl visited the Segal household in what she understood to be both an apology and an explanation (165). Though fourteen-year-old Segal was initially asked to leave due to her youth, she continued to bear witness by eavesdropping from around the corner. This moment represents a complex layering of witness-bearing: Leibl testifies to his own experience while Segal becomes a witness not only to his story, but to her parents' reactions to his testimony. Leibl's compulsion to share his testimony beyond the courtroom, specifically with his friends, demonstrates the urgent need to create new witnesses to carry forward this history—a role Segal would later embrace. Through these experiences, the text clearly demonstrates how Segal experienced a transference of trauma through her parents.

TRANSFERENCE OF TRAUMA

Elizabeth Rosner explores the biological transmission of trauma across generations through epigenetic inheritance. She writes, "Which is to say, my generation's DNA carries the *expression* of our parents' trauma, and the trauma of our grandparents' too. Our own biochemistry and neurology have been affected by what they endured. Epigenetics researchers are looking at the ways that the experiences of starvation, grief, and shock pass forward into the future" (Rosner 7). This understanding of inherited trauma moves beyond psychological and social transmission into the realm of biological memory, where the body itself becomes an archive of historical trauma.

The scientific evidence supports this perspective: children of survivors demonstrate altered cortisol production, a hormone crucial for regulating the body's stress response through both the immune and nervous systems.

This biological manifestation of inherited trauma aligns with Hirsch's concept of "postmemory," where the transmission of traumatic knowledge and experience occurs so deeply that it creates memories in its own right. However, while Hirsch primarily focused on psychological and cultural transmission, epigenetic research suggests a literal biological inscription of ancestral trauma. This intersection of biological and psychological inheritance complicates traditional understandings of trauma transmission. The reduced cortisol production in survivors' children represents what Caruth might call a "wound that speaks," a physical manifestation of historical trauma that continues to express itself in subsequent generations. This biological echo of past trauma challenges conventional temporal boundaries between past and present, suggesting that traumatic experiences leave traces not only in narrative and memory, but in the very substance of heredity.

Ettie Zilber's memoir demonstrates the complex interplay between direct and inherited trauma. Her narrative illustrates Hirsch's "postmemory" when she writes, "Sometimes, I get a feeling as if I had lived through the dark days of my parents' trauma—with fleeting fears and thoughts. As some of us, particularly those born shortly after liberation, may say; 'We feel as if we experienced the Holocaust'" (130). This articulation of temporal collapse, where past trauma intrudes into present consciousness, is particularly poignant given her birth in a displaced persons camp and her status as firstborn.

Her naming after her grandmother who was murdered in Birkenau in 1944 represents what Young terms "received memory," where remembrance becomes both tribute and burden (131). The weight of this memorial practice is amplified through her mother's persistent efforts to maintain connections with survivors and collect photographs of murdered relatives. The creation of a portable shrine of photographs demonstrates what Alison Landsberg describes as "prosthetic memory"—physical links to traumatic pasts that move with the family through space and time (135). The starkness of inherited trauma emerges in moments like her mother's response about family medical history: "they had no time to develop a disease; they were killed young" (146).

Zilber's childhood in 1950s Brooklyn reveals the complexities of postwar Jewish identity. When asked about her birthplace, she "had to publicly acknowledge that she was born in Germany," leading to cruel taunts of "Nazi" from classmates (142). This experience led to what she describes as "a preference of being with other children of survivors or immigrants and a desire to hide her Jewish identity from those that were not like her" (136). She had to conceal not just her Judaism, but "the languages she spoke, the foods she ate, and the traditions she upheld in her household" (133).

The transmission of trauma manifests in her description of self-testing behaviors. She recalls walking to school on a freezing day, allowing her toes to freeze to her boots despite having extra socks, "to test her ability to survive just as her mother had survived a death march" (150). Her mother's reaction of shock to this revelation underscores the complex ways trauma echoes across generations.

The domestic sphere becomes a site of what Laub terms "witness by adoption" as Zilber describes her father's "wrath that often seemed to be unprovoked" and her mother who "lost sleep because of nightmares that would frighten her to awake." Her mother's coping mechanism—she "was never idle" and would "delve into cleaning the house or gardening to distract herself" from painful memories (145)—demonstrates trauma's manifestation in perpetual activity. The transference of nightmares from mother to daughter culminates in Zilber's own dreams where she becomes "the hero, saving her family from the impending doom" (146), illustrating what Ernst van Alphen calls the "inherited right to remember," where subsequent generations not only carry trauma, but attempt to master it through imagination.

This careful integration of Zilber's direct testimony with trauma theory reveals how second-generation survivors embody what Hartman terms "witnesses by adoption," carrying forward not just memories, but the very mechanisms of trauma and survival. The interweaving of her precise language with theoretical frameworks helps us understand how personal narrative illuminates broader patterns of intergenerational trauma transmission.

Zilber's account demonstrates the complex psychological inheritance of Holocaust trauma through everyday behavioral patterns. Her understanding of her parents' emphasis on punctuality and education as survival-based behaviors demonstrates what Laub calls "knowing without knowing," an inherited understanding of trauma's imperatives without direct experience. The concentration camps' requirement for perfect timing as "an act of life or death" becomes transformed into a familial mandate for precision in all things (157). Her powerful testimony reveals a core dynamic in survivor families:

> I could never ask them for help with my mundane problems, which could never be compared to the problems and suffering they had endured. I also never wanted to burden them with my disappointments or difficulties—or anything negative; after all, they had it worse, and my petty problems paled by comparison. I don't remember if they ever articulated this attitude, but I certainly absorbed it, as did so many of the Second Generation that I read about. (159)

This self-silencing exemplifies what psychiatrist Yael Danieli terms the "conspiracy of silence," where children of survivors internalize a prohibition against expressing their own pain, creating what she calls a "double wall" of silence between generations. The internalization of this dynamic demonstrates what Rachel Yehuda describes as "implicit trauma transmission," where survival behaviors are passed down without explicit instruction. This transmission manifests in another crucial testimony from Zilber:

> I also felt that since they had suffered so much, I had to shield them from further suffering, so I never wanted to tell them any bad news and always brought home excellent report cards. I always wanted to make them happy, almost as if to make up for their suffering. Teenage rebellion did not exist—at least not overtly. (159)

The absence of teenage rebellion reflects what Epstein terms "children of the Holocaust," where normal developmental processes are altered by the weight of historical trauma. Her role as protector inverses the traditional parent-child relationship, creating what psychoanalyst Martin Bergmann calls "transposition of roles," where children of survivors often feel responsible for their parents' emotional well-being.

Through Zilber's detailed account, we see how "postmemory" operates not just through stories and images, but through deeply ingrained behavioral patterns and unspoken emotional contracts between survivors and their children. Her testimony provides crucial insight into how historical trauma shapes family systems and individual identity formation in subsequent generations.

Like Zilber, Emily Wanderer Cohen's memoir explores second-generation trauma through her relationship with her survivor mother, Mutti, in America. Her narrative demonstrates the "unclaimed experience" of trauma, where past experiences intrude violently into the present. This manifestation appears in Wanderer Cohen's description of her mother's sudden shifts in behavior: "We would be having a conversation and it was like a switch would flip. She became enraged-yes, rage is the right word—and I knew what was coming." She later recognizes, "Reflecting back on those times, I think Mutti left the present and went back to Germany in her mind, to the concentration camps and the terror she experienced in them" (Wanderer Cohen 3).

The physical abuse through the flyswatter (45) represents what Yehuda terms "intergenerational transmission of trauma," where survivors can unconsciously recreate trauma dynamics. Wanderer Cohen's insight that "victims can become perpetrators" while she assumed "the role of the victim," "acting out"—the unconscious repetition of traumatic patterns. Her understanding that her mother's violence might stem from an inability to fight back against the Nazis reveals the complex ways trauma can transform within family systems.

The preoccupation with possessions illustrates Hirsch's "postmemory." This emerges in Mutti's response to a lost bracelet: "'Well, don't you dare think we'll replace it. You don't deserve nice things. You clearly can't take care of them'" (13). The prohibition against striped clothing (30) and strict rules about sandwich portions—"The portion of meat and cheese to bread had to be less than 1:1" (58)—demonstrate what Hoffman calls "embodied knowledge" of survival, where concentration camp experiences become encoded in everyday practices.

The demand for perfection and comparison of suffering exemplifies what Laub terms "the imperative to tell" conflicting with the impossibility of fully conveying trauma. When Wanderer Cohen "demonstrated any imperfection," her mother's response involved comparing their suffering—her status as a survivor against her daughter's perceived failures in "a much easier world" (14). This dynamic reflects what Epstein identifies as the "double bind" of second-generation survivors, caught between honoring their parents' suffering while attempting to establish their own identity.

The discovery of her mother's hidden past through the unexpected letter (65) and subsequent research reveals the "collective memory" of trauma, where individual memories are shaped by larger historical forces. The contrast between Mutti's joyful prewar personality—"You know, they were both always laughing and having fun! Your mother was so full of life—and she was funny!" (79)—and her postwar self demonstrates what Lawrence Langer terms "deep memory" versus "common memory," where trauma creates an unbridgeable divide between past and present selves.

Wanderer Cohen's evolution from hiding her mother's survivor status to eventually understanding her own trauma inheritance illustrates what Dan Bar-On calls "the legacy of silence." Her initial attempt to avoid being "different" (115) and later realization that the Holocaust "was just something that happened to Mutti that I had to deal with" (116) shows the gradual process of what Susan Rubin Suleiman terms "conscious remembering," where second-generation survivors come to understand their own relationship to historical trauma.

This careful analysis reveals how intergenerational trauma operates through what Nicolas Abraham and Maria Torok call "transgenerational haunting," where unprocessed trauma creates patterns that echo through generations, ultimately leading Wanderer Cohen to recognize how she "passed it down to her children" (118).

In her parenting, Wanderer Cohen consciously struggles against reproducing traumatic patterns, finding it "extremely difficult" (15) to avoid her mother's harsh responses to imperfection. This illustrates what psychoanalyst Abraham terms "phantom transmission," where unconscious traumatic patterns persist even when consciously recognized. The challenge of breaking these patterns demonstrates what Hoffman calls the "paradox of indirect knowledge," where inherited trauma feels both foreign and intimately familiar.

Her relationship patterns reveal what attachment theorist Mary Main identifies as "disorganized attachment," stemming from her mother's emotional unavailability. Cohen's insight that she sought relationships with emotionally unavailable men or those who "wanted to have control over her, like her Mutti" (49) demonstrates what trauma theorist Vamik Volkan calls "chosen trauma"—where survivors and their children unconsciously recreate traumatic dynamics in their intimate relationships. Her recognition of these patterns through conversations with other second-generation survivors illustrates "witnessing to witness," where shared testimony enables deeper understanding of trauma's impact.

The psychological inheritance of her mother's hypervigilance manifests in "unclaimed experience"—anxiety, self-doubt, and fear of leaving safe spaces. Wanderer Cohen's childhood memory of "begging to take part in activities" only to be paralyzed by fear because "her Mutti had convinced her that the world was a horribly dangerous place" (41) demonstrates what Helen Epstein terms "traumatic worldview," where the child inherits the survivor's sense of persistent danger. Her ongoing struggles with travel anxiety and last-minute cancellations (42) show how "postmemory" continues to shape daily life choices.

The concept that there cannot be a "post-Holocaust" for her powerfully illustrates what LaCapra calls "founding trauma," where historical trauma becomes constitutive of identity. Her understanding that "her survivorship is directly linked to her mother's suffering" demonstrates what Bar-On terms "the legacy of silence," where trauma's impact continues even without direct discussion. Her conscious effort after her mother's death in 2014 to "avoid becoming her Mutti," symbolized by her vow to never use a flyswatter, reveals what Susan Rubin Suleiman calls "conscious working through"—the intentional effort to transform inherited trauma patterns.

This analysis reveals how what Gabriele Schwab terms "haunting legacies" operate across generations, requiring conscious effort to transform rather than transmit traumatic patterns. The ongoing presence of Holocaust trauma in Wanderer Cohen's life demonstrates "durational time," where traumatic past continues to shape present and future experiences.

Another second-generation survivor influenced by her maternal upbringing was Susan H. Brown. She wrote a book of poems based on her experiences and understanding of what it means to be a second-generation survivor. Brown's hope was to convey this message to her children. This, in and of itself, is of importance as she tried to find a way to express her own upbringing to her children and how, in turn, her childhood could have impacted them. Her poems are not simply a history of events, but rather an emotional rollercoaster that evokes more questions than answers, possibly a symptom of her becoming a psychologist. Her poems follow a chronological path while intertwining her family's Holocaust experiences. At a very young age, her father was taken by the government of Hungary for his political beliefs and held for five years. He was released only when the Soviet Union fell. When he returned to their home, she wrote that he turned to his wife and asked, "Which one is mine?" (16). This question is reminiscent of Polak's story in the orphanage—the inability to recognize one's loved ones. This story sets the tone of suffering within Brown's family structure, a narrative often devoid of deeper connections, possibly due to the potential for pain and abandonment.

Her story is one of instability, especially regarding home. Brown's parents made the decision to move from Hungary to Austria and finally to the United States. She writes about the losses she experienced during each of these moves and the parts of herself that she was forced to leave behind because her parents were trying to escape their traumatic pasts. During these moves, she lost connections to people, language, culture, and Judaism itself. At the age of ten, Brown said goodbye to Annus, her nanny. Throughout Brown's early life, this woman had filled the void of affection that her parents were unable to fill: "My nanny, my mother, my love, my happy memory" (Brown 46). Annus fulfilled the role of mother for as long as she was permitted, but much of Brown's childhood was spent as an only child in a world where she did not belong. It would be sixteen more years before Brown could reunite with Annus. The reunion created a blur between past and present: "I zigzag through time zones" (47). However, it was Annus who had become the small, vulnerable person who needed care, and when they parted, Brown understood they would never meet again.

From a trauma theory perspective, this passage illustrates several key concepts in the intergenerational transmission of trauma. The multiple relocations represent not just physical displacement, but also psychological fragmentation—a common experience for children of survivors who must navigate their parents' attempt to outrun their traumatic pasts. These moves create what trauma theorists call "disrupted attachment patterns," where the child experiences repeated severance of meaningful connections. The relationship with Annus is particularly significant in trauma theory. Her role as a substitute maternal figure suggests what theorists term "compensatory attachment," where children seek emotional nurturing from alternative sources when trauma prevents their parents from providing it. The sixteen-year separation and final reunion with Annus represents what trauma theorists call "temporal disruption," where traumatic experiences cause time to be experienced nonlinearly, as evidenced by Brown's description of "zigzagging through time zones." The role reversal in their final meeting—where Annus becomes the one needing care—illustrates what theorists describe as the "recursive nature of trauma," where patterns of care and loss repeat themselves across generations and relationships, but with shifted dynamics. This cycle of separation and loss echoes her parents' traumatic experiences, showing how trauma patterns can replicate themselves even in different contexts.

Brown wrote a poem about her mother's life, and through these words it becomes evident that Susan viewed her mother primarily as a woman defined by suffering. The poem begins with "With quiet rage..." and continues with her tale of survival in Bergen-Belsen (53). She poignantly writes, "To leave her family behind, She bears a child"—this child being Susan herself. Yet when writing about herself as this child, she does not claim this personhood, suggesting both her sense of having had no choice in her existence and her guilt that her mother left behind her family for her own survival. She ends the ode to her mother with what could be interpreted as stark observations of emotional absence, perhaps masking her unfulfilled hopes: "She doesn't mourn, She doesn't pray, No hope, no tears, She dies bereft of speech" (54). Her mother could not express emotions, her "curiosity lost" and her drive for life absent (53). As a daughter, this created tension and an inability to relate to her own mother in a world where her family represented her only cultural connection and means of communication.

Her father had hoped to connect with his only child through music but found that she did not live up to his expectations. When they listened to a rousing classical music composition, he asked his daughter to identify the composer, only to be disappointed by her incorrect response. Although only a child at the time, she understood that she had humiliated him (32). Brown had also left behind her Jewish roots. While she does not explicitly state this began with her parents, she provides glimpses suggesting their approach to surviving Europe influenced this departure. One revealing anecdote describes her mother furnishing their new house in Vienna when their landlady remarked, "I have more of these carpets in the attic, they belong to some Jews" (26). According to the poem, her mother remained silent in response to this painful comment. Brown then transitions to her school experience, where she was placed in a Protestant class and had to keep her true religion secret (26). In both instances, the poem reflects how silence became central to Brown's understanding of the Holocaust, as she learned to remain silent about her Jewish identity to protect herself. Her family's behavior demonstrates the continuing impact of Nazi ideology. It was not until her college years that Brown began "to shed my secret Jewishness" and chose to study psychology, hoping it would "resolve the conflict of my identity" (3).

From a trauma theory perspective, this passage illuminates several key aspects of intergenerational trauma transmission. The mother's emotional numbness ("doesn't mourn ... doesn't pray") represents what trauma theorists call "affect dysregulation," where survivors lose the ability to process and express emotions normally. This creates a profound impact on the next generation, as children of survivors often struggle to develop healthy emotional expression when their primary caregivers are emotionally unavailable. Her father's attempt to connect through music, resulting in shame and disappointment, exemplifies what theorists term "disrupted attachment patterns." His response to her musical ignorance suggests his own traumatic perfectionism being projected onto his child—a common phenomenon where survivors' high standards and need for control stem from their experiences of complete powerlessness during the Holocaust.

The theme of silence—particularly around Jewish identity—demonstrates what trauma theorists call "conspiracy of silence," where traumatic experiences remain unspoken but powerfully shape family dynamics. Brown's forced Protestant identity and her mother's silence in the face of antisemitism show how trauma can lead to what theorists term "adaptive surviving," where victims learn to suppress their authentic selves to ensure survival. This suppression often passes to the next generation as learned behavior. Brown's ultimate turn to psychology represents what theorists call "posttraumatic growth," or the potential for healing and transformation through understanding one's trauma. Her decision to study psychology suggests an attempt to intellectually master what she could not emotionally process in childhood, a common pattern among second-generation survivors.

Of course, Brown could not entirely escape her Jewish identity as a child. She was an outsider in various aspects of her life, with language being a primary marker of difference. Having left Hungary in the fourth grade to move to Vienna, she wondered if anyone would speak Hungarian with her, and although she learned German, it remained a foreign tongue. This sense of linguistic alienation would reemerge when she was nineteen years old: "My acquired language sounds like them, And yet, they detect, My otherness so easily" (33). Brown's identity struggles manifested in her changing her name three times throughout her life, perhaps to connect with new surroundings or to escape her and her parents' past. Born as Zsuzsi in Hungary, she became Susi in Vienna, and finally settled on Susan. While such transitions are common in assimilation, her original name Zsuzsi carried special significance as a link to her paternal aunt, a survivor who had lost part of herself when her husband was murdered. Unlike other second-generation survivors who were named after murdered relatives, Brown carried the name of a living survivor, yet this connection brought its own unique burden.

In her poem "She and I," Brown explores the deep interconnectedness created by sharing a name with her aunt. Despite her aunt having her own daughter, Brown describes herself as the perceived successor, while the actual daughter is "cast aside." When she references their shared characteristics, attributing them to genes, she raises a profound question about the nature of inherited trauma: is she referring to physical appearance, the transmission of trauma, or perhaps an inseparable combination of both? Brown draws parallels between their experiences, particularly focusing on the loss of a father—temporary in her case but permanent in her aunt's.

This comparison becomes a watershed moment in understanding their shared trauma. As the poem progresses, Brown begins to merge their identities, using collective pronouns: "Our willful disregard to conform," "our world," and "our similarities" (63). This linguistic choice suggests she cannot separate her identity from her aunt's—she sees herself as a continuation of someone who mourns lost loves and a vanished culture.

This complex relationship with her namesake aunt illustrates how Brown feels unable to fit in with her cousins, a situation beyond her control. The name becomes both a bridge to her family's past and a barrier to her own independent identity. This struggle with belonging reaches a dramatic climax when she rebels by dating a child of a Nazi, bringing this relationship home to her family. From a trauma theory perspective, this passage illuminates the concept of "postmemory," where the second-generation individual carries memories of experiences they never directly had. Brown's changing names represent what theorists call "identity fragmentation," common among children of survivors who must navigate multiple cultural and linguistic worlds. Her relationship with her aunt demonstrates what trauma theorists term "traumatic fusion," where boundaries between self and other become blurred due to shared trauma histories.

The linguistic alienation she experiences—speaking a language perfectly yet being detected as an outsider—represents what sociologists call "unheimlich" or "uncanny" experience, where one is simultaneously familiar and foreign. This duality is particularly poignant for second-generation survivors who must navigate between their parents' world and their present reality.

> I meet his parents, the father who was a Nazi-because
> It was the war. He meets my parents. My mother
> Shudders thinking of her family in Israel. His mother
> Says nothing, all question tied up in her apron. (43)

Brown's relationship with the child of a Nazi represents a complex psychological dynamic. She writes that he was "atoning for the sins of his father" through his relationship with a survivor's daughter, noting that

"We both silently accept our roles" (43). While this might appear as typical teenage rebellion on the surface, Brown's writing suggests something deeper—an unconventional attempt to understand her parents' experiences. Their connection transcends the personal, rooted in their shared inheritance of Holocaust-related trauma, though from opposite sides. Their joint participation in Vietnam protests and love rallies further illustrates how they attempted to process their inherited trauma through social activism.

The relationship exemplifies what trauma theorists call "traumatic reenactment," where subsequent generations unconsciously recreate aspects of historical trauma in an attempt to master it. Their mutual acknowledgment of their "roles" suggests a conscious engagement with their parents' historical positions, but transformed into something potentially healing rather than destructive. Brown's persistent sense of displacement—never fully belonging anywhere—illustrates what theorists term "cultural liminality." In each new location, she acquired the surface markers of belonging (language, cultural knowledge), yet remained fundamentally an outsider. This outsider status extended even to her own home, where she could not fully identify as a survivor. The incident with her father and the composer, her religious concealment in Vienna, and her linguistic struggles in each country all demonstrate what sociologists call "multiple marginality"—the experience of being simultaneously an outsider in multiple contexts.

This experience of perpetual outsidership among second-generation survivors reveals a crucial distinction from their parents' experience. While both generations faced displacement and cultural adaptation, the nature of their alienation differs fundamentally. The parents' displacement was concrete and historical—they were physically forced from their homes, compelled to learn new languages, and subjected to direct trauma. In contrast, their children's displacement is more psychological and existential—they inherit the emotional impact of their parents' trauma without the direct experience.

The intergenerational difference in experiencing displacement adds another layer to what trauma theorists call "postmemory." While survivors experienced a clear break from their past lives, their children exist in a constant state of in-betweenness—not fully part of their parents' world of trauma and survival, yet not fully integrated into their contemporary society either. This creates what psychologists term "identity diffusion," where the individual struggles to develop a coherent sense of self across different cultural and historical contexts.

CONCLUSION

The central argument challenges the very notion of "post-Holocaust" as a temporal marker for subsequent generations. This challenge rests on a sophisticated understanding of trauma that goes beyond simple chronology. For second—and third-generation survivors, the Holocaust isn't a historical event that preceded their existence, but rather a constitutive element of their identity from birth. This fundamentally changes how we must think about temporal relationships to historical trauma.

Jacobs' observation that "the traumas of the past remain embedded in the psychic life of victims" points to what trauma theorists call "embodied memory," the way trauma manifests not just in conscious recollection, but in unconscious behaviors, emotional patterns, and even physical responses. This embodiment of trauma in subsequent generations creates what we might call a "continuous present" of the Holocaust experience, rather than a "post-Holocaust" period.

The passage makes a crucial distinction between physical threat and psychological presence. While the immediate danger of the Holocaust ended in 1945, the psychological threat continues to exist within the minds of survivors' descendants. This persistent psychological presence manifests in various ways: hypervigilance, inherited fear responses, and what psychologists term "anticipatory trauma"—the expectation of future persecution based on historical experience.

The concept that these later generations "endure their own traumas" from being descendants adds another layer of complexity to trauma theory. This suggests a form of compound trauma where inherited trauma interacts with and shapes personal experiences of trauma. This interaction creates what we might call a "trauma echo chamber" where historical and contemporary experiences amplify each other.

The implications for historical study are significant. Traditional historical methodologies often rely on clear temporal boundaries and cause-effect relationships; however, the ongoing psychological presence of the Holocaust in subsequent generations suggests we need new methodological approaches that can account for what we might call "temporal collapse"—where past trauma continues to actively shape present experience in ways that defy simple chronological categorization.

This understanding challenges us to develop new terminology beyond "post-Holocaust" to describe this ongoing relationship with historical trauma. Perhaps we need terms that capture the continuous nature of this experience—something like "trans-generational Holocaust experience" or "continuous Holocaust impact"—though even these terms might not fully capture the complexity of this phenomenon.

CONCLUSION

This book examines the conceptual shift of studying and teaching the Holocaust as an ongoing event rather than a historical event when engaging with survivors and their descendants. It investigates how this pedagogical framework transforms our understanding of Holocaust memory and trauma, affects survivors and their descendants, and potentially reshapes public policy and commemorative practices. By challenging the notion of the Holocaust as "past," this work engages with critical questions about historical continuity, collective responsibility, and the living legacy of genocide.

In examining the complex nature of Holocaust trauma and its transmission across generations, this research demonstrates the fundamental inadequacy of traditional historical periodization, particularly the term "post-Holocaust," in capturing the lived experience of survivors and their descendants. Through analysis of diaries, memoirs, generational accounts, and the Tabak family case study, we see how trauma persists and transforms rather than ending at a historically designated moment. The traditional framing of our era as "post-Holocaust" suggests closure and historical distance, implicitly positioning the Holocaust as a completed historical event. This book interrogates this temporal boundary, arguing that the ongoing effects of the Holocaust—including intergenerational trauma, unresolved questions of justice, and contemporary antisemitism—necessitate reconceptualizing the Holocaust as a continuing phenomenon, the impacts of which reverberate through present social, political, and cultural systems. This shift challenges conventional historiography that sets clear boundaries between past and present. By examining how Holocaust memory is continually reconstructed and recontextualized, we can better understand how historical events continue to shape contemporary consciousness and identity formation.

The evidence reveals multiple dimensions of temporal complexity in Holocaust experience. The Tabak family case study illuminates how trauma interweaves across generations, creating complex patterns of inheritance, response, and adaptation that defy simple chronological understanding. Diary writers create what amounts to a permanent present of the Holocaust—their narratives preserve voices either silenced by genocide or forever altered by survival. For those who perished, these texts represent their final connection to humanity, while for survivors, they document the beginning of a lifelong journey with trauma. Memoir analysis shows how the impossibility of "returning" to pre-Holocaust life challenges linear concepts of time and recovery. The labels of "survivor" or "victim" become core identity markers that shape all subsequent experience. Perhaps most significantly, examination of generational accounts reveals how descendants inherit not just memories, but also traumatic responses, creating what we might call an "inherited temporality" where the Holocaust is not past event but ever-present reality.

Teaching the Holocaust as a continuing event fundamentally transforms educational approaches. Rather than presenting the Holocaust as a discrete historical period (1933–1945), this framework encourages educators to trace ongoing consequences, including persistent mechanisms of dehumanization that continue to operate in contemporary contexts, connecting historical antisemitism to present manifestations; unresolved questions of justice and restitution that continue to shape legal and political landscapes; the living memory preserved in survivor testimonies and their descendants, which challenges historical closure; and architectural and physical reminders that continue to exist in European landscapes. This approach moves beyond factual historical knowledge to emphasize ethical engagement and moral responsibility, asking students to consider their own relationship to this history and its ongoing implications. Traditional Holocaust education typically emphasizes chronological frameworks, presenting the events as having clear beginning and end points. This approach, while providing necessary historical context, inadvertently reinforces the notion that genocide belongs to history rather than living memory. Additionally, standard curricula often focus primarily on perpetrator chronology rather than victim experience of time, leaving students with incomplete understanding of how genocide disrupts temporal continuity for those who experience it.

The framing of the Holocaust as a continuing event has profound implications for survivors and subsequent generations. For survivors, this approach validates their lived experience that the Holocaust did not "end" with liberation, but continues to shape their lives through trauma, loss, and disrupted family histories. For descendants of survivors, this framework acknowledges intergenerational trauma and the inheritance of Holocaust memory. Recent trauma research demonstrates how extreme traumatic experiences produce biological, psychological, and social effects that transmit across generations, challenging traditional understandings of historical boundaries. However, this approach may also present challenges. Some survivors and descendants may prefer a clear delineation between past and present as a coping mechanism, finding it difficult to navigate daily life when the Holocaust is framed as ongoing rather than historical. This tension requires sensitive navigation by educators and policymakers.

This research carries important implications for both scholarship and practice. For historians, it suggests the need for new methodological approaches that can account for trauma's ongoing influence on both the creation and interpretation of historical sources. For educators and practitioners, it demands more trauma-conscious approaches to working with survivors and their families, recognizing that each trauma retelling involves real psychological cost. Contemporary trauma theory helps explain why conventional historical frameworks that emphasize closure may be inadequate when dealing with extreme historical violence. Traumatic experiences resist narrative integration and temporal containment, existing in what trauma theorist Cathy Caruth describes as a state of "belatedness" where past events continue to intrude upon the present. Recent advances in epigenetics suggest that trauma can induce biological changes that may be inherited by subsequent generations, providing a scientific foundation for understanding the Holocaust's continuing biological impact. This perspective helps explain why traditional pedagogical approaches focusing solely on historical facts may fail to capture the Holocaust's ongoing psychological and social dimensions.

Conceptualizing the Holocaust as a continuing event has significant implications for public policy, including ongoing debates about compensation for Holocaust victims and their heirs, which become reframed not as historical reconciliation, but as addressing continuing injustice; policies prohibiting Holocaust denial, which gain renewed justification as addressing ongoing rather than historical harms; contemporary humanitarian crises, which may be more directly connected to Holocaust precedents; and memorial sites and museums, which might shift from preserving historical memory to addressing continuing societal conditions. This framework potentially strengthens arguments for ongoing vigilance against antisemitism and other forms of discrimination, positioning these not merely as historical lessons, but as continuing societal responsibilities.

The conceptual shift from "post-Holocaust" to "continuing Holocaust" inevitably encounters resistance from various quarters. This book examines who resists this reconceptualization and why. Traditional historians may resist based on methodological concerns about historical specificity and periodization. Political actors seeking to close chapters of historical responsibility may prefer bounded historical narratives. Some survivors and descendants may resist for psychological reasons, needing closure for their own healing. Educational institutions may find it challenging to implement curricula that resist clear historical boundaries. Conversely, those who might benefit from this shift include advocates for ongoing justice for Holocaust victims and their descendants, those working against contemporary antisemitism who see direct connections to Holocaust history, educators seeking deeper ethical engagement from students, and trauma researchers and therapists working with intergenerational trauma. This analysis reveals how theoretical frameworks are never neutral, but are embedded in social and political contexts with concrete implications for individuals and communities.

More broadly, this work points toward new frameworks for understanding genocide—frameworks that can account for trauma's continuous nature, its intergenerational transmission, and its nonlinear temporality. By moving beyond simplistic periodization, we can better comprehend how genocidal trauma shapes both individual lives and collective memory. Ultimately, this research argues for a fundamental shift in how we conceptualize and study genocide. Rather than treating it as a discrete historical event, we must understand it as an ongoing process that continues to actively shape reality for survivors and their descendants. Only through such understanding can we hope to prevent future genocides while properly honoring and supporting those who continue to live with genocide's lasting impact.

The Holocaust does not exist in the past tense for survivors and their families—it remains a present reality that shapes their daily lives, their relationships, and their understanding of themselves in the world. Our scholarship and practice must evolve to reflect this profound truth. Teaching the Holocaust as a continuing rather than historical event fundamentally transforms our understanding of history, memory, and responsibility. This conceptual shift has profound implications for survivors, descendants, educators, and policymakers, challenging conventional boundaries between past and present. By engaging with trauma theory, examining power dynamics, and considering policy implications, this book provides a comprehensive framework for understanding how we might teach, commemorate, and respond to the Holocaust, not as a closed historical chapter, but as a continuing presence that demands ongoing ethical engagement and responsibility.

BIBLIOGRAPHY

PRIMARY SOURCES

Alter. n.d. "Understanding the Difference Between PTSD and Trauma." alterbehavioralhealth.com/blog/understanding-the-difference-between-ptsd-and-trauma

Améry, Jean. *At the Mind's Limits: Contemplations by a Survivor on Auschwitz and Its Realities.* Indiana University Press, 1980.

Berg, Mary. *The Diary of Mary Berg: Growing Up in the Warsaw Ghetto.* Edited by S.L. Schneiderman, Oneworld, 2018.

Bitton-Jackson, Livia. *I Have Lived a Thousand Years: Growing up in the Holocaust.* Scholastic, 1997.

Bluman, Barbara R. *I Have My Mother's Eyes: A Holocaust Memoir Across Generations.* Ronsdale Press, 2009.

Brown, Susan H. *Circles: A Legacy.* Hermann Press, 2020.

Bukiet, Melvin J., editor. *Nothing Makes You Free: Writings by Descendants of Jewish Holocaust Survivors.* W.W. Norton and Company, 2002.

Czerniakow, Adam. *Warsaw Diary of Adam Czerniakow: Prelude to Doom.* Translated by Stanislaw Staron, edited by Raul Hilberg, Josef Kermisz, and Stanislaw Staron, Elephant Paperbacks, 1999.

Delbo, Charlotte. *Auschwitz and After.* Translated by Rosette C. Lamont, Yale University Press, 1995.

"Eichmann trial—Session No. 68, 69." *YouTube*, uploaded by Yad Vashem and Israel State Archives, 25 Oct. 2012, https://www.youtube.com/watch?v=m3-tXyYhd5U.

Epstein, Helen. *The Long Half-Lives of Love and Trauma: A Memoir.* Plunkett Lake Press, 2017.

Frank, Anne. *The Diary of a Young Girl.* Translated by B.M. Mooyaart-Doubleday, Bantam Books, 1986.

Geclewicz Raz, Mirla. *The Birds Sang Eulogies: A Memoir.* Library of Congress, 2019.

Ginz, Petr. *The Diary of Petr Ginz: 1941–1942*. Translated by Elena Lappin, edited by Chava Pressburger, Atlantic Monthly Press, 2007.

Kaplan, Chaim Aron, and Yisrael Gutman. *Scroll of Agony: The Warsaw Diary of Chaim A. Kaplan*. Translated by Abraham I. Katsh, Indiana University Press, 1999.

Ka-Tzetnik 135633. *Shivitti: A Vision*. Translated by Eliyah Nike De-Nur, Harper and Row, 1989.

Klisman Ellis, Lori. *4,456 Miles: A Survivor's Search for Closure: Awakening Her Daughter's Search for Understanding the Holocaust*. Arkett Publishing, 2019.

Lang, Berel. "Is It Possible to Misrepresent the Holocaust?" *History and Theory*, vol. 34, no. 1, 1995, pp. 84–89.

Laskier, Rutka. *Rutka's Notebook: A Voice from the Holocaust*. Yad Vashem, 2008.

Leitner, Isabella. *Fragments of Isabella*. A Laurel Book, 1978.

Lengyel, Olga. *Five Chimneys: A Woman Survivor's True Story of Auschwitz*. First Academy Chicago Publishers, 1995.

Levi, Primo. *Survival in Auschwitz*. Translated by Stuart Woolf, Simon and Schuster, 1996.

Lipiner, Lucy. *Lusia's Long Journey Home: A Young Girl's Memoir of Surviving the Holocaust*. Usher Publishing, 2013.

Loridan-Ivens, Marceline. *But You Did Not Come Back: A Memoir*. Translated by Sandra Smith, edited by Judith Perrignon, Atlantic Monthly Press, 2016.

Mermelstein, Mel. *By Bread Alone: The Story of A-4685*. Mel Mermelstein, 1993.

Müller, Filip. *Eyewitness Auschwitz: Three Years in the Gas Chambers*. Translated by Susanne Flatauer, Ivan R. Dee, 1999.

Nyiszli, Miklos. *Auschwitz: A Doctor's Eyewitness Account*. Translated by Tibère Kremer and Richard Seaver, Arcade Publishing, 2011.

Polak, Joseph. *After the Holocaust the Bells Still Ring*. Urim Publications, 2014.

Rabinek Epstein, Franci. *Franci's War: A Woman's Story of Survival*. Penguin Books, 2020.

Ringelblum, Emmanuel. *Notes from the Warsaw Ghetto: The Unflinching, Classic First-Hand Account*. Edited and translated by Jacob Sloan, iBooks, Inc., 2006.

Roskies, David G., editor. *Voices From the Warsaw Ghetto: Writing Our History*. Yale University Press, 2019.

Rosner, Elizabeth. *Survivor Café: The Legacy of Trauma and the Labyrinth of Memory*. Counterpoint Press, 2018.

Segal, Sarah. *An Heiress of Holocaust: How My Family Survived the Holocaust and the Lasting Effects on My Life.* eBookPro Publishing, 2020.

Sierakowiak, Dawid. *The Diary of Dawid Sierakowiak: Five Notebooks from the Łódź Ghetto.* Translated by Kamil Turowski, edited by Alan Adelson, Oxford University Press, 1998.

Venezia, Shlomo. *Inside the Gas Chambers: Eight Months in the Sonderkommando of Auschwitz.* Translated by Andrew Brown, edited by Jean Mouttapa, Polity Press, 2009.

Wanderer Cohen, Emily. *From Generation to Generation: Healing Intergenerational Trauma Through Storytelling.* Morgan James Publishing, 2018.

Wiesel, Elie. *Night.* Translated by Marion Wiesel, Hill and Wang, 2006.

Wiesenthal, Simon. *The Sunflower: On the Possibilities and Limits of Forgiveness.* Schocken Books, 1998.

Zilber, Ettie. *A Holocaust Memoir of Love and Resilience: Mama's Survival from Lithuania to America.* Amsterdam Publishers, 2019.

SECONDARY SOURCES

Abraham, Nicolas, and Maria Torok. *The Shell and the Kernel: Renewals of Psychoanalysis, Volume 1.* Edited by Nicholas T. Rand, University of Chicago Press, 1994.

Agamben, Giorgio. *Remnants of Auschwitz: The Witness and the Archive.* Translated by Daniel Heller-Roazen, Zone Books, 2002.

Améry, Jean. *On Suicide: A Discourse on Voluntary Death.* Translated by John D. Barlow, Indiana University Press, 1999.

Barkat, Amiram. "Who Counts as a Holocaust Survivor?" *Haaretz*, 18 April 2004, https://www.haaretz.com/1.4781806.

Bauer, Yehuda. *A History of the Holocaust.* Revised Edition, Franklin Watts, 2001.

Berg, Philip S., and Michael Berg. *The Zohar: The Complete Original Aramaic Text.* New York, The Kabbalah Centre, 2007.

Berlant, Lauren. *The Female Complaint: The Unfinished Business of Sentimentality in American Culture.* Duke University Press, 2008.

Bernard-Donals, Michael. *An Introduction to Holocaust Studies.* Routledge, 2005.

Bowlby, John. "Separation Anxiety: A Critical Review of the Literature." *The

International Review of Psycho-Analysis, vol. XLI, 1960.

Carp, Matatias. *Holocaust in Romania: Facts and Documents on the Annihilation of Romania's Jews 1940–1944.* Translated by Sean Murphy, edited by Andrew L. Simon, Simon Publications, 2000.

Caruth, Cathy. *Trauma: Explorations in Memory.* Johns Hopkins University Press, 1995.

Celan, Paul. *The Meridian: Final Version-Drafts-Materials.* Translated by Pierre Joris, edited by Bernhard Böschenstein and Heino Schmull, Stanford University Press, 2011.

Cvetkovich, Ann. *An Archive of Feelings: Trauma, Sexuality, and Lesbian Public Cultures.* Duke University Press, 2003.

Danieli, Yael. "Psychotherapists' Participation in the Conspiracy of Silence about the Holocaust." *Psychoanalytic Psychology,* vol. 1, no. 1, 1984, pp. 23–42.

de Certeau, Michel. *The Practice of Everyday Life.* Translated by Steven Rendall, University of California Press, 2011.

Dov Kulka, Otto. *Landscapes of the Metropolis of Death: Reflections on Memory and Imagination.* Translated by Ralph Mandel, The Belknap Press of Harvard University Press, 2013.

Eichenbaum, Howard. "Memory on Time." *Trends in Cognitive Sciences,* vol. 17, no. 2, Feb. 2013, pp. 81–88.

Elliott, Mark. "Andrei Vlasov: Red Army General in Hitler's Service." *Military Affairs,* vol. 46, no. 2, Apr. 1982, pp. 84–87.

Epstein, Helen. *Children of the Holocaust: Conversations with Sons and Daughters of Survivors.* Penguin Books, 1988.

Erikson, Kai Theodor. *Everything in Its Path: Destruction of Community in the Buffalo Creek Flood.* Simon and Schuster, 1978.

Fabian, Johannes. *Time and the Other: How Anthropology Makes Its Object.* Columbia University Press, 2002.

Fackenheim, Emil L. *To Mend the World: Foundations of Post-Holocaust Jewish Thought.* Indiana University Press, 1994.

Falconer, Rachel. *Hell in Contemporary Literature: Western Descent Narratives Since 1945.* Edinburgh University Press, 2007.

Febvre, Lucien. *A New Kind of History: From the Writings of Lucien Febvre.* Translated by K. Folca, edited by Peter Burke, Harper and Row, 1973.

Feldman, Jackie. *Above the Death Pits, Beneath the Flag: Youth Voyages to Poland and the Performance of Israeli National Identity*. Berghahn Books, 2010.

Felman, Shoshana, and Dori Laub. *Testimony: Crises of Witnessing in Literature, Psychoanalysis and History*. Routledge, 1992.

Fine, Ellen S. "The Absent Memory: The Act of Writing in Post-Holocaust French Literature." *In Writing and The Holocaust*, edited by Berel Lang, Holmes and Meier, 1988.

Fogg, Shannon L. "'Everything Had Ended and Everything Was Beginning Again': The Public Politics of Rebuilding Private Homes in Postwar Paris." *Holocaust and Genocide Studies*, vol. 28, no. 2, Fall 2014, pp. 277–307.

Frankl, Viktor E. *Yes to Life: In Spite of Everything*. Beacon Press, 2020.

Fresco, Nadine. "Remembering the Unknown." *International Review of Psycho-Analysis*, vol. 11, no. 4, 1984, pp. 417–27.

Friedlander, Saul. *Memory, History, and the Extermination of the Jews of Europe*. Indiana University Press, 1993.

Friedman, William J. "Memory for the Time of Past Events." *American Psychological Association*, vol. 113, no. 1, 1993, pp. 44–66.

Garbarini, Alexandra. *Numbered Days: Diaries and the Holocaust*. Yale University Press, 2006.

Greenspan, Henry. *On Listening to Holocaust Survivors: Beyond Testimony*. 2nd ed., Paragon House, 2010.

Gross, Jan T. *Fear: Anti-Semitism in Poland after Auschwitz*. Random House, Inc., 2006.

Gruner, Wolf. *The Holocaust in Bohemia and Moravia: Czech Initiatives, German Policies, Jewish Responses*. Translated by Alex Skinner, Berghahn Books, 2019.

Gubkin, Liora. "From Empathetic Understanding to Engaged Witnessing: Encountering Trauma in the Holocaust Classroom." *Teaching Theology and Religion*, vol. 18, no. 2, Apr. 2015, pp. 103–20.

Hartman, Geoffrey H. *The Longest Shadow: In the Aftermath of the Holocaust*. Indiana University Press, 1996.

Heller, D. "Themes of Culture and Ancestry Among Children of Concentration Camp Survivors." *Psychiatry*, vol. 45, no. 3, 1982, pp. 247–61.

Herman, Judith. *Trauma and Recovery: The Aftermath of Violence—From Domestic Abuse to Political Terror*. Basic Books, 1997.

Hilberg, Raul. *Perpetrators, Victims, Bystanders: The Jewish Catastrophe 1933–1945*. Harper Perennial, 1993.

Hirsch, Marianne. *The Generation of Postmemory: Writing and Visual Culture After the Holocaust.* Columbia University Press, 2012.

Hirsch, Marianne, and Leo Spitzer. "The Witness in the Archive: Holocaust Studies/ Memory Studies." *Memory Studies*, vol. 2, no. 2, 2009, pp. 151–70.

Hoberman, J. "Horniness Meets Horror in Stalags." *The Village Voice*, April 8, 2008.

Hoffman, Eva. *After Such Knowledge: Memory, History, and the Legacy of the Holocaust.* PublicAffairs, 2004.

Holliday, Laurel. *Children in the Holocaust and World War II: Their Secret Diaries.* Pocket Books, 1995.

Huener, Jonathan. *Auschwitz, Poland, and the Politics of Commemoration 1945–1979.* Ohio University Press, 2003.

Huyssen, Andreas. *Present Pasts: Urban Palimpsests and the Politics of Memory.* Stanford University Press, 2003.

Ioanid, Radu. *The Holocaust in Romania: The Destruction of Jews and Gypsies Under the Antonescu Regime, 1940–1944.* Ivan R. Dee, 2000.

Jacobs, Janet. *The Holocaust Across Generations: Trauma and Its Inheritance Among Descendants of Survivors.* New York University Press, 2016.

Jonkisz, Jakub. "Consciousness: Individuated Information in Action." *Frontiers in Psychology*, vol. 6, no. 1035, July 2015.

Kassow, Samuel D. *Who Will Write Our History? Rediscovering a Hidden Archive from the Warsaw Ghetto.* Vintage Books, 2009.

Kliymuk, Alexander. "The Construct Ostjuden in German Anti-Semitic Discourse of 1920–1932." *Scripta Judaica Cracoviensia*, vol. 16, 2018, pp. 97–108.

Krystal, Henry, and J. H. Krystal. *Integration and Self-Healing: Affect, Trauma, Alexithymia.* Analytic Press, Inc., 1988.

LaCapra, Dominick. *Writing History, Writing Trauma.* Johns Hopkins University Press, 2014.

Landsberg, Alison. *Prosthetic Memory: The Transformation of American Remembrance in the Age of Mass Culture.* Columbia University Press, 2004.

Lang, Berel, editor. *Writing and the Holocaust.* Holmes and Meier, 1988.

Levinas, Emmanuel. *Time and the Other.* Translated by Richard A. Cohen, Duquesne University Press, 1987.

Leys, Ruth. *From Guilt to Shame: Auschwitz and After.* Princeton University Press, 2009.

Lifton, Robert J. *Death in Life: Survivors of Hiroshima.* University of North

Carolina Press, 1991.

Littell, Franklin H. *The Crucifixion of the Jews: The Failure of Christians to Understand the Jewish Experience*. Mercer University Press, 2017.

Main, Mary, and Judith Solomon. "Discovery of an Insecure-Disorganized/Disoriented Attachment Pattern." *Affective Development in Infancy*, edited by T. B. Brazelton and M. W. Yogman, Ablex Publishing, 1986, pp. 95–124.

Marchetti, Giorgio. "Consciousness: A Unique Way of Processing Information." *Cognitive Processing*, vol. 19, 2018, pp. 435–64.

McGoldrick, Monica, and Randy Gerson. 1985. *Genograms in Family Assessment*. New York: Norton.

Nora, Pierre, editor. *Rethinking France: Les Lieux de Mémoire, Volume 4: Histories and Memories*. Translated by David P. Jordan, Richard C. Holbrook, Deke Dusinberre, Christine Haynes, John Goodman, Daniel Hall, Richard S. Levy, Gayle Levy, Teresa L. Fagan, and Sarah Maza, University of Chicago Press, 2010.

Northoff, Georg. "Do Cortical Midline Variability and Low Frequency Fluctuations Mediate William James' 'Stream of Consciousness'? 'Neurophenomenal Balance Hypothesis' of 'Inner Time Consciousness.'" *Consciousness and Cognition*, vol. 30, 2014, pp. 184–200.

Oumano, Elena. "A Cognitive Behavioral Therapy Model: Integrating Anxiety and Phobia Coping Strategies into Fundamentals of Public Speaking College Courses." U.S. Department of Education, 2005.

Patterson, David. *Along the Edge of Annihilation: The Collapse and Recovery of Life in the Holocaust Diary*. University of Washington Press, 1999.

Patterson, David. *Open Wounds: The Crisis of Jewish Thought in the Aftermath of the Holocaust*. University of Washington Press, 2006.

Patterson, David. *The Shriek of Silence: A Phenomenology of the Holocaust Novel*. University Press of Kentucky, 2014.

Pennebaker, James W., and Sandra K. Beall. "Confronting a Traumatic Event: Toward an Understanding of Inhibition and Disease." *Journal of Abnormal Psychology*, vol. 95, no. 3, 1986, pp. 274–81.

Rothberg, Michael. *Multidirectional Memory: Remembering the Holocaust in the Age of Decolonization*. Stanford University Press, 2009.

Rubenstein, Richard L. *After Auschwitz: Radical Theology and Contemporary Judaism*. 6th ed., Bobbs-Merrill, 1966.

Sak, Jarosław, and Magdalena Suchodolska. "Elazar de Wind." *National Library of*

Medicine, 2020. Journal of Neurology, vol. 268, no. 6, 2020, pp. 2297–98.

Schwab, Gabriele. *Haunting Legacies: Violent Histories and Transgenerational Trauma.* Columbia University Press, 2010.

Scott, James C. *Domination and the Arts of Resistance: Hidden Transcripts.* Yale University Press, 1992.

Spicer, Ellis. "'One Sorrow or Another': Narratives of Hierarchical Survivorship and Suffering in Holocaust Survivor Associations." *Holocaust Studies: A Journal of Culture and History,* vol. 26, no. 4, 2020, pp. 442–60.

Suleiman, Susan R. "The 1.5 Generation: Thinking about Child Survivors and the Holocaust." *American Imago, vol. 59, no. 3: Postmemories of the Holocaust, Fall 2002, pp. 277–95.*

"Trauma." American Psychological Association, accessed on August 21, 2024, https://www.apa.org/topics/trauma#:~:text=Trauma%20is%20an%20emotional%20response,shock%20and%20denial%20are%20typical.

Trouillot, Michel-Rolph. *Silencing the Past: Power and the Production of History.* Beacon Press, 1995.

Tuchman, Aryeh. "Generational Changes in the Holocaust Denial Movement in the United States." *Deciphering the New Antisemitism,* edited by Alvin H. Rosenfeld, pp. 350–72.

Turner, Victor. *The Ritual Process: Structure and Anti-Structure.* Aldine De Gruyter, 1995.

Tydor Baumel, Judith. "Hannah Szenes (Senesh)." *Jewish Women's Archive,* 27 Feb. 2009, https://jwa.org/encyclopedia/author/tydor-judith.

Urynowicz, Marcin. *Adam Czerniaków 1880–1942. Prezes getta warszawskiego (Adam Czerniaków 1880—1942. The Chairman of the Warsaw ghetto).* Warsaw, 2009, pp. 326–33, 338–41.

van Alphen, Ernst. *Caught by History: Holocaust Effects in Contemporary Art, Literature, and Theory.* Stanford University Press, 1997.

van der Kolk, Bessel A. *The Body Keeps the Score: Brain, Mind, and Body in the Healing of Trauma.* Penguin Books, 2014.

Volkan, Vamik D. "Transgenerational Transmissions and Chosen Traumas: An Aspect of Large-Group

Identity." *Group Analysis,* vol. 34, no. 1, 2001, pp. 79–97.

Wardi, Dina. *Memorial Candles: Children of the Holocaust.* Translated by Naomi Goldblum, Routledge, 1992.

Waxman, Zoë. *Writing the Holocaust: Identity, Testimony, Representation.* Oxford Historical Monographs, Oxford University Press, 2008.
Wiesel, Elie. *The Accident.* Hill and Wang, 1985.
Wiesel, Elie. *All Rivers Run to the Sea: Memoirs.* Schocken Books, 1996.
Wiesel, Elie. *One Generation After.* Translated by Lily Edelman and Elie Wiesel, Schocken Books, 2011.
Wieviorka, Annette. *The Era of the Witness.* Translated by Jared Stark, Cornell University Press, 2006.
Winnicott, Donald W. "The Concept of the False Self." *The Collected Works of D. W. Winnicott: Volume 7, 1964–1966,* edited by Lesley Caldwell and Helen Taylor Robinson, Oxford Academic, 2016, pp. 27–32.
Wyschogrod, Edith. *Saints and Postmodernism: Revisioning Moral Philosophy.* University of Chicago Press, 1990.
Yehuda, Rachel, and Amy Lehrner. "Intergenerational Transmission of Trauma Effects: Putative Role of Epigenetic Mechanisms." *World Psychiatry,* vol. 17, no. 3, Oct. 2018, pp. 243–57.
Yellow Horse Brave Heart, Maria. "The Historical Trauma Response among Natives and Its Relationship to Substance Abuse: A Lakota Illustration." *Healing and Mental Health for Native Americans: Speaking in Red,* edited by Ethan Nebelkopf and Mary Phillips, Altamira Press, 2004, pp. 7–18.
Young, James E. *At Memory's Edge: After-Images of the Holocaust in Contemporary Art and Architecture.* Yale University Press, 2000.
Young, James E. *Writing and Rewriting the Holocaust: Narrative and the Consequences of Interpretation.* Indiana University Press, 1988.
Zeitlin, Froma I. "The Vicarious Witness: Belated Memory and Authorial Presence in Recent Holocaust Literature." *History and Memory,* vol. 10, no. 2, Fall 1998, pp. 5–42.

NOTES

1. During this period in Romania, the family, which consisted of a father, a mother, and their children, was considered the most important facet of life.
2. The term *Ostjuden* was originally used to categorize Eastern European Jewish immigrants in Germany at the start of the twentieth century. It began as positive term utilized to view the "romanticized world of their [German Jews] Eastern European coreligionists" (Kliymuk 97). However, the term has unfortunately evolved (or devolved) with its use by German antisemites who would use it for other Eastern Jews in Germany (97–98).
3. Czernowitz, where Frieda would eventually move to, was occupied on July 6. A pogrom was carried out, killing 2,000 Jews, and an additional 300 were shot two days after occupation (Carp 22).
4. Some students ask Frieda if she knew Anne Frank personally. Had students been taught geography or about the Holocaust in greater depth, they may have understood the unlikely nature of this question.
5. The Iron Guard and Ion Antonescu forced King Carol II to abdicate on September 6, 1940. With the shift in power, antisemitism took on new meanings, including the expulsion of Jews from the workforce, the plundering of Jewish stores, and the physical abuse of Jews (Ioanid 44–45). Although a part of the Axis alliance, some Nazis were shocked at the grotesque torture and murder of the Jews, and a complaint was filed to the Romanian chiefs of staff (Carp 22).
6. JewishGen is a nonprofit organization that specializes in Jewish genealogy.
7. This pilgrimage, much like those with other second-generation survivors, exhibits the complexity of transference of trauma but even the idea of having a place to pilgrimage and hold a connection to was incredibly powerful. David's hope to understand his mother a bit more and understand where she came from and who she is now is linked to this decision because her roots, including the Holocaust, are still a large part of who Frieda is. David had never met his biological grandmother, and Frieda hardly remembers her birth mother from when she was a child.
8. For some, including Carl Hirsch, a rumor of these certificates would save

him. He was a professional, an engineer, and while heading into the ghetto he asked a major if he would qualify to stay, and the major confirmed. He was saved from the ghetto (Hirsch and Spitzer 2011: 128).

9. On November 15, 1941, the deportations to Transnistria ceased, and only 20,000 Jews remained in the city (Hirsch and Spitzer 2011: 185). The deportations would resume in June 1942 (190). With these new roundups, Popovici's authorization cards were no longer valid.

10. Romania, having joined the Axis powers in 1941, would be forced to accept its defeat at the hands of the Soviet Union and the Allies. On August 24, 1944, Romania signed the agreement waiving its rights to continue military operations against the Allied forces and agreed to fight with the Allies (Armistice Agreement 1944).

11. LaCapra's concept of "truths," mentioned in future chapters, comes into play with regard to family legends.

12. Vlasovites, those that defected from the Red Army to serve Nazi Germany, were often Red Army POWs. They were called this after the Red Army hero, General Andrei Vlasov, who was captured by the Nazis in July 1942. In 1944, Vlasov trained those who had defected, but only one division became operational in April 1945. After the war, the Soviet Supreme Court tried Vlasov for espionage, sabotage, and treason. Interestingly, ideologically he was not an antisemite and encouraged his men not to engage with racial slurs (Elliott 84–86). As Mark Elliott claims, Vlasov became a pawn, "first by Stalin, then by Hitler. Vlasov was a pawn in the epic struggle just like the lowliest POW or forced laborer" (87).

13. A nine-year-old non-Jewish boy left his home on July 1, 1946, without his parents' knowledge. When he returned on July 3, to avoid being punished, he claimed that he was kidnapped and held hostage by the Jewish Committee. The police went to investigate along with a crowd of Poles from the Ludwikow steel mill. Although the boy's story unraveled, a shot was fired, and the violence began. The civilians and police killed forty-two Jews and injured forty others (Gross).

14. Liora Gubkin wrote, "From Empathic Understanding to Engaged Witnessing: Encountering Trauma in the Holocaust Classroom," in which Gubkin addresses the concern of teaching the Holocaust and the response that may ensue. Within the American educational system, administrators must cater to a variety

of cultures, and there is concern for emotional harm or discomfort, which introduces the idea of trigger warnings (Gubkin 103). Teachers, as I would imagine Frieda would view herself in this situation, attempt to protect and shelter their students from what is at the heart of the Holocaust—terror and trauma. Once in eighth grade, students are teenagers and are viewed as more emotionally apt (however good or bad). Thereby, their ability to process history is more developed, much like how Frieda attempted to shield her own children.

15. The establishing of survivor groups is a dominant feature of the Holocaust survivor community. As Ellis Spicer stated, "Furthermore, the quest for recognition by the child survivors forming their own group does not just indicate the desire to be recognized by the survivor community but by society at large" (Spicer 450). Frieda has already accomplished this sense of recognition through her speaking throughout her community, but it could also link to her original belief that she did not suffer like others had and, in turn, was not a true Holocaust survivor. With in-person groups, a survivor would share their story of survival, and that may invoke painful memories or self-doubt.

16. According to the CODOH's Facebook page, the group's mission is, "The aim of this site is to promote intellectual freedom with regard to this one historical event called 'Holocaust.'" In reality, the group works to deny the Holocaust. Aryeh Tuchman wrote, "In 1991, [Bradley] Smith hit on a strategy that would catapult Holocaust denial to a much larger audience. He created the Committee on Open Debate on the Holocaust (CODOH), whose mission was to place advertisements denying the Nazi genocide of European Jewry in college student newspapers" (Rosenfeld 357).

17. These events are being referred to as "wartime events" because the term "genocide" was not coined yet by Raphael Lemkin, and thereby many diarists refer to the events that they witnessed as a part of war.

18. Two well-known Jewish survivors who could not reconcile their relationship with God due to their experiences were that of Primo Levi and Richard Rubenstein; however, these two individuals only represent a very small sampling of those who could no longer maintain a relationship with God. This will be analyzed further in the memoirs chapter.

19. Of course, there are those survivors who became Holocaust scholars. Although these individuals engage with the Holocaust from a scholarly perspective, they maintain the unique perspective of a survivor. Within the

memoir chapter, survivors who are also Holocaust scholars will be discussed further.
20. The *Judenrat*, a Jewish council in the Warsaw Ghetto, was established prior to the ghetto's formation in October 1940. The *Judenrat* was forced to carry out the Nazi decrees and maintain daily life within the ghettos, including food distribution, medical care, housing, police, and deportations.
21. On January 20, 1942, the Wannsee Conference, hosted by Reinhard Heydrich and including fifteen Reich officials, was held to coordinate the "Final Solution to the Jewish Problem." This gathering of top Nazi officials would lead to the expansion of the concentration camp and extermination camp system.
22. The Vichy government came into power in June 1940 until August 1944, stemming from the armistice with Nazi Germany. This armistice would place Philippe Pétain in power and allow for German troops to occupy the northern half of France. This authoritarian structure permitted the government to deport foreign Jews to concentration camps and partake in other antisemitic policies and attacks, like the removal of Jews from civil service and the thieving of Jewish property.
23. The Arrow Cross was the Hungarian fascist group that was established in October 1944 until April 1945. It maintained an emphasis on the value of agriculture, and was anti-capitalist, anti-Communist, militantly antisemitic, adhered to Hungarian nationalism ideologies, and was pro-Nazi. It was under the Arrow Cross that roughly 80,000 Jews were deported from Hungary in a death march to Austria, and thousands more murdered in the capital city of Budapest.
24. Kol Nidre prayers open the Day of Atonement services.
25. We can assume Berg is specifically referring to the Warsaw Ghetto. This data is not entirely provable as there are no records that reflect death by suicide or the religious affiliations of those who committed suicide; however, the individuals committed suicide needed someone to remember them, and Mary Berg attempted to do just that.
26. A *pipel* was a young boy selected by a *Kapo* (a prisoner selected by the guards to oversee work details in the Nazi camp system). The boys were servants and were often given extra rations, but at the cost of abuse, including sexual abuse.
27. This is not to mention the horrors of liberation, such as the rapes that occurred at the hands of the Russians at Auschwitz-Birkenau by the

"liberators." Tragically, this would be true at many camps that housed women.
28. It must not be forgotten that her mother had suffered in a different way. Her husband and daughter were deported and she had to maintain a household with her other two children without a patriarch. Although this does not dismiss her actions, they are not acknowledged in her memoir.
29. The *Sonderkommando* were mostly Jewish men forced to assist in the processes related to the crematoria at the death camps. Members of the *Sonderkommando* were renewed every three months; the old members were murdered to prevent them from becoming witnesses.
30. Additionally, children and grandchildren of survivors do not have the same experiences, and this case study represents only those who have willingly written a memoir, much like the survivors from the previous chapter.
31. This is not to say that second—and third-generation survivors all live their lives focused on the Holocaust or that they cannot have happy lives, but that the Holocaust has impacted who they are and will continue to do so throughout their lives.
32. At this time the relationship of other family dynamics, such as aunts, uncles, and cousins, has not been written about enough in generational memoirs and therefore will not be included in this study.
33. Epstein does not classify her book as a memoir; however, as mentioned with survivor's memoirs, she is telling her life story as a second-generation survivor. It is possible that she does not utilize this definition because of the period in which it was written, 1979—a period in which Holocaust memoirs were becoming popular, but second-generation survivors were not writing memoirs, nor were considered a topic within Holocaust studies or psychology. In 1997 and 2021, Epstein published two books that she does label "memoirs," including *Where She Came From: A Daughter's Search for Her Mother's History* and *The Long Half-Lives of Love and Trauma*.
34. Even the "before" is influenced by the Holocaust. Those who were murdered are often remembered primarily as Holocaust victims, and second—and third-generation survivors learn of these family members primarily as individuals who were murdered. Additionally, those who reminisce about the pre-Nazi years are influenced by their experiences from 1939 onward. The potential to romanticize those earlier days is heightened due to the horrendous and ineffable nature of the Holocaust.

INDEX

abandonment, 98, 100, 122, 147
Abraham, Nicolas, 110, 120, 145
absent memory, 116
acting out, 91, 108, 109, 113
active witness chain, 136
acts of postmemory, 127
after?, 80–85
after memory, 81
After the Holocaust the Bells Still Ring (Polak), 121
Agamben, Giorgio, 53, 58, 88, 90, 96, 97, 98; *Remnants of Auschwitz* by, 47
Along the Edge of Annihilation (Patterson), xiii, 47, 52
Alphen, Ernst van, 46, 58, 81, 142
America: immigration to, 90; Tabak, F., in, 5, 12, 32; Tabak, S., in, 28, 30, 37; Weinschenker family in, 28–31
American Psychological Association (APA), xii
Améry, Jean (Hans Mayer), 88, 91, 98, 113; on suicide, 106–9; on torture, 106–7
analysis: of diaries, 43–44, 45, 155; of trauma, xi, 155, 157
An Archive of Feelings (Cvetkovich), 48
Anne Frank's Diary, 14, 47, 171nn4–5
anticipatory trauma, 153
antisemitism, 13, 28, 33, 37, 93, 150; contemporary, 155, 158; postwar antisemitism, 90–91
anti-world, of Auschwitz-Birkenau, 87
APA. *See* American Psychological Association
ASPCA, 36–37
Assmann, Aleida, 82
Auschwitz and After (Delbo), 78, 84
Auschwitz-Birkenau, ix, x, 47, 48, 81, 112, 138; anti-world of, 87; Delbo in, 87–88; Dov Kulka in, 82–84; Kilsman Ellis in, 133; Tabak, F., in, 18, 20

Bakhtin, Mikhail, 96
bare life, 90
Bar-On, Dan, 145
Bassarabian/Moldavian Jewish Roots, 36
Bauer, Yehuda, on suffering, 19
Beall, Sandra Kliher, 79
bearing witness: burden of survivor guilt and, 95–105; privilege of, 98–104; of second-generation survivors, 115, 117, 136–37; of Segal, 120, 138–40; of third-generation survivors, 136–37; of Wiesel, 103–5; to the witness, 139; without witnessing, 135–40
belatedness, of narrative experience, 44, 154, 157

Berg, Mary, diary of, 59–60, 61, 63; on holidays, 67–68; on suicide, 72, 74–75, 174n25
Bergen-Belsen, 99, 125, 126, 148
Berlant, Lauren, 48
Bernard-Donals, Michael, 52
biographical commission, 101
biological impact, of Holocaust, 157
biological inheritance of trauma, 110, 114
biological memory, 140
The Birds Sang Eulogies (Geclewicz Raz), 119
Birkenau. *See* Auschwitz-Birkenau
Blanchot, Maurice, 47, 96
Bloch, Ernst, 99–100
Bluman, Barbara Ruth, 120
"the body keeps the score," 108
Borowski, Tadeusz, 113
borrowed memories, 116
Bowlby, John, 93
Britton-Jackson, Livia, 92
Brown, Susan H., memoir of: cycle of separation and loss in, 148; Jewish identity relating to, 149–50; pain and abandonment in, 147; poems relating to, 147–51; relationships relating to, 146–53; relocations in, 147–48
Browning, Christopher, 90
Buchenwald, 92
Bukiet, Melvin Jules, 137–38
bureaucratic retraumatization, 134–35

calendar time, 52

Caruth, Cathy, xii, 87, 98, 100, 109, 141, 157; on trauma, 46, 50, 52, 70, 91, 108, 117; *Unclaimed Experience* by, 44; on wounds of consciousness, 89, 91, 107
Caught by History (van Alphen), 46
CBT. *See* cognitive behavioral therapy
Celan, Paul, 101, 113
cemetery, Poland as, 90
certificates, for Jews, 23, 171n8
childhood, killing of, 61
children: deaths of, 63; defense mechanism of, 63; Delbo on, 84; as future, 58; meaning of, 58–63; murder of, 58; in orphanages, 60; starvation of, 60
children, diaries of, 58; Berg, 59–60, 61, 63, 67–68, 72, 74–75; Fishken, 61–62; Laskier, 61, 63; Rudashevski, 66–69; Sierakowiak, 62–63, 67; Szenes, 64–66
children of the Holocaust, 143
Children of the Holocaust (Epstein), xi
child survivors, 5, 19. *See also* Polak, Joseph
choiceless choices, 60, 70, 109
chosen trauma, 146
chronological narratives, of survivors, 118
chronological privilege, 52
chronotype, 96
citizenship changes, of families, 26–27, 32
CODOH. *See* Committee for Open Debate on the Holocaust

cognitive behavioral therapy (CBT), 83
collapse, temporal, 78–79, 154
collapse of witnessing, 49, 62, 81, 97, 108, 109, 110, 111
collected memory, 49, 88, 91, 104, 108, 112, 120
collected memory preservation, 58
collective guilt, 106
collective historical consciousness, 45
collective memory, 120, 121, 158
collective memory frameworks, 105
collective memory rupture, 89
collective trauma, 49
commandant (*Kommandatura*), ix–x
commemorative practices, 155
Committee for Open Debate on the Holocaust (CODOH), 39–40, 173n16
common memory, 145
Communism, 13
compartmentalization, 103
complete witnesses, 96
compound trauma, 153
concentration camps. See *specific camps*
concentration camp syndrome (KZ syndrome), xii
connection: to Holocaust, 4; to humanity, 156; Polak relating to, 124
connective histories, 51
consciousness, 3–4, 119. See also *specific topics*
conscious remembering, 145
conscious working through, 146
conspiracy of silence, 143
contemporary antisemitism, 155, 158

contested memory, 90
continuing Holocaust, 155, 157–58
continuous dispossession, 135
continuous Holocaust impact, 154
continuous traumatic present, 129, 153
conventional historical frameworks, 157
"co-owners of the traumatic event," 135
cortisol production, altering of, 140–41
crematorium, 98, 102
crisis of representation, 98
crisis of testimony, 70
crisis of witnessing, 52, 58, 109
crying wound, 100–101
cultural liminality, 152
cultural memory, 82
cultural memory transmission, 134
cultural shock, 31–32
Cvetkovich, Ann, 48
Czechoslovakia, 33
Czerniaków, Adam, 60, 68, 69; as hero, 71; suicide of, 70–75; in Warsaw Ghetto, 58–59, 72
Czernowitz (in Romania): Jews of, 23–24; mass killings in, 14–15; Popovici as mayor of, 23–24, 30, 171n8, 172n9; Ukrainian soldiers in, 25; Weinschenker family in, 11–12, 23, 25–26, 30, 172

death, 88, 106; of children, 63; of father of Wiesel, 103–4; of soul, 54; of Tabak, E., 17; of Weinschenker, Chaim, 37; of Weinschenker, Clara, 37

death experience, of Delbo, 87–88
death guilt, 109, 114
death imprint, 88
Death in Life (Lifton), 47
death time, 53
deep memory, 46, 145
dehumanization, 94
Delbo, Charlotte, 78, 84; in Auschwitz, 87–88; death experience of, 87–88; emptiness of, 89; return experience of, 88
denial, of Holocaust, 137, 158
De-Nur, Yehiel (Ka-Tzetnik 135633), 96–97
dialectic of trauma, 50, 112
diaries, xiv, 14, 53, 55–57, 75–76, 171nn4–5; analysis of, 43–44, 45, 155; as historical documentation, 44, 48; life preservation with, 43; as symbol of resistance, 44; temporal continuity relating to, 47, 48; as witnesses to historical events, 43; writing of, 46–52, 156. See also *Anne Frank's Diary*; children, diaries of
differential trauma response, 126
direct witness. See *superstes*
discomposure, 10
disconnect, temporal, 129
disorganized detachment, 146
displaced persons, 40, 93, 152
displaced persons camps (DP camps), 33, 94
displacement, temporal, 80, 128
disrupted attachment patterns, 148
dogs, fear of, 36–37

double bind, of second-generation survivors, 145
double killing, 136–37
double-reality, xi–xii, 115
double-wound, 91
Dov Kulka, Otto, 82–84, 97–98, 112
DP camps. *See* displaced persons camps
Dreyfus, Lucien, 55, 57
dual temporal imprisonment, 74–75
durational time: Langer on, 92–99, 121; survivor experience of, 44, 62, 64, 89, 92–99, 121–22, 126, 146

Eastern European Jewish immigrants (*Ostjuden*), 12, 171nn2–3
Eichmann trial (1960s), 79, 95, 139
Einsatzgrippen D, 14–15
embodied memory, 107, 153
emigration, 94
emotional response to terrible event, trauma as, xii
empathic unsettlement, 52, 122; LaCapra on, 48, 66, 97, 107, 114, 117, 120
emptiness, of Delbo, 89
encapsulating narrative structure, 120
epigenetics, 140, 157
Epstein, Helen, xi, 119–20, 143, 145, 146, 175n33
erasure, of Jews, 21, 55, 57, 90
Erikson, Kai, 49
everyday resistance, 50, 51
exclusionary thinking, 20
exile consciousness, 92
existence, post-Holocaust relating to, 56, 57

INDEX / 181

experiences, 41, 87–88, 151; of durational time, 44, 62, 64, 89, 92–99, 121–22, 126, 146; narrative, belatedness of, 44, 157; of post-Holocaust, xiv, xv–xvi, 32, 62–63; of Tabak, F., in Holocaust, 8, 15–16, 31–32, 35–36, 40, 172n14; temporal, 53, 96; transgenerational Holocaust experience, 154; of trauma, x–xii, 41, 60, 81; unclaimed, 50, 70, 81, 108, 113, 146
explicit time, 3
extreme situation, 111

failed experience, of trauma, 81
Falconer, Rachel, 81
false self adaptation, 92
familial projection, 134
families, 155–56; citizenship changes of, 26–27, 32; of survivors, xi, 21; of Szenes, 64–65. *See also* Weinschenker family
Febvre, Lucien, 48
Feldman, Jackie, 127, 130
Felman, Shoshana, 101; on crisis of witnessing, 52, 58, 109; on testimonies, 88, 92, 112; *Testimony* by, 44, 45, 96; on trauma, 47, 135
Final Solution, 59
Fine, Ellen, 116
first-generation survivor memoirs, 77–80, 118, 123, 138, 175n32
Fishken, Sarah, 61–62
founding trauma, 62, 64, 87, 89, 120, 146
fractured moral time, 71
frameworks. See *specific topics*

Frank, Anne, 47–48
Frankl, Viktor, on suicide, 107–9
Fresco, Nadine, 90, 120
Friedländer, Saul, 49, 112
From Guilt to Shame (Leys), 48
frozen timeframes, 132

Garbarini, Alexandra, 43, 46, 51
gas chambers, ix, 98, 103, 112
Geclewicz Raz, Mirla: *The Birds Sang Eulogies* by, 119; Poland pilgrimage of, 131–32
generational memoirs, time within, 118–20
generational transmission, of memory, 128
The Generation of Postmemory (Hirsch), 44
Generations of Shoah International (GSI), 36
genocide, ix, 114, 156–59; diary writing and, 46; *after* genocide, 7; time relating to, xiii; understanding of, xvi, 57
German government, restitution from, 30
Gestapo, 87
ghetto, 19, 23. *See also* specific ghettos
ghost in the family system, 111
Ginz, Petr, 47–48, 50–51
God, relationship with, 46, 81, 173n18
Goldin, Leyb, 53–54, 55, 73
Greenspan, Henry, xiv, 2, 9
grey zone, 88, 91, 101–2
Gross, Jan, 90–91

Gruner, Wolf, 50
GSI. *See* Generations of Shoah International
guardianship. See *shamor*
guilt: collective, 106; death guilt, 109, 114; of survivors, 20, 38–39, 65, 85, 95–105
guilt without fault, 65

halacha (Jewish lineage), 116
Halbwachs, Maurice, 58, 80, 89, 108, 120, 121
Hartman, Geoffrey H., 50, 60, 71, 82, 92, 109, 120, 134; *The Longest Shadow* by, 45
haunting legacy, 116
An Heiress of Holocaust (Segal), 120
Herman, Judith, 49, 61, 63, 112
heterological historian, 55
heterotemporal reality, 98
hidden transcripts, 50
hierarchy of suffering, 19–20
Hilberg, Raul, 71, 117
Hirsch, Marianne: on heterotemporal reality, 98; on point of memory, 122; on postmemorial working through, 120; on postmemory, 44, 47, 90, 116–18, 127–29, 133, 134, 141
historical consciousness, collective, 45
historical documentation, 31, 44, 48
historical frameworks, conventional, 157
historical periodization, 155
historical studies, 154
historical trauma, 93, 143, 153
historical trauma response, 110, 114
historical truth, testimonial evidence and, 78
historical witness, 95
history, 87; conclusion to, 75–76; holidays as framework of time, 63–69, 174n24; meaning of children relating to, 58–63; received, 46, 90, 108; suicide, 45, 70–75; time constructs relating to, 45, 52–57; understanding of, x–xi; writing of, 43–52
history of repetition, 136
Hitler, Adolph, 22, 136
Hoffman, Eva, 88, 108, 114; *After Such Knowledge* by, 118; on exile consciousness, 92; on memory, 81, 127, 145; writings of, 10, 96, 118, 145
holidays, as framework of time: personal holidays, 63; religious holidays, 63–69, 174n24
Holocaust, 28; biological impact of, 157; connection to, 4; as continuing phenomenon, 155, 157–58; denial of, 137, 158; end of, x, 44, 54, 86, 153; finite period for, 55; as "is," 85; as ongoing event, 155; past, present *vs.*, 157–59; teaching of, 156, 159
Holocaust diarists, 56, 75–76
Holocaust diary (Dreyfus), 55
Holocaust experience, 41
Holocaust experiences, of Tabak, F, 8, 15–16, 31–32, 35–36, 40, 172n14
The Holocaust in Bohemia and Moravia (Gruner), 50
Holocaust scholars, on memoirs, 79–80

Holocaust Testimonies (Langer), 44
Holocaust testimony, 95
home. *See* return home
homeland, absence of, 31, 32–33, 94
homelessness, 27, 32–33, 93
hopelessness, 45
Huener, Jonathan, 90
humanitarian witness, 58
humanity, 27, 54, 82; connection to, 156; returning to, 63, 86, 156; time via, xiii
Hungarian Arrow Cross, 65, 90, 174n23
Huyssen, Andreas, 82, 117

ibed atzmo ladaat (to lose oneself), 74
identity, 95, 149–50
identity diffusion, 153
I Have My Daughter's Eyes (Bluman), 120
imperative to tell, 47
implicit time, 3
implicit trauma transmission, 143
impossibility, of post-Holocaust, 48, 56–57, 69–70, 75–76, 80, 85, 128, 133
impossibility of return, 130, 131
impossible history, of trauma, 87
impossible witness, 49
imposter syndrome, 5
imprisonment, dual temporal, 74–75
incurable life-long disease, 121
inheritance, paradoxical, 90
inheritance of trauma, 110, 114, 127
inherited hypervigilance, 131–32, 153
inherited memory, 116

inherited memory images, 128
inherited right to remember, 142
inherited temporality, 156
inherited trauma, 119, 141
inherited witness, 135
inner time consciousness, 3
intellectual witness, 82, 109
intergenerational obligation, 104
intergenerational survivors, xiii, xv, 9, 15–16
intergenerational transmission of trauma, 15, 110, 117, 118, 147, 152–53, 155, 158
intimate publics, 48
An Introduction to Holocaust Studies (Bernard-Donals), 52
invasions, 12–13, 22
irreconcilable memory, 91

James, William, on stream of consciousness, 3
Jewish Council. See *Joodse Raad*
Jewish Federation, 16
JewishGen, 22, 171nn6–7
Jewish identity, of Brown, 149–50
Jewish lineage. See *halacha*
Jews: certificates for, 23, 171n8; of Czernowitz, 23–24; erasure of, 21, 55, 57, 90; of Poland, 49; stereotype of, 13; Vel'd'hiv roundup of, 86–87
Jonkisz, Jakub, on consciousness, 3–4
Joodse Raad (Jewish Council), 125
Jordan (doctor), 18
Judaism, 86
Judenrat, 58, 68, 174n20

justice, 158

kairological time, 97
Ka-Nzetnik 135633. *See* De-Nur, Yehiel
Kaplan, Chaim, 47, 49–50, 54–55, 68
Kielce pogrom, 27, 90–91, 172n13
killing: of childhood, 61; mass, in Czernowitz, 14–15
KL. See *konzentrationslager* system
Klisman Ellis, Lori, 133
knowing without knowing, 142–43
Koffler, Salo (uncle), 13
Kommandatura (commandant), ix–x
konzentrationslager system (KL), 64
Krystal, Henry, on trauma studies, xii, 112
KZ syndrome. *See* concentration camp syndrome

LaCapra, Dominick, 49, 53, 110; on empathic unsettlement, 48, 66, 97, 107, 114, 117, 120; on founding trauma, 62, 64, 87, 89, 120, 146; on trauma, 60, 62, 81, 91, 108, 109, 113, 123, 129; *Writing History, Writing Trauma* by, 44
Landsberg, Alison, 82, 141
Landscapes of the Metropolis of Death (Dov Kulka), 82
Langer, Lawrence, 51, 52, 60, 81, 87, 104; on deep memory, 46, 145; on durational time, 92–99, 121; *Holocaust Testimonies* by, 44; on tainted memory, 49, 92, 99, 109

language, 18, 29, 31
Laskier Rutka, 61, 63
Laub, Dori, 78, 91, 112, 142–43; on collapse of witnessing, 49, 62, 81, 97, 108, 109, 110, 111; *Testimony* by, 44, 45, 96; on trauma, 47, 60, 88, 122, 135
legacy of silence, 145
Leibl, 139–40
Leitner, Isabella: as Hungarian Jewish survivor, 90; immigration to America, 90
Lengyel, Olga: medical block work of, 101; survivor guilt of, 100–101
Levi, Primo, 85–86, 88, 91, 111, 113
Levinas, Emmanuel, 102
Leys, Ruth, 48, 65, 71, 88, 90
liberation and freedom, as meaningless, 92
lieux de memoire (sites of memory), 51, 81
life preservation, with diaries, 43
Lifton, Robert Jay, 47, 53, 70, 88, 109, 114
liminal period, during pilgrimage, 129
liminal space, 129
the limit of representation, in trauma narratives, 49, 53
linear temporality, 119
Lipiner, Lucy, 93
living testimony, 135
Łódź Ghetto, 62, 71
The Longest Shadow (Hartman), 45
Loridan-Ivens, Marceline, memoir of, 84–85, 91, 109–11, 175n28
Luisa's Long Journey Home (Lipiner), 93

Marchetti, Giorgio, 4
Marine Flasher, SS, 30
mass extermination, 98
massive psychic trauma, 112
mass killings, in Czernowitz, 14–15
maternal support, of Clara Weinschenker, 25–28, 32–34
Mayer, Hans. *See* Améry, Jean
McGoldrick, Monica, 111
meaning: of children, 58–63; in suffering, 16
meaningless, of liberation and freedom, 92
mediated trauma sites, 132
medical block work, of Lengyel, 101
memoirs, xiv, 4–5, 43, 155–56; definition of, 77; of first-generation survivors, 77–80, 118, 123, 138, 175n32; of generational survivor, 115–18, 175nn30–31; Holocaust scholars on, 79–80; temporal hierarchy relating to, 78; as temporal link to those murdered, 79; time within generational, 118–20; value of, 77–78; witnessing role of, 79. *See also specific memoirs*
memorial, for Szenes, 66
Memorial and Museum Auschwitz-Birkenau, ix
memorial candles, 22, 115, 138–39
Memorial Candles (Wardi), xi–xii
memorial disruption, 129
memorial journeys, 129
memorial-museum space, 132
memorial object, 120
memorial time, 128
memory, 95, 118, 131, 132; generational transmission of, 128; imagination relating to, 138; loop of, 123; nonlinear transmission of, 78; of third-generation survivors, 137–38, 175n34. *See also specific memory*
memory and narrative structure, of multigenerational Holocaust testimonial, 4; explicit time with, 3; implicit time with, 3; inner time consciousness with, 3; stream of consciousness with, 3
memory gap, 132
memory reconstruction, 127
memory-work, 125
meridian time, 101
Mermelstein, Mel, 92
methodology, for multigenerational Holocaust testimonial, 2–3
minds in mourning, 88
Moldova (once Romania), 22
Molotov-Ribbentrop Pact with Russia, 14
moral time, of the camps, 98
mortality, 54
motherhood concept, 34, 37
Müller, Flip, 111, 113
multidirectional memory, 45, 82, 90
multigenerational Holocaust testimonial, 1; memory and narrative structure, 3–4; methodology for, 2–3; reflections on, 40–41; writing approach for, 4–5
multiple interview process, xiv

multiple marginality, 152
murder, 79; of children, 58; by Nazis, 45; of Szenes, 65
Muselmänner, 105–6

"The nameless ones! It's them. Them! All those anonymous ones! Write their name: K. Tzetnik!," 96
narrative, 118
narrative closer, 53, 173n19
narrative experience, belatedness of, 44, 157
narratives: artificial, 53; encapsulating structure of, 120; redemptive, 109; of trauma, 49, 53. *See also* memory and narrative structure, of multigenerational Holocaust testimonial
Nazis, 136; destruction by, 31–32, 68; goal of, xiii, 20; murders by, 45; Russians *vs.*, 39
near trauma, xii
Neu Freimann DP camp, 33
"Never Again," 79, 138
Night (Wiesel), 14
nightmares, dreams with, 86, 174n27
nonlinear transmission, of memory, 78
non-synchronicity, 99–100
Nora, Pierre, 128
Northoff, George, on inner time consciousness, 3
Numbered Days (Garbarini), 46
Nuremberg Race Laws, 72
Nyiszli, Miklos, 111–12, 113

object trauma, 134
object witnessing, 134
1.5 generation phenomenon, 127
Oneg Shabbat archive, 51, 73
On Listening to Holocaust Survivors (Greenspan), 2
ordinary men, 90
orphanages, 60
Ostjuden (Eastern European Jewish immigrants), 12, 171nn2–3
Oumano, Elena, 83–84

pain, 90, 110, 147
paradoxical inheritance, 90
paradoxical legacy, 108, 114
paradoxical time, 88
paradox of indirect knowledge, 145
paradox of survival, 113
Patterson, David, xiii, 47, 52, 55–57, 59
Perpetrators, Victims, Bystanders (Hilberg), 71
personal holidays, 63
phantom pain, 90, 110
phantom transmission, 145
pilgrimage, 126, 130, 133–35; concept of, xv, 21–22, 171nn6–7; of Geclewicz Raz, 131–32; liminal period during, 129; motivation for, 127; of Polak, 125; by second-generation survivors, 125, 127; temporal, 128; trauma of, 131
pipels, 81, 174n26
poems, of Brown, 147–51
pogroms, 27, 28, 90–91, 172n13
point of memory, 122

Polak, Joseph, 5; abandonment of, 122; *After the Holocaust the Bells still Ring* by, 121; as bearing witness, 137; at Bergen-Belsen, 125; as child survivor, 121–22; father of, 123–24; in inescapable loop of memory, 123; at *Joods tehuis*, 121; "Lost Train" to Troebitz from Bergen-Belsen relating to, 121; pilgrimage of, 125; separation and reunion with mother of, 122

Poland, 59, 131–32; as cemetery, 90; Jews of, 49; Kielce pogrom in, 27, 90–91, 172n13; life in, 26–28, 32; return to, 93; Weinschenker family in, 26–28, 32

Popovici, Traian, as Czernowitz mayor, 23–24, 30, 171n8, 172n9

post-Holocaust, ix, 40, 65, 72, 155; bearing witness without witnessing, 135–40; concept of, xv–xvi, 45–46, 55, 96, 119, 132, 146, 153; conclusion to, 153–54; to continuing Holocaust, 158; existence relating to, 56, 57; experience of, xiv, xv–xvi, 32, 62–63; false construct of, xv–xvi; impossibility of, 48, 56–57, 69–70, 75–76, 80, 85, 128, 133; Jewish diaspora relating to, 94; pilgrimage to Europe, 125–35; straddling generations, Polak relating to, 121–24; Tabak, F., concept of, 1, 8, 9–10, 34; time within generational memoirs, 118–20; transference of trauma, 140–53; trauma in generational survivor memoirs, 115–18, 175nn30–31

post-memorial affect, 129
post-memorial future, 58
post-memorial succession, 120
post-memorial vision, 132
post-memorial work, 134
post-memorial working through, 120
postmemory, 44, 47, 90, 116–18, 127–29, 133, 134, 141
postmemory gaps, 90
post-traumatic stress disorder (PTSD), xi
postwar antisemitism, 90–91
pre-Eichmann testimony, 95
pre-Holocaust Romania, 21
present pasts, 82
privilege: of bearing witness, 98–104; chronological, 52
"A Prologue that Could Also Be an Epilogue" (Dov Kulka), 82
prosthetic memory, 82, 141
psychic closing off, 109
psychic numbing, 47, 89, 92
psychological issues from trauma, Epstein on, xi
PTSD. *See* post-traumatic stress disorder

Rabinek Epstein, Franci, memoir of, 98–100
rebuilding, 86–87, 93
received history, 46, 90, 108
received memory, 141
recursive nature of trauma, 148

redemptive narrative, 109
reflections, on multigenerational Holocaust testimonial, 40–41
religious holidays, 63–69, 174n24
religious practice, of Clara Weinschenker, 33
remembrance, 142, 145. See also *zakhor*
Remnants of Auschwitz (Agamben), 47
reparations, 95
resistance, individual, 51
restitution, from German government, 30
retraumatization. *See* bureaucratic retraumatization
retrospective testimony, 52
return experience, of Delbo, 88
return home: attempt to, 91–95; Levi on, 85–86; nightmares relating to, 86, 174n27; possibility of, 93; unfulfilling dream of, 85–91
returning, to humanity, 63, 86, 156
Ricoeur, Paul, 97
Rifka (Frieda's aunt), 9–10, 21
Ringelbaum, Emanuel, 49, 71, 72
ritual reenactment of survival, 127
Romania, 25, 171n1; German invasion of, 22; language of, 31; pre-Holocaust, 21. *See also* Czernowitz
Rosner, Elizabeth, 136–37, 140
Rothberg, Michael, 45, 49, 88, 108
Rudashevski, Yitskhop, 66–69
ruins of memory, 104–5
Rumania Armistice Agreement, 24, 172n10

Rumkowski, Chaim, 71
rupture, of time, xiii, 56–57
Russians: Nazis *vs.*, 39; Romanians welcome of, 25
Russian soldiers, 25

Saints and Postmodernism (Wyschogrod), 55
Schwab, Gabriele, 116, 146
Scott, James C., 50, 51
secondary trauma activation, 131
secondary traumatization, 130
secondary witnessing, 127
second-generation memoirs, 118
second-generation survivors, xi, xiii–xiv, 9, 10, 119–20; as bearing witness, 115, 117, 136–37; double bind of, 145; first generation relating to, 115, 117; memory relating to, 137–38, 147, 175n34; pilgrimage of, 125, 127
second-generation trauma, of Wanderer Cohen, 144
second Holocaust, 112, 136
second wound, 122
Segal, Sarah, on bearing witness, 120, 138–40
"Sensibility and History" (Febvre), 48
separation and loss, cycle of, 121, 148
separation anxiety, 93
shamor (guardianship), 135, 136
Sierakowiak, Dawid, 62–63, 67
silence, 143, 145
Silencing the Past (Trouillot), 57
site of memory. See *lieux de mémoire*
sites of memory transfer, 128

site-specific memory activation, 126
Skype, 2, 7, 13
social death, 88
Sonderkommando, 101–3, 111, 112, 113, 140, 175n29
souls: death of, 54; destruction of, 45; of diarists, 56; as lost, 45
Soviet Union: as antisemitic, 13; invasion by, 12–13
speculative memory work, 134
Spicer, Ellis, 10, 19–20
stable truth, 55
starvation, 53–54, 60, 67, 73–74
state of exception, 88, 109
stereotype, of Jews, 13
stream of consciousness, 3
Stutthof sign, 134
After Such Knowledge (Hoffman), 118
suffering, 55; hierarchy of, 19–20; meaning in, 16
suicide, 7, 45; Améry on, 106–9; Berg on, 72, 74–75; of Czerniaków, 70–75; Frankl on, 107–9; *ibed atzmo ladaat* relating to, 74; Loridan-Ivens on, 109–10; *Muselmänner*, 105–6; unprecedented trauma of, 105–6, 111–13
Suleiman, Susan Rubin, 127, 145, 146
superstes (direct witness), 135, 136
Survivor Cafe (Rosner), 136
survivor chronological narratives, 118
survivor frameworks, 136
survivor groups, 36, 173n15
survivors, x; child, 5, 19, 121–22; dreams of, xiv; durational time experienced by, 44, 62, 64, 89, 92–99, 121–22, 126, 146; families of, xi, 21; guilt of, 20, 38–39, 65, 85, 95–105; intergenerational, xiii, xv, 9, 15–16; passing of, 115; past and present of, 88. *See also* second-generation survivors; third-generation survivors
survivorship, ix–xv, 41
survivor's paradox, 92
survivor testimony, memory, identity, historical witness relating to, 95
survivor-writer's struggle, 104
suspended time, 53
symbol of resistance, diaries as, 44
syndrome: imposter, 5; KZ, xii–xiii
Szenes, Hannah: diary of, 64–66; memorial of, 66; murder of, 65; religious holidays of, 64–65; survivor guilt of, 65

Tabak, David (son), xiii, 21, 22, 34, 35, 36–37
Tabak, Edward (husband): background of, 17–18; death of, 17; life with, 16–17, 34
Tabak, Frieda: in America, 5, 12, 32; Auschwitz-Birkenau visit by, 18, 20; in book club, 35–36; as case study, 1–2; Clara as stepmother of, 11–12, 25; documentation relating to, 31; education significance to, 11, 24, 40; family photograph of, 30; fear of dogs relating to, 36–37; Feige as birth mother of, 8–9, 10, 22; flashbacks of, 6–7; Holocaust

Tabak, Frieda *(continued)*
    experiences shared by, 8, 15–16, 31–32, 35–36, 40, 172n14; homelessness of, 27, 32–33; indoctrination of, 24; intergenerational transmission of trauma relating to, 15; language skills of, 18, 29; loneliness of, 20; material possessions relating to, 5–6; motherhood concept of, 34, 37; on post-Holocaust concept, 1, 8, 9–10, 34; reestablishment of, 32; rehearsed story of, 3, 7; in Romania, 5, 13, 17, 21–22, 171n1; in school, 33–34; self-preservation of, 18; tolerance taught by, 35; in Transnistria, 15; trauma of, 38–40; as Weinschenker, Freda, 7; as Wishner, Frieda, 7
Tabak, Mark (son), xiii, 8–9, 13–14, 21–22, 38; bar mitzvah of, 17
Tabak, Stanley (son), xiii, 8; in America, 28, 30, 37; in Poland, 27–28, 32; profession of, 13–14; stories from, 10–12, 25–27
Tabak family case study, 155–56
Tadek, suicide of, 72
tainted memory, 49, 92, 99, 109
temporal anchoring, 80, 132
temporal boundary, 155
temporal collapse, 78–79, 154
temporal continuity, with diaries, 47, 48
temporal delay, of trauma, 82
temporal disconnect, 129
temporal displacement, 80, 128
temporal disruption, 88, 96, 111, 130
temporal experience, 53, 96
temporal haunting, 81
temporal hierarchy, 78
temporality: inherited, 156; linear temporality, 119; traumatic, 120
temporal pilgrimage, 128
temporal rupture, 92, 93, 103
temporal stasis, in Holocaust memory transmission, 132
testimonial. *See* multigenerational Holocaust testimonial
testimonial anxiety, 126
testimonial dialogues, 119
testimonial evidence, historical truth and, 78
testimonial life, 51
testimonial objects, 88, 90
testimonial practices, 50
Testimony (Felman and Laub), 44, 45, 96
testimony of survival, 112
testimony's crisis, 92
testis (third-party witness), 135, 136
theology of witness, 105
Theresienstadt, 20, 29, 85
third-generation memoirs, 118
third-generation survivors, xv; as bearing witness, 136–37; first generation relating to, 115, 117; memory relating to, 137–38, 175n34
third-party witness. *See testis*
third time, 97
time, 46, 81, 125; durational, 44, 62, 64, 89, 92–99, 121–22, 126, 146; event chronology relating to, 52; within generational memoirs, 118–20;

holidays as framework of, 63–69, 174n24; humanity via, xiii; inner time consciousness, 3; preservation of, 47; rupture of, xiii, 56–57; Wiesel on, 77, 78–79, 84. See also *specific topics*

time constructs, 45, 55–57; calendar time, 52; chronological privilege, 52; death time, 53; limits of representation, 53; narrative closer, 53, 173n19; reconceptualization relating to, 54; starvation relating to, 53–54, 60; suspended time, 53; time of absence, 53

time of absence, 53

"the time of the Other," 102

time of the remnant, 98

to lose oneself. See *ibed atzmo ladaat*

Torok, Maria, 110, 120, 145

torture, Améry on, 106–7

traditional historical periodization, 155

transference of trauma, 145–53; cortisol production relating to, 140–41; epigenetics relating to, 140–41; self-testing behaviors relating to, 142; Zilber relating to, 141–44

transferential relation to the past, 110

transgenerational haunting, 145

transgenerational Holocaust experience, 154

transgenerational memory work, 131

transgenerational phantom, 120, 123

transgenerational trauma, 119; transformation of, 130; transmission of, 129

transgenerational witness, 128

transmission. See *specific transmissions*

transmission, of memory: generational, 128; nonlinear, 78

transmission of roles, 143

transmitted trauma, 135–36

Transnistria, 15, 23

trauma: aftermath of, 88; analysis of, xi, 155, 157; Caruth on, 46, 50, 52, 70, 91, 108, 117; damage with, 20; defense mechanism with, 47; direct and inherited, 141; as emotional response, xii; experience of, x–xii, 41, 60; failed experience of, 81; Felman on, 47, 135; in generational survivor memoirs, 115–18, 175nn30–31; through generations, xv–xvi, 15, 133; inherited, 119; LaCapra on, 60, 62, 81, 91, 108, 109, 113, 123, 129; Laub on, 47, 60, 88, 122, 135; legacy of, 137; lifelong journey with, 156; near trauma, xii; new methodological approaches to, 157; of pilgrimage, 131; post-traumatic stress disorder, xi; proof of, 95; psychological issues from, xi; space and time relationship to, 125; temporal delay of, 82. See also transference of trauma; specific traumas

trauma, through transcribing: after?, 80–85; attempt to return home, 91–95; bearing witness and burden of survivor guilt, 95–105; conclusion to, 113–14; first-generation survivor memoirs, 77–80, 118, 123, 138, 175n32;

trauma *(continued)*
  suicide, 105–13; unfulfilling dream of return to home, 85–91
Trauma and Recovery (Herman), 49
trauma echo chamber, 153
trauma narratives, the limit of representation in, 49, 53
trauma spiral, 130
trauma studies, Krystal on, xii
traumatic dissociation, 63
traumatic immediacy, 52
traumatic memory, 117, 123
traumatic perfectionism, 149
traumatic realism, 49, 88, 108
traumatic reenactment, 152
traumatic rupture, 122–23
traumatic temporality, 120
traumatic worldview, 146
trauma time, 90
Tree of Life Synagogue (Pittsburgh), 28
Troebitz, 126
Trouillot, Michel-Rolph, 57
Turner, Victor, 129–30

Ukrainian soldiers, in Czernowitz, 25
unclaimed experience, 50, 70, 81, 108, 113, 146
Unclaimed Experience (Caruth), 44
"unheimlich" (uncanny) experience, 151
United States Holocaust Memorial Museum, 14
USC Shoah Foundation, 16

Van der Kolk, Bessel, 48–49, 108

Vel'd'hiv roundup, of Jews, 86–87
Venezia, Shlomo, as *Sonderkommando*, 101–3
verification moments, 134
vicarious witnessing, 116
Vichy government, 64–65, 86, 174n22
Vilna Ghetto, 67
voluntary death, 106

Wanderer Cohen, Emily, memoir of, 118; mother relationship with, 144–46; parenting issues of, 145; second-generation trauma of, 144; survivorship of, 146
Wannsee Conference, 59, 174n21
Wardi, Dina, xi–xii, 9, 115–16, 139
Warsaw Ghetto, 29, 67; Czerniaków in, 58–59, 72; Golden diary relating to, 53; *Judenrat* in, 58, 174n20; Kaplan diary relating to, 49
Warsaw Ghetto Uprising, 59
wartime events, 45, 173n17
Waxman, Zoë, 50
Weinschenker, Chaim (father), 9, 25–26, 27, 32, 37
Weinschenker, Clara (stepmother), 11–12; in America, 28–31; in Czernowitz, 23, 25–26, 30, 171n8, 172n9; death of, 37; family citizenship changes by, 26–27, 32; family protected by, 25–28, 32–34; maternal support of, 25–28, 32–34; in Poland, 26–28; religious practice maintained by, 33
Weinschenker, Frieda. *See* Tabak, Frieda

Weinschenker, Milo. *See* Tabak, Stanley
Weinschenker family: in America, 28–31; in Czernowitz, 23, 25–26, 30, 171n8, 172n9, 172n11–12; in Germany, 32; in Poland, 26–28, 32
Westerbork, 125
Wiesel, Elie, xiii, 14, 40, 45, 136–37; on bearing witness, 103–5; on father's death, 103–4; on temporal anchoring, 80; on time, 81; watch found by, 80–81; on writing, 77, 78–79, 84
Wiesenthal, Simon, 90
Wieviorka, Annette, 95–96
Wind, Eliazar de, on KZ syndrome, xii–xiii
Winnicott, Donald, 92
Wisconsin Historical Society, 30
Wishner, Frieda. *See* Tabak, Frieda
Wishner Feige (birth mother), 8–9, 10, 22
witness, 43, 44, 45, 49, 52, 58, 62. *See also specific topics*
witness by adoption, 120, 142
witnesses of the witnesses, 128
witnessing role, of memoirs, 79
witness testimony, 71

wound of consciousness, 89, 91, 107
wound of the mind, 107
wounds, 91, 100–101, 122
wounds that speak, 141
writing: approach of, for multigenerational Holocaust testimonial, 4–5; danger in, 51; of diaries, 46–52, 156; of history, 43–52; trauma of, 44
Writing and Rewriting the Holocaust (Young), 55–56
Writing History, Writing Trauma (LaCapra), 44
writing trauma, 44
Wyschogrod, Edith, 55

"Yad Hannah," 66
Yehuda, Rachel, 110, 113–14, 143
Yellow Horse Brave Heart, Maria, 110–11, 114
yellow star, 23
Yiddish, 29
Young, James E., 46, 49, 52, 55–56, 64, 108, 120

zakhor (remembrance), 135, 136
Zilber, Ettie, memoir of, 133–35, 141–44
Zionism, 64

ABOUT THE AUTHOR

Sarah Seiselmyer-Snyder holds a PhD in history of ideas with a concentration in Holocaust studies from the University of Texas at Dallas. She specializes in public memory, testimony, and intergenerational trauma within genocide studies. She currently is a visiting scholar at the Center for the Study of Genocide and Human Rights at Rutgers University. Additionally, she teaches history, memory studies, and anthropology classes at Ithaca College and Goodwin University, and is developing curricula on the Bosnian Genocide while coediting a volume, *Genocide Studies: Through the Eyes of Intergenerational Survivors*. Her background includes conservation work at the Memorial and Museum Auschwitz-Birkenau.

www.ingramcontent.com/pod-product-compliance
Lightning Source LLC
Chambersburg PA
CBHW070315240426
43661CB00057B/2656